ROBERT HULL

# THE
# LANGUAGE
# GAP

How classroom dialogue fails

METHUEN    London and New York

First published in 1985 by
Methuen & Co. Ltd
11 New Fetter Lane,
London EC4P 4EE


Published in the USA by
Methuen & Co.
in association with Methuen, Inc.
733 Third Avenue,
New York, NY 10017

Typeset in Great Britain by
Scarborough Typesetting Services
and printed by
Richard Clay (The Chaucer Press),
Bungay, Suffolk

*British Library Cataloguing in
Publication Data*

Hull, Robert
The language gap: how classroom
dialogue fails.
1. Language and languages — Study and
teaching (Secondary) — Great Britain
I. Title
407′.1241    P57.G7

ISBN 0–416–39390–X
ISBN 0–416–39400–0 Pbk

*Library of Congress Cataloging in
Publication Data*

Hull, Robert.
The language gap.
Includes index.
1. Teacher–student relationships –
England – Case studies.
2. Interaction analysis in education –
Case studies.
3. English language – Remedial
teaching – Case studies.
4. Comprehension – Case studies.
5. Language and education – England –
Case studies.
I. Title
LB1033.H76   1985   371.1′ 02
84–27219

ISBN 0–416–39390–X
ISBN 0–416–39400–0 (pbk.)

# CONTENTS

# ACKNOWLEDGEMENTS

Particular thanks are due to the staff and pupils of Bognor Regis School, where I was allowed to wander more or less at will for a year and a half, in and out of classrooms, meetings, and conversations. The support of teaching staff went well beyond the kind of tolerance that an intruding observer might hope for.

I owe a special debt also to Barry Cooper; whatever clarity the book might have derives in good measure from him. John Fines, Heather Thomas and Ray Verrier have been assiduous readers and listeners, and their support and encouragement have been invaluable.

I am grateful to the following for permission to reproduce copyright material:

Addison-Wesley Publishers Ltd for the page from *Mathematics for Schools* by H. Fletcher and A. Howell on p. 61;
C. V. Burgess for two pages from *Burgess Composition, Book 2* on p. 97 and p. 111;

Daphne Kerslake and the Mathematical Association for the test material in the *Mathematics in Schools* article, 'Visual mathematics' on p. 64;

George Philip and Son Ltd for two maps from *Groundwork Geographies, Europe* by N. Jackson and P. Penn on p. 190 and p. 192;

Schofield & Sims Ltd for the pages from *Beta Mathematics 3* by T. R. Godard and A. W. Grattridge on pp. 58–9;

Ward Lock Educational Co. Ltd for the tables from 'Teachers' perception and children's reading in secondary schools' by T. Dolan on pp. 208–9.

# PREFACE

This book derives ultimately from conversations with a small group of 14- and 15-year-old boys and girls in a comprehensive school, whom I used to take for 'Supplementary English'. They opted for this because they found routine academic work for CSE difficult, and for four lessons a week they were able to work on language-related problems arising in their main subjects – problems with reading, note-taking, essays, and so on. Their lessons with me consisted mainly of informal talk about what they were doing, or failing to do, and they discussed their difficulties with revelatory candour. It seemed that they were quite often unable to cope: episodes like the following were as common as they were baffling.

D was doing some physics as part of a CSE general science course. He read a passage of textbook prior to attempting a question. One paragraph began: 'If the pulley system were a "perfect machine", i.e. composed of weightless and frictionless strings and pulleys . . .'. This short interchange took place:

Self: Is there such a thing as a perfect machine?
D:    Yes.
Self: Where?
D:    There.
      (Pointing to the diagram of a pulley system.)
Self: Could you make one?
D:    No.
Self: Do you know anyone who could?
D:    Yeah, David, he's good at physics.

M showed me an English exercise he'd done on apostrophes of possession, and read aloud these unconsciously poetic lines:

the barber of the pole
the spectators of the rattle
Keats of the poems
the Bishop of the voice
children of faces
women of eyes

F was wrestling with a page in her office practice text. It finished with the question: 'Do you think the undertaking was a fair one?' She called out, 'I want to know what undertaking is – a graveyard is it?'

A asked if he could go outside 'to record clouds'. He had some ominous-looking sketches and a list of cloud-types that might have been jotted down in the university lecture room, except for the spelling. Ten minutes later he came back baffled. He clearly wasn't up to observing clouds and couldn't see any cloud on his list. The 'colominusbus' weren't there, or the others. Someone spat on him from an upstairs window, too.

The informality of the lessons, allied to the idea that we were looking for difficulties not obvious to their teachers, made it likely that uncertainties which might normally stay hidden would come to the surface. It was not just the extent to which this occurred that was remarkable, but the nature of the problems themselves; it suggested that the failure they were experiencing with schooling went deep indeed. Some of the questions they asked me seemed quite rudimentary: 'Which way is clockwise?' 'Is descending going up?' 'Is glucose a plant?' At the same time they made seemingly bizarre errors in comprehension. 'Animals harbour insects' meant they ate them. 'The lowest bridge-town' was a slum on a bridge. 'Flushing (22,000)' meant they caught 22,000 fish there. Expressions such as 'molten iron', 'physical feature', 'factor', 'western leader' were often insuperable obstacles to comprehension.

And yet, as soon as one did stop to think – and to look and listen – some of the bizarre quality faded, and became explicable. A perfect machine might well be as good a machine as can actually be made; the language of exercises in English isn't always meaningful; specialist words like 'undertaking' are likely to be taken in their usual sense, despite the odd results, if their technical sense is unfamiliar. And so on. What began to seem odder than their odd responses was the assumption, implicit in the way their textbooks and questions and worksheets handled subject language, that correct responses would be widely available, and that errors like thinking that 22,000 refers to numbers of fish were bizarre and would not normally be made.

This seemed like a step towards understanding something of their predicament. But it often entailed seeing their tasks not as things for them to do but as things for them to be unable to do. It seemed that without intending to teachers gave them work which underlined for them the fact of their failure. The cheery resilience with which they none the less confronted probable defeats was admirable, but it also seemed worrying that they were apparently not much perturbed, and appeared for the most part to accept their role as non-copers. Perhaps they disguised their concern, and perhaps they did not accept what was happening to them – which was that they seemed to be drifting to the edge of the school's working life – and developed a kind of sang-froid as resistance. Certainly, they evinced a marked detachment from their school work.

At the clearest pitch of disavowal this expressed itself in humour. It was even guiltily entertaining at times. They were not, apparently, merely protecting themselves. They occasionally found it genuinely funny that they sometimes 'hadn't a clue' about what was going on, and had to get through lessons pretending they were in touch, 'copying up notes' from the board and not knowing what country they were about, for instance. The sense that there was often something appropriate and not just cathartic in their humour seemed not only to suggest that their encounters with secondary school knowledge might often have been unfruitful but also to hint that the base level of their problem was not this or that text or concept and its difficulty, but the whole of the relation between them and their own learning.

Many teachers will have arrived at this conclusion, or rather premise. It is a basic stress in Douglas Barnes' influential paper 'Language in the secondary classroom',[1] and in his book *From Communication to Curriculum*,[2] and his outlook colours much that follows. But to try to emphasize the teaching relation, rather than look at knowledge or pupils separately and in isolation, seems difficult, particularly when the thrust of efforts to remedy problems connected with children's encounters with 'academic' school knowledge seems often to lie in new remedial programmes – courses in reading skills, for example – that are added to existing curricula. It seems less often urged that attention could be paid at the level of the school itself, to the nature of particular pupils' negotiations with the particular talk, reading, worksheets and question papers that are offered them there.

I directed my attention to precisely this issue during a period of eighteen months or so when I was able to work as a non-teaching researcher in a large mixed comprehensive school. 'The' issue itself, of course, is hardly formulable in a precise way, and certainly at the beginning of my researcher time in the school I was aware only that school subject languages seemed to be, in certain obscure respects, rather too frequently unavailable to those who encountered them. Even so, such an awareness, however nebulous it might appear to those who prefer issues clearly stated from the start, was quite enough as a personal incentive. Moreover, to attempt to pin down a line of interest prematurely might have meant that the research undertaken in the school where I did not teach would be less continuous with the earlier informal enquiries conducted as part of routine school teaching. This, I think, made it a more practical enterprise, but not only that. I should also argue that the theoretical suggestions are as a result grounded in an acquaintance with – and a commitment to – the practice of teaching in a way in which not all educational theory is grounded, and that the practical orientation latent in the observer's stance makes for a view which is overall more theoretical rather than less. In other words, a tight relation between practising and theorizing conduces both to good practice and to good theory.

Perhaps for this reason it would be as well to indicate where, in this book, the fieldwork – in the sense of 'formal research period' – begins and ends, since there is a short passage at the beginning, and a chapter at the end, which derive from teaching rather than 'doing research'. The remedial work already referred to was, as I made clear, from lessons of my own. The worksheets discussed in the first part of the introductory chapter were some I found on staffroom coffee tables in schools I taught in. The 'routine lesson' which is described in the second part of the introductory chapter is the first account drawn from the research school itself, and was in fact one of the first lessons observed there. The whole of the rest of the book, up to the final chapter, is a study of what occurred in lessons and conversations in the research school, and of the text-books, worksheets and question papers I was very freely given or allowed to see. Two episodes of observation in a remedial class turned into something like teaching; these are the narratives about B in Chapter 4. Apart from this, I did no teaching in the research school. The last chapter, on 'dialogue', is, however, an attempt to pay reflexive attention to some teaching of my own in a different school. It tries to take note of what went wrong – some of the things that went wrong at least – in a piece of 'open' enquiry. It seemed not only appropriate to return to teaching from watching, but also fair to the teachers whose work had been scrutinized critically to discard any residual presumption of having special powers of detachment.

This is, therefore, a teachers' book, written by a schoolteacher for schoolteachers; it suggests that teachers need to look afresh at what they do, not primarily through the lens of a theory of learning or philosophical persuasion that has been gathered outside the classroom and brought to it, but through their own undervalued and under-used intuitive skills and their empathizing observation

xiv THE LANGUAGE GAP

of children learning – or not learning. It starts from the sense that features which are accepted by teachers as being natural expressions of the way language is handled for learning are often better questioned; what seems to be clear may be in shadow. The body of the book then consists essentially of an attempt to describe the teaching relation as it seemed to express itself to one observer through the way pupils negotiated with books, talk, worksheets and so on. It is not an attempt to describe the school at work in any broad or rounded way. Most of the lessons and work described come from the lower end of the school, and there are no lessons in PE, modern languages or drama. And since I tried to portray the narrative structure of what happens in classrooms, I have drawn on relatively few lessons. This, and the focus on aspects of the teaching relation, means that there is no attempt to convey the novelist's or documentary-maker's dimensions of school reality. Missing from the account, therefore, are many things that are warm and vital about the school. It might seem in some ways a mean and curmudgeonly picture unless these restrictions of focus are allowed for. What follows is therefore essentially a series of views of learning seen through the same preoccupation, views that are intended, like walking round a building, to gather towards one apprehension, not be merely repetitive.

## References

1 D. Barnes, 'Language in the secondary classroom', in D. Barnes, J. Britton and H. Rosen (eds), *Language, the Learner, and the School* (Harmondsworth, Penguin, 1969).
2 D. Barnes, *From Communication to Curriculum* (Harmondsworth, Penguin, 1975).

# 1
# INTRODUCTORY

**Routine questions**

Boys and girls in school meet knowledge in various ways. Not the
least common encounter, significant for their careers in school and
their futures beyond it, is with written questions. For example,
this question was given to some fourth-year pupils in a comprehensive school in which I taught:

> Define ten of the following terms, giving as many details as
> possible:
> (a) Hypothesis
> (b) Pre-coded questions
> (c) Pilot study
> (d) Culture
> (e) Social structure
> (f) Hierarchy
> (g) Embourgeoisement
> (h) Stratification

   (i)   Peer group
   (j)   Patrilineal
   (k)  Socialization
   (l)   Conditioned
  (m)  Subliminal advertising
   (n)  Infant mortality
   (o)  Demography.

The fourth-year pupils' view of the question might be that it was easy or difficult, fair or unfair, and so on. The teachers who set it might say it was intended to test their grasp of certain key ideas, to stretch them, or give the hardworking but slow pupil a chance, and so on. They might also say, self-critically, that there was too much to do in the time given, or that some of the ideas were dealt with in lessons rather sketchily.

These hypothetical but familiar perspectives on the question, even when they are critical, seem to take for granted that it is a natural expression of the relation between a particular piece of learning and particular learners. Those outside the particular teaching relation might well see the question differently in some ways, but still see it as essentially 'natural'. Parents might perhaps be impressed by the ideas their children can handle, and other teachers might note how some concepts overlap with areas in their own subjects, or some styles of questioning seem to be common to various subjects.

And yet, if the question were discussed casually over coffee in any secondary school staffroom, it is quite likely that its natural, taken-for-granted status would not be merely endorsed; it might well be put in question in some way. A certain unease about the 'difficulty' of the terms or the ideas might surface. English teachers might ask whether children need to learn definitions at all. A sceptic might express doubt as to whether this mode of questioning ultimately issues from an egalitarian concern to make academic knowledge accessible to everyone. A sociology teacher, in a reflexive moment, might wonder whether the teacher had written questions with a sociologist's special awareness of the social meaning of what he has done, or just 'written some questions'.

Quite informally, the question might thus be moved from a context of thought where it seems merely natural, to a context in which its naturalness is no longer taken for granted. Differing viewpoints emerge about what the question does or implies, or is an example of, or is connected with, and so on. Its 'meaning' becomes somewhat problematic, discoverable – if at all – only by seeing it in relation to other features and issues. And, of course, in the process of looking at its relation to other features or issues, these also become somewhat problematic.

Thus, a natural view would accept pupils' performance on the question as simply revealing their ability. A more critical perspective, having noted the 'difficulty' of the language, might ask whether it does not rather work to hide how pupils might think and what they can do. The notion of their capacities, which in the natural commonsense attitude is seen as being revealed by answers to such questions, thus itself becomes problematic.

Of course, there is no presumption that putting features of language use in question in this way necessarily leads to the uncovering of some concealed truth about them, only that a shift away from 'the natural attitude of commonsense', in which we suspend 'doubt concerning the existence of the outer world and its objects' and 'the possibility that the world could be otherwise than as it appears',[1] makes such uncovering possible. It therefore seems important to confront the most routine features of school learning and consider them as if routine descriptions and characterizations did not exhaust their meaning, as if, in some respects, they could be other than they appear to be or are said to be. The kind of casual remark over coffee that I have referred to may be important in so far as it temporarily shelves assent to institutional definitions of what constitute appropriate questions, pieces of text, contents, concepts, and so on, and creates the possibility of seeing things in less taken-for-granted ways. And it does seem to be the routine feature in isolation which most often draws comment, rather than larger matters like courses, theories, and general aims and the like. Worksheets, texts, teachers' talk inside and outside lessons, children's talk and writing are all subjected to comment, which may either endorse taken-for-granted, natural perspectives, or seek for other less visible meanings.

What meanings or interpretations might then be given to the following questions, first in the natural attitude that takes them for granted, then in some other perspective? They are drawn from a twenty-five-question mock 'O'-level paper, set in a different comprehensive school.

> Why would a marriage with a 'hen-pecked' husband *not* demonstrate symmetry?
> How do sexual relations strengthen a marriage?
> What are the *TWO* main interpretations of 'respect for life'?
> How can marriage cure a person's inner loneliness?

Sixteen questions are about marriage, so that one interpretative comment on the question paper may be that it is a way of finding out whether boys and girls have developed certain helpful attitudes to sexuality and marriage. One might also say that it is necessary that schools attend to these things, and handle with sensitive concern issues like loneliness, respect, 'mutuality', and so on. Moreover, to ask these questions in the way other questions are asked in school helps to give the subject credibility.

At the same time the paper will produce other meanings for other readers. Some might ask about the difficulty of ideas like 'symmetry' or 'inner loneliness'. English teachers might ask whether children need to learn definitive views about how sex helps marriage, or nagging doesn't. A sceptic might express doubt as to whether this mode of questioning ultimately issues from a humanizing concern to make religious knowledge available to all those who do not have it. A religious education teacher, in a quiet moment, might wonder whether the teacher has spoken about the religious and moral life in terms that sufficiently respect it.

In response to such feelings of disquiet, reasons could be produced, explaining the need for papers like these to be in the form they are because of the way syllabuses and exams are and the way university entrance requirements are, and, perhaps, the way pupils are. This itself might be seen as a way of taking for granted the relations between examining bodies, schools and the universities. It might be pointed out that teachers in various ways contribute to the work of examining bodies – by devising Mode 2 and Mode 3 courses, for instance – so that the relation between boards and teachers is not a one-way influence. In this way different perspectives are produced which take the question paper out of its natural context, as something with self-evident meaning.

I shall pursue one kind of question further, since it was put in different form by some teachers reading the paper. They asked, in effect, whether the questions did not somehow reveal a view of fourth-year pupils as unlikely to learn or think productively about sex, harmony in marriage, respect for life, and so on, except through some pre-cast conceptual scheme that essentially tells them about such things; and whether that view does not entail assuming that children are not able to conduct their own moral searches or grasp the basic intellectual purposes of religious education.

## A routine lesson

At about the time the teachers put these questions, I observed a lesson – one of the first in the research school – which in some ways seemed to point to the issues they had raised. Second-year pupils discussed with their teacher the question: 'Why is there so much evil and suffering in the world today?' Two days later I talked about it with two girls (C and R). Almost immediately C said that she felt they'd 'needed a few days to think about it. It was too serious a question just to do like that.' R said, 'She only gave us two minutes. It's a hard question . . .'. They argued about whether they wrote what they really thought – C did, R did not. They also felt that a teacher of RE should 'see their doubts', and not propagandize – 'go on about women's lib and evolution', both suspect, apparently. 'She dismisses you . . . she tells you things are wrong . . . you *can't* get things wrong in RE.' I was not alert enough at the time to ask what she meant, perhaps through assuming that children of that age are not likely to mean a great deal by such a remark, and that it referred to marks, tests, and so on. In retrospect, it suggests not only a capacity for true seriousness and a willingness to exhibit it, but an impressive clarity about the purpose of their work in RE. Their insistence that doubts are important, propaganda irrelevant, and being wrong impossible, is a version of their work imbued with a natural gravity and intellectual self-respect.

Somehow the lesson had not seemed to acknowledge the possibility of such seriousness. The question was written on the board at the beginning of the lesson and then some administrative matters were mentioned, to do with work marked and work missing: 'Does David E exist? He's only got one mark this term. He'll get two E's for his assessment.' The homework was to finish all unfinished work. The teacher also had to write end-of-term assessments in the pupils' homework report books. Then she said, after the talk about homework but before doing assessments, 'Close your books. Put down your pens. Don't pick them up till I tell you – I'm waiting for pens to go down.' She played the tape of a song about news, and then paraphrased it orally, commenting on the general depressingness of the news: 'After quarter of an hour you turn off – yuk.' Then she said, 'Now, I'm going to ask you a tough question', and read aloud the question she had written on the board. 'When I give you your books back, make sure the play's finished – then I want you to write down what you think – no talking.' A brief half-minute of quiet followed. 'Right, no talking from anyone, thank you. . . . Right, get on quietly please. . . . I'm not telling you again, no talking.' She then began to move round the room, writing in the assessments.

R wrote, at this point, 'I think the reason there is evil and suffering in the world is because of what Adam and Eve did. They rejected God as their master . . .'. But she remarked two days later, in the conversation with C, 'It wasn't me anyway. . . . I write what she wants us to write.'

The lesson continued with pupils writing and teacher circulating doing assessments.

P1:  Miss, shall . . .
T:   I want you to put down what you think is the answer.
P1:  About the future?
T:   No. I want you to say only why you think that there is so much evil and suffering in the world today. . . . Boys, I said I want your ideas not your neighbour's.

(Two or three minutes later the assessment-round was completed.)

T: Now, tell me what kind of things you've written down.
P2: People wanting more money.
P3: People demanding their rights.
   (The teacher wrote these on the board.)
T: More, please.
P4: To teach us good from bad.
T: You mean . . . we disobey . . . you mean man's disobedience to God . . . is that what you mean?
P4: Yes.
   (Pause)
T: Come on, girls.
P5: People fight for what they haven't got.
T: Well, that's covered in the first. . . . Come on . . . oh dear, not a patch on yesterday's class.
P6: Terrorist groups.
P7: Guerrillas.
   (All these contributions were written on the board.)
P8: Governments keeping money.
T: [Indistinct]
P9: God teaching us a lesson.
   (c. ten-second pause)
T: Come on.
P10: Revenge.
T: Good one.
P11: Vandalism.
P12: Racial discrimination.
T: OK, now, pens down. Listen hard. All the people who gave me those answers, out of all of them, not one answered my question – WHY? What you've done is given an accurate breakdown, but you haven't told me WHY! Clare got nearest.

Had the earlier mock exam questions been written by this teacher, and not by someone else in a different school, one might have seen the meaning of the written questions as somehow connected with the style of the lesson. Even allowing for the distraction of assessments, for possible tiredness, or the inevitable off-form lesson, there seem to be certain resemblances between them – in particular in the way that, despite the maturity of reflection that two 12-year-old pupils can bring to such issues, pupils are implicitly invited to contribute very little to the discussion from their own stores of self-awareness. But perhaps the fact that the resemblance – if it is admitted – is between practices in different schools makes it more suggestive, and allows one to ask whether there may not be discernible certain basic similarities about the way knowledge is handled in different contexts which are not clearly seen because they too are part of teaching's natural, taken-for-granted world.

One feature of this world that is frequently commented on is the relative isolation of teachers in classrooms. Just as routine, but less often noted, is that questions relating to learning and its innermost workings tend not to be the most urgent professional concerns of teachers or their superiors. Merely to teach can even mean somehow, by an odd paradox, not to be noticed as a teacher. Colin Lacey, for example, describes how an anonymous young classroom teacher was transformed into a respected public personality by assuming responsibility for a judo team.[2] If this image is writ large, there is, on the one hand, the relatively remote habitat of the classroom and the infrequently observed behaviour there of teacher and pupils, and, on the other, the close and familiar public world of discipline and exam results and the things the comprehensive stands for in social terms – games, exchange visits, discos, parent association functions, drama and music presentations, charity efforts, and so on. It can come to seem that the question of how, in a particular school, pupils actually do learn and how they cope with school subjects lies in shadow somewhere in a well-lit world.

Part of the teacher's natural outlook may be that questions of learning are always important in the life of the school: curriculum reform takes place, departmental policies are carefully thought out, teachers are more professional than they used to be, pupils are seen as individuals and their progress carefully monitored. It seems to follow that how pupils actually learn and confront knowledge must be under detailed and continuous scrutiny.

To sense how much truth there might be in such an outlook, it seems necessary first to see it as a framework of assumptions, and in so doing step outside it. One then might look at 'the learning that takes place in classrooms' without assuming *a priori* that something called 'learning' is taking place, so that even if it is – assuming that 'it' is describable and recognizable – one may see it more clearly.

I shall try to look at some examples of school learning from the standpoint of a different presupposition, which is that routine features of language use have meanings which are not self-evident, but that parts of these meanings may become available when single features are seen in relation to other features, and set in a context of how knowledge is customarily handled within a particular kind of teaching relation. It seems necessary to begin with, and stick close to, examples, to narratives of lessons and their culmination or continuation in questions, essays, worksheets, and so on, and also to grasp something of how pupils and teachers see these things.

# References

1 A. Schutz and T. Luckmann, *The Structures of the Life-World*, trans. R. M. Zaner and H. T. Engelhardt (London, Heinemann, 1974), p. 36.
2 Colin Lacey, *The Socialization of Teachers* (London, Methuen, 1977), p. 148.

# 2
# MEETING AN IDEA

## Artesian wells

The first two narratives, which deal with how pupils meet one particular idea – the artesian water notion – at two levels in the school, attempt a number of ways of looking at the encounter in order to come to some sense of its difficulty for pupils, and of the general quality of their involvement with it. This seems to necessitate treatment at some length: the language of textbook and worksheet, the teacher's own talk, pupils' comprehension, the register terms of the topic, pupils' own views about their grasp of it, and so on, all seem important. And since the subject is geography it seems to raise in almost dramatic fashion the question of the relation between subject language and the external empirical world that pupils negotiate with as it is coded and processed in their own language.

I shall look initially at the first-year work, which was on the Great Artesian Basin, Australia. The first lesson I observed was the second devoted to this topic. A worksheet had been given out the day before and the class (twenty-nine mixed-ability first years) had to 'use the notes in the textbook' to describe how artesian wells work. The artesian principle was re-explained orally before they began. The teacher described the drawing on the board, which was reproduced on the worksheet, as a 'cross-section', and compared it with a cut sandwich-cake. He said there were two kinds of rock: one with 'large spaces between the grains . . . like a sponge', called 'porous' rock (this word was written on the board and appeared in both the worksheet and the textbook). In the other kind the grains were close together and water did not 'get into it'. He went on to describe the subterranean movement of water. All this was revision of work done in the previous lesson, and my notes refer to the teacher's 'very clear explanation' and the 'very clear worksheet'.

The teacher then described how the clouds lose their moisture before they reach the artesian basin, comparing their drying-out with clothes on a line in the wind: 'Will there be a lot of moisture or a little?' His tone was colloquial: 'What he [a farmer] does is drill a hole. . . . What's going to happen if there's a dry summer?' There was mention of 'artesian' and 'sub-artesian water', and of the 'Eastern and Western Highlands'.

To some extent, then, the written language of the textbook was supported by oral explanation which drew on the pupils' real world ('sponge', 'clothes drying'); this talk was colloquial in idiom and easy in tone. There were signs, in short, of an oral style that spoke directly to his audience.

Afterwards, I talked to a boy who had not been very attentive, doodling during some of the explanation and thumbing through the textbook, though he said he 'listened' for the last half. I asked him questions about the textbook and worksheet language. He thought 'the rainfall is light' meant it came down 'gently'; he was unsure about 'pastures', but thought the 'plants were poor' because 'there wasn't much water'. When I asked whom it would matter to, he said 'farmers', because they 'can't feed cattle'. When I asked if he could draw a simple sketch of the kind of reservoir that was referred to, he drew the following, with the strata flat.

*Figure 1*

He then altered it to:

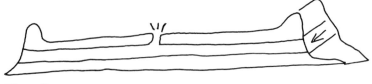

*Figure 2*

He referred to pressure, but 'wasn't sure what caused it', and was not sure what 'porous' or 'sub-artesian' meant.

Evidently, though he gave me what my notes referred to as a 'coherent explanation' of some aspects of the artesian concept (which did not include a view of how the pressure was caused), he could not handle some of the key terms, nor the written passage in which they were embedded. I wondered how far such kinds of difficulty presented themselves for other pupils.

Using some of the questions I had discussed with him, which had been based on the passage picked by the teacher to provide pupils with help for their explanation, I drew up the set of questions below. They were given to seventy-five pupils in a block of three first-year mixed-ability classes, comprising one of the four all-ability vertical divisions of the year-group, all taught by the same teacher using the same syllabus, worksheets and textbook.

In your book about Australia, there were some sentences about the Great Artesian Basin. They are typed out underneath, with some questions. Read them through, and then answer the questions.

'The Great Artesian Basin is about twelve times the size of England. Rainfall is light and pastures are poor. Water is obtained from artesian wells. Water enters the porous rock and seeps through to the lower part of the basin, where it is trapped between the layers of non-porous rock, turning the porous rock into a reservoir.'

*Questions*

1 Which of these four sentences, A, B, C, or D, has the same meaning as 'the rainfall is light'?
   (A) Not much rain falls there.
   (B) Rain falls gently there.
   (C) The rain glitters in the sun when it falls.
   (D) There is a lot of rain there.
2 What are *pastures*? Why are the pastures 'poor'?
3 What does 'porous' mean?
4 *What* 'turns the porous rock into a reservoir'? (Read the last sentence for the answer.)
5 What does 'non-porous' mean?
6 Try to do a simple sketch of the kind of reservoir that is mentioned.
7 What kind of people in Australia do you think would be specially interested in artesian wells?
8 Has finding water in dry places anything to do with artesian wells?
9 Can water ever get through rock?
10 Name a place where you could find artesian wells.
11 Do you think the Great Artesian Basin is bigger or smaller than England?
12 Is it bigger or smaller than the county you live in?
13 What do you think 'pressure' is? Has it got anything to do with artesian wells?

The questions were intended not so much to test the pupils' grasp of the artesian concept as to explore the extent to which they successfully handled the kind of language in which the concept was embedded. It involved testing their grasp of bits of language that do not seem intrinsically technical nor to belong to the register of geography (terms such as 'rainfall' and 'pasture').

The boy I had interviewed had taken 'rainfall is light' in the sentence 'rainfall is light and pastures are poor' to mean 'it falls gently': so did twenty-six other first years. The responses to Question 1 were as follows: (A)42, (B)26, (C)3, and (D)4. The (B) answers were produced, presumably, by pupils' attending to their own experience of 'light' rainfall, and they might have been thrown back on this because the notion of measuring amounts of rainfall – and hence the specialist sense here of 'light' – is not familiar to them.

Responses to Questions 1 and 2 together produced a small paradox. Ten of the pupils who answered (B), (C) or (D) in Question 1 none the less referred to small amounts of rainfall when answering Question 2. It might be thought that pupils who explain 'correctly' in Question 2 why the pastures are poor would choose (A) in Question 1, on the assumption that if they correctly explain 'the cause' of the poor pasturage they would choose a meaning for 'rainfall is light' that expresses the causal relation they know. But this is to assume that their successful handling of one piece of the language surrounding 'artesian' means that they 'understand' it, and well enough to deploy it successfully in other contexts – because they appear to know the reason for the poor pastures, as expressed in the answer 'rainfall is light', they know the meaning of 'rainfall is light'. In fact, all but one of the Question 2 answers that demonstrate this paradoxical response avoid the term 'light', and use expressions like 'little rain', 'no rain', 'not much rain' or 'little rainfall'. They appear to have grasped the (causal) import of the whole sentence without knowing what the first half means in isolation; their grasp of the whole appears to precede their grasp of the parts.

A similar bias towards their own empirical experience (assuming that 'light' does recall empirical situations) might account for why twenty-six pupils said 'no' when asked, 'Has finding water in dry places anything to do with artesian wells?' It may be that 'find' suggests 'come upon accidentally', or even that 'dry' contradicts 'light rainfall'. They do not seem to sense that, within this content, in the complex of language round 'artesian', 'drill' (a word they use very frequently, in the drawings for Question 6, for example) is roughly synonymous with 'find', and 'dry' with 'light rainfall'. Their own real-life empirical meanings for 'find' seem to be recalled in such sentences as: 'Yes, it could have if water was leaking from a hole in the ground.' It may also be that for some pupils 'drill' is not a human activity and so not an aspect of 'finding': 'Water pressure itself could "drill" a hole through rock.'

Questions 3 and 9 were framed with a view to possibly producing paradoxical answers. 'What does "porous" mean?' is a typical 'checking they know the meaning of terms' question. 'Can water ever get through rock?' then uses a phrase that might well be used in answer to Question 3. There were two true contradictions, where pupils used the expression 'go (or get) through' in Question 3, then said explicitly, 'No, it can't ever get through rock' in Question 9. Six other pupils implied a distinction between 'sink *into*', 'soak into', 'holds', and so on in Question 3, and 'get through' in Question 9. These apparently paradoxical responses were consistent in keeping 'through' for passing 'out of' one stratum into another. In this sense of 'through', if water goes 'through' porous rock, it goes out of it, into the non-porous layer. One pupil, using this meaning in labelling a diagram, put 'POROUS – stored (doesn't soak through)' and then 'NON-POROUS – soaks through'. Very logical, and an instance of what words can do when cut loose from their empirical mooring. (Many other pupils talked of 'porous' as meaning 'hold in', and so on; I only mention here the expressions for 'porous' in Question 3 that accompany a 'no' to Question 9.)

This restricted sense for 'through' is interesting, but puzzling. It overlooks the fact that for water to be *held* in, it has to *get* in, and so pass through rock. Thus it seems to envisage water as being in the rock to start with. It is worth noting here how potent everyday phrases like 'get through' and 'soak in' must be as a means of recalling a broad range of specific empirical situations. Whether or not the 'soak into' situations are kept distinct, as empirical types, from the 'get through' situations, there is the possibility anyway that the terms' very potency may disturb the distinction by later recalling what is inappropriate. This may be one reason why teachers tend to distrust the use of pupils' own language for describing, or embodying, technical concepts. The potency and ambiguity of everyday language are really one and the same thing. Because of its very plasticity, ordinary language perhaps needs continuously to be resituated, to be made meaning-ful by being re-placed in empirical situations. When this empirical relocation is, as here, not available, language seems to take on a formalistic life of its own. Some pupils, for example, when told that porous rock is 'sponge-like', push the analogy further than they would be likely to if they handled chalk or sandstone, and write that such rock is also 'spongy', 'looks like a sponge', and 'is soft'. Though 'soft' is geologically appropriate for 'chalk', it will sum up different and inappropriate everyday empirical situations, unless the relative 'softness' of chalk is also given an empirical dimension, and hence a meaning.

The absence of empirical support for language within geogra-phy might then be responsible for the fact that the use of everyday language tends to exhibit 'empirical bias'; that is, pupils will employ such plastic everyday expressions in terms of real-life situations they know, rather than in terms of the formal concepts they are only beginning to grasp. The diagrams drawn for Ques-tion 6 help to make this clear. One boy wrote, persuasively: 'The water seeps through the porous rock and because the non-porous rock does not let water through the water collects and forms a reservoir.' As a piece of complex thinking-in-language this was coherent; the teacher presumed he understood, thinking of the reservoir as formed 'in the porous rock', yet his drawing, shown below, shows that this 'through' is 'through and beyond'. Non-porous rock allows water to enter to form a reservoir, but not to 'go through'.

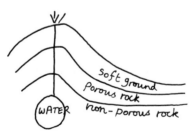

*Figure 3*

The language is appropriate, but the diagram shows an inappro-priate empirical projection for it. There are two categories where one has been used (soft and porous), and the drilling is done from the highest point. The reservoir, in non-porous rock, collects, with an unempirical neglect of gravitation, to form a balloon – not a puddle-shaped thing.

In other diagrams, the pupils' empirical images for 'holds' are also revealed as inappropriate. One boy wrote, 'Porous means rock that holds water.' His drawing reveals this:

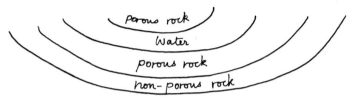

*Figure 4*

His slip (perhaps he half-recalls the phrase 'trapped between layers of non-porous rock') is crucial, but he seems to have no empirical awareness to draw on that would alert him to it. Three other pupils also drew this version.

For a third version, 'porous lets water through' and 'trapped between layers of non-porous rock' seems to produce an uncomfortable compromise:

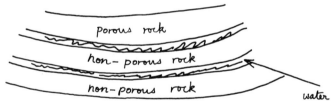

*Figure 5*

A variant of the following occurred three times:

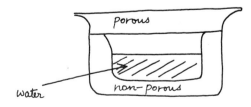

*Figure 6*

One of these three was oddly labelled 'water soaking through non-porous to stop at porous rock'.

Six drawings out of the twenty-seven suggest an inappropriate empirical projection for the language; a further three (Figure 6), envisaging a cavernous gap between strata, produce a central and gratuitous feature. As a group they exhibit the consequences for language of presuming that appropriate language points to the appropriate 'facts' of the empirical world.

## The 'difficulty' of the written text

I shall now consider some linguistic features of the passage quoted earlier, as these might relate to its difficulty. This is not to imply, objectivistically, that experienced difficulty inheres in bits of language, but to point to features that for those pupils at that time seemed not to be grasped.

'Artesian', in the lessons I saw and in the worksheets and text-book selections covered, was not related to 'Artois'; while not creating difficulties, this might serve to mystify slightly. 'Basin', a crucial metaphor, sums up the kind of topographic knowledge that, to judge from pupils' language and drawings, they often did not possess. 'Rainfall', as a quantifying notion, presumes knowledge of a complex measuring operation; this knowledge seemed unavailable in the 'gentle' rainfall answers. A well is here not the familiar well of old houses and pictures in story-books, but a more abstract and mechanical principle, as in physics. It thus subsumes, and presupposes the understanding of, both 'pressure' and 'basin'. 'Porous' they find difficult, as we have seen. 'Reservoir' is a familiar word in a new sense, and this might have been troublesome: in fact, almost all the pupils asked to do a sketch successfully produced the worksheet-type of diagram, although teachers had expected sketches of ordinary reservoirs. That this did not happen might be related to the lack of above-ground reservoirs in this part of the country.

The tone of the passage is impersonal in the sense that it is about what happens to water, and human agency is unstressed. Thus, the passive 'is obtained' does not locate the drilling of wells in the context of human need. One other tonal feature, common in worksheets and texts, is the lack of any signal that a new term is to be encountered: the first textbook mention of 'artesian wells', which occurred in the sentence 'water is obtained from artesian wells', was unaccompanied by a signal such as 'these are called'. The absence of this tonal or phatic gesture, small though it is, seems through its frequency to express a reluctance to take the pupils' situation into account.

The word 'pastures' did not occur in the spoken language of the two lessons, or in the worksheets. It is thus part of the subject, but not 'part of the subject' – as much school language may be. How pupils come to cope with such language is an interesting question. Assessment, for instance, which purports to draw on the subject only, may frequently, as here, draw on some kind of 'cultural capital' that lies behind it. In so far as a subject is defined by its routine, conventionalized practice, it will perhaps tend not to see its own inverted commas, to forget that 'geography' presupposes usages, terms and syntactic structures which, while they contribute to defining what geography is, are often anterior to it and certainly wider than it, and as such, of course, they may not be explicitly taught. Here 'pastures' may be available only to pupils who have already derived their knowledge of this bit of geography outside 'geography' from elsewhere. And many pupils were uncertain about 'pastures': 'pastures are where not much rain falls'; 'pastures are bits of green round the reservoirs'; 'pastures are fields where crops are grown'; 'pastures are light rainfall'; 'pastures are bits of wet land – not good because not much rain'.

It seems important to note in passing how well such pupils do cope in this context with an evidently unfamiliar word. Each of the answers I describe as uncertain may also be seen as pointing to some relevance in the complex scheme they are encountering. Thus, they are right in suggesting that 'not much rains falls' or that they are 'bits of wet land', in the sense that they link two ideas appropriately ('pastures' and 'little rain' or 'wet land') though their usages are not assuredly idiomatic. Not knowing 'pastures', they are particularly unlikely to formulate sensible predicates with 'pastures' as subject. Yet they apparently begin the process of fitting a new word into a scheme whose other features are also often strange. It could be seen as a primary success with a complex of technical language.

A final feature of this text that might be noted is the absence of subordinating connectives. The causal implication of 'and' in 'Rainfall is light and pastures are poor' will be noted only by those who already understand the concept well enough to attribute causality to it. Both this kind of dependence on other contexts, and that relating to terms like 'pastures', make it clear that an adequate reading of such a passage may depend on a prior grasp of parts of the concept. It may be as appropriate then to see understanding as a precondition of right reading as to see it the other way round. Rather than 'the' meaning 'of' a passage – as if it inhered in the print on the page – one might speak of a range of attributable meanings, summoned for different readers by different cues in the passage.

What is difficult about the passage, then, is not intrinsic, but a matter of relations, its lack of expressive fit with the purposes and meanings of its readers. It is unlikely, in particular, that such readers as these pupils will bring with them an already formalized, elliptical, concise model of the artesian notion with which to interpret whatever they read because, of course, they are working towards that model, partly through reading. The catch seems to be that here their reading deals precisely with the concise model which they can only yet work towards.

### Other language for artesian

What other language, written or spoken, supported the pupils' attempts to interpret this book language? I have suggested that the spoken language of one lesson had supportive colloquial features. Apparently so. A distinction needs to be drawn, though, between a seemingly supportive feature which is merely an oral paraphrase of the 'abstract', conceptual language used to articulate the model, and features which are genuinely the language of speakers not yet in a position to see a notion in terms of that finished, formalized, elliptical version. The teacher's mention of 'artesian and sub-artesian', of 'Eastern and Western Highlands', his focus on the mechanics of porosity and evaporation and pressure, alongside a relative unconcern for the human location of the problem, suggested an oral gloss that reproduces the features of the finished model, rather than, say, a re-articulation of his own original coming-to-terms with the notion, and certainly rather than an imaginative elaboration or extension of the kinds of language that pupils may be using.

The language of the worksheets also suggests strongly the dependence of its colloquial explanatory features on text which stresses formal features without having moved with the pupils from ordinary to conceptual language. For example: 'Water in the porous layer (aquifer) can be reached, provided that there is sufficient water pressure to push the water up, by an artesian well.' The delayed 'by an artesian well' might account for the drawing shown below, in that the idea of reaching water by means of sinking a well is somewhat dissolved by so separating 'well' from 'reach' that the link may not be perceived, while the idea of 'pushing water up' is emphasized, and then left in isolation in the text and then in the drawing.

*Figure* 7

The worksheet continues: 'This is drilled through the top impermeable layer down to the porous layer.' The water itself, moreover, 'is too salty for irrigation, but can be used for watering huge herds of cattle'. Pupils might well have inferred, from '*pastures* are poor' that the water *was* used for irrigation. And, of course, 'watering cattle' is likely for some to be the same 'watering' as in 'watering the roses'.

'Rainfall' was used in the sense of a quantified amount six times on the first page of a worksheet handed out a week previously. Phrases like 'rainfall between 1000 and 1500 millimetres a year' were read by all the pupils. The same worksheet deals in these terms with the climatic context of artesian wells: 'In this area the forests thin out into TROPICAL GRASSLAND known as SAV-ANNA. To the south-east of this area, south of the TROPIC of CAPRICORN, the temperatures are a little cooler and in this region the grasslands are known as TEMPERATE GRASS-LANDS.'

The model of the artesian concept seems clear. Its main features are: discontinuous layers of rock; a binary division into porous and non-porous; water travelling underground and accumulating; pressure forcing water upwards; a hole being drilled (a 'well' *or* 'a pump'); inadequate or malnutritious grass; and not enough rain.

There is a good deal of mechanics here, and pupils seem to have to take on trust these aspects of the concept. One might argue that it is for Nuffield science to deal with porosity thoroughly, yet there is no need to take such mechanics on trust; children may well have what Barnes calls 'action-knowledge'[1] relating to water movement, percolation, soaking, pressure, and so on. Not to work from this or foreground it is a way of assenting to the articulation of a piece of knowledge in formalistic terms.

The model's formalistic character emerges clearly in relation to 'porous'. A binary division into porous and non-porous is an abstraction from the varying degrees of porosity or permeability exhibited by different rocks. Children who have not gathered their own experiences of such differentially soakable rocks and soils are at this point, in dealing with porous *or* non-porous, dealing only with language. The same applies to the levels and boundaries between strata. The empirical experience of boundaries in strata is potentially available, and is less a matter of such sharp discontinuity than the diagram indicates. The geological diagram, if it is not derived from some empirical experience, is 'abstract' without being abstract*ed* by individual children. This formalistic language may well be the *object* of children's thinking in respect, similarly, of wells, pumps, pastures and rainfall; and I mean here only when 'they know the meaning' of the words.

The implication of discontinuity in the word 'layers', and made clear especially by the diagrams, is likely to be remedied not empirically but by later written language, if at all. Thus an 'O'-level geology text (Bradshaw, *A New Geology*), inevitably

more specialized in such respects than a geography text, has this
to say about chalk:

> Although the lower layers contain up to half their volume of
> clay and have a greyish colour, the greater majority of the chalk
> is dazzling white in colour with less than 1% of non-calcareous
> material.[2]

Any adult or child who has walked down a chalk scarp with his
eyes open knows this colour shift well enough, but the mundane
truth of it has somehow become annexed to a specialist content
reserved for 16-year-olds, and it has gathered accretions like the
chemistry flavour of 'non-calcareous' and the reference to volume; this, despite the fact that the essential absurdity of implying
severe discontinuity is available to the naked eye.

Is the pupils' language a support or remedy? I have suggested
that half-apprehensions of the artesian concept are inferrable from
what pupils write in their own words, out of their own experience. Yet the opportunity to construct a personal model is restricted. The worksheet already referred to set two tasks: the first,
a missing-word exercise, and a sentence–answer group of questions which needed either factual or register-word recall answers:
'What type of vegetation grows in the Mediterranean-type
climate?' The other asked pupils to copy (merely) a diagram and
the sentence, quoted above, beginning 'Water in the porous layer
(aquifer) . . .'.

The exercise books for one of the sets I looked at contained
three short pieces of writing for this topic, all copied or dictated.
There was no small-group discussion. This is clearly extreme –
from the difficult textbook to the 'academic' worksheets, the
narrow writing assignments and the absence of pupil talk. Yet,
though it is unusually dry, this might seem in some ways typical of
the secondary school's way of handling knowledge. Two things,
in particular, might seem typical: one is the model for a topic to
assume the reified character it has here, and for the written
language that explains it to be derived from it, in terms of its
mode of conceptualization, its selection of criterial concerns, and
the restriction to and implicit insistence on register terms. Second
is the relation of pupils' language to this. Their role here is

reduced essentially to the recapitulation of text. Essentially, they have done little else; even their own explanations of the artesian concept have been attempts to attribute meaning to a complex of technical language. And of course through this, in the single sentence–answer questions, in the multiple-choice and missing-word answer questions, their own activity as learners of geography is developing towards, or anticipating, their future role as candidates whose exhibitions of knowing take these forms. The future teacher of geography is perhaps also learning that geography for schoolchildren is essentially a matter of coping with forms of expression, rather than with the relation between them and the empirical world.

## Pupils' views of the language of 'artesian'

These comments may illuminate, and themselves be given substance by, what pupils said in discussions with me. I talked with four first years from a mixed-ability group, having asked the teacher to select 'average to bright' pupils.

Our discussion had been first about the English lesson homework they had to do, which was 'different because you're thinking about it over the weekend, it's fun'. An articulate girl is speaking:

P1:   But with geography or history or maths you haven't got to sort of think about it, you've just got straightforward sums. You know, you just do 'em. An' geography, you know, you've just . . . you haven't really got to think how you know about artesian water. You've just got to look it up in the dictionary or the library or som'ink, just copy it up. You don't have to think 'em you can't think of lots of different ways to write about artesian water because only one way's right . . .

I said I wasn't quite sure what she meant, and her friend (P2) helped me out.

P2:   She said there's only artesian, there's only one thing and it can't be . . . it's right. In English there's a witch and a witch can either be, um, . . . a space witch or a water witch. But artesian water can only be artesian water it can't be anything else . . . you know.

That artesian water 'can only be one thing' which is 'right' and which is 'looked up' and 'copied' suggests that for them the concept exists as a set of language forms, rather than as a way of handling the empirical, everyday world.

I was interested in their confident-sounding use of the phrase 'artesian water'. They had all done artesian water two or three weeks earlier. What was it, then? I wasn't sure, I said.

P3: It's ground water.
P4: It's water which comes out the artesian well and . . . they dig them.
Self: What's an artesian well?
P3: It's water from out the ground.
P2: In Australia they dig the wells because they need the water and it rises through the ground.
Self: Why is it called artesian?
P2: Because it's purified as it comes through the layers of the ground.

It seemed evident as we went on that register phrases like 'ground water' concealed a lack of awareness of how water got into the ground, and that, similarly, 'their own' terms like 'rises [through the ground]' were attempts at finding words of their own to fit in with the technical language.

I wondered if an artesian well was like an ordinary well.

P2: No . . . it's sort of . . . an underground stream.
P3: It's like a sort of underground spring and it's in a sort of hole or something and it builds up into a sort of lake or something like that . . . very slowly.

The 'sort of' expressions perhaps suggest less an uncertainty over what terms to use than an awareness that terms seem not to penetrate to the reality of what is being talked about. In contrast with the girls' earlier confidence, tonally very marked, with 'artesian water' and 'ground water', this might be thought to reveal an intuitive scepticism as to the grounds of such talk.

In the model represented by the teacher's talk, the diagrams and the basin metaphor, what allows the water to rise is 'pressure'. Yet the nature and source of such pressure is apparently inaccessible. I asked how the water 'got out'.

P1: They dig down.

P4: Pressure . . . forcing it up.

Self: Pressure of what? What causes it?

P3: No . . . it's just underground pressure . . . heat or something forcing it up.

Self: Heat perhaps? Is it? If I was in your class and you were four geography teachers together deciding what to do to help me understand . . . what would you say to me? What would you do . . . or draw or . . .?

P4: It depends how we've been taught though.

Self: Yes, OK, it depends how you've been taught.

P2: They're called the basins, the artesian basins, so you'd draw a . . . like a big dip in the ground and the layers of ground and the pressure, 'cos it's only a spring and it goes through the layers of the ground and comes up into this basin and forms up a lake.

(The 'lake' here is above ground, it seems.)

Self: Where does the pressure come from?

P3: Underground.

P4: We haven't been taught that . . .

P2: He didn't ask us . . . he just asked us . . . why it was so important.

P4: What it was . . .

Self: So do you think you know what it is, an artesian well?

P1: Yes, we know what it is, but . . .

P2: We know what it is but we don't know how it's formed . . . sort of thing.

P3: Yea . . . mmm. It's an underground source of water.

Self: Well, aren't all springs underground sources of water, unless . . .?

P3: Well you can get them come [sic] out of rocks, just smash the rocks holding the rock and water.

I returned to 'pressure' again. Where did this pressure come from?

P3:  Well, probably the water's been building up underground, there's nowhere for it to go . . . so it finds a weak spot in the earth's crust and spurts out.

P2:  But we haven't been taught pressure or how it appears. We've just been taught what is artesian water and why it's important in Australia. I put it's important for livestock, you know.

I asked where the water in this area came from if it was a dry area.

P1:  I don't know.

P2:  Well, when it rains it seeps through the layers and sort of forms a lake underground and this is when the spring floats up through the layers . . . it's the natural source of rainwater.

Again, there is the interesting contrast between the uncertain use of a familiar word, 'floats', and the confident return to register in 'the natural source of rainwater'. But the notion of water being conveyed from distant wetter uplands through inclined strata, the notion presupposed in the diagrams, was apparently unavailable. They were forced to find explanations like 'must get big rainstorms' to account for why rain that fell in a 'dry area' was nevertheless enough to produce artesian wells. The model they were using was only part of the teacher's model, and the missing bits were those that might be thought central to 'artesian' – the transporting of water along inclined 'basin'-shaped strata, and the resulting pressure in the central and deep sections. If this formalized model was offered as a simplified account, pupils simplified it further, almost out of existence.

It emerged that the grandmother of one of the girls had been to Australia and she'd said that 'when the rain comes down it really pelts, not a little bit like we have here'. I asked if she'd mentioned this at the time. No. Why didn't she?

P1:   Don't really know.

P4:   It doesn't [indecipherable two (?) words] homework.

P2:   We don't think of that, you don't talk about it.

I asked if sometimes, in other classes as well, there were things they knew about and could mention but didn't, like the girl's grandmother being in Australia and talking about rain.

P3:   You haven't got time to mention them.

Self:   Why haven't you got time?

P2:   Well, there's your homework and you do that at home so when you get to school you do a different work.

Perhaps she meant there would be time at home.

She then expanded on what she said in a way that hints at how influential is teachers' control over definitions of knowledge.

P2:   You don't think it is all that important really, 'cos they're not teaching you it.

Self:   What kind of thing isn't important?

P1:   Like why the water comes out of the earth.
      (This speaker a moment or two later pointed again at time as a factor.)

P2:   You have restricted time in class . . . and the teacher wants to get all the work through.

The peripheral value for pupils of these points of individual contact with subject content – points of entry, even, as they might be considered – emerges in what they say about how such knowledge is seen by others – pupils and teachers. Other pupils would ignore them; teachers would encourage, but in a way that seems nearer to tolerance than positive endorsement. I asked why they wouldn't mention their own bits of knowledge.

P2:   Well, it gives *me* an idea of artesian wells . . . but you don't think it's important to other children. . . . They wouldn't tell you if they knew anything about . . . so why would you tell? . . . you're giving . . .

P3:   Yea, they wouldn't be interested, they'd sit there yawning.

Self:   What about the teacher?

P4:   He'd be quite interested.

P2:    Yea, he'd encourage you to find out about these things.
       He'd say, 'That's good', then he . . . he wouldn't say
       much because he wants you to carry on. But he wouldn't
       put you off by saying you didn't have to find out about that
       . . . he likes you to find out as much as possible.

P2 here is evidently learning to accept without question the
contradiction between the educationist's insistence on the value of
finding things out for yourself and the constraints of working
within courses and timetables: 'he likes you to find out as much as
possible', but 'he couldn't say much because he wants you to
carry on'.


## The 'grammar' of 'artesian'

Wittgenstein makes a distinction which might fruitfully be introduced at this point. He suggests that propositions, or more often
the components of propositions, may be distinguished by use of
the terms 'grammatical' and 'empirical'.[3] An empirical proposition, like 'everybody has a fault', might be falsified by the
discovery of a flawless being, so that its truth-value depends
'partly on the rules of usage of the words contained in them and
partly on the empirical data'. A purely grammatical proposition,
like 'every rod has length', would only be falsifiable if the rules
of usage and the meanings of the words themselves changed.
   This dual feature of propositions makes it possible to treat that
part of an empirical proposition that is to do with its 'grammar'
(in Wittgenstein's sense) as if it were the only part. What looks
like an empirical statement − 'chalk is porous' − can effectually
come to be treated as a grammatical proposition. The proposition
is empirical because chalk can be defined independently of porosity;
porosity isn't entailed by chalk, as length is by rod. Like 'everyone has a fault' it is logically falsifiable; for instance, the frozen
chalk landscapes of immediately post-glacial times were presumably not porous, but despite this, if lessons on chalk landscapes,
artesian wells and so on handle statements like 'chalk is porous' as
if they needed no empirical anchoring or corroboration, such
statements will tend to become purely grammatical, and the

child's grasp of the concept 'artesian' will consist in the ability to deal with the grammatical complex clustering round that word. Any empirical knowledge the child might possess tends to be beside the point.

This may also be what Merleau-Ponty meant when he referred to the possibility that language might come to be 'placed before language'.[4] In this context, a film of language which is apparently grammatical, but is in fact formalistic, might come to be placed 'before' a language which is certainly grammatical but which is rescued from formalism by virtue of its having kept in close touch with those empirical realities that the child encounters. Such a grammar is formal, not formalistic.

Merleau-Ponty observes that in such a formalistic situation, 'I have the feeling of dealing only with words' and 'expression has failed'.[5] His analysis of this impasse – which seems to me especially pertinent here – proceeds from a distinction he makes between the 'constitutive' features of language on the one hand, and the 'sedimented' or 'constituted' language on the other.[6] The latter is 'the language the reader brings with him', or 'language as an institution', an example of which is the ('constituted') complex of language that surrounds the ideas of artesian and porous.

The constitutive features of language are those which 'establish a new signification in a linguistic apparatus constructed with old signs'.[7] They do so, moreover, on two distinct levels: in literary language and in everyday speech. The latter emphasis is what seems particularly important here. If everyday speech has 'constitutive' features analogous to those of literature, such speech is a crucial source of meaning. Traditionally, in pedagogic contexts pupils' everyday speech is not considered constitutive. It is not in what pupils actually say and write that the teacher looks for knowledge, but in the degree of correspondence between what they say and write and the constituted forms.

Merleau-Ponty, on the other hand, stresses the heuristic value of everyday speech. In an insight which seems of special relevance here, he observes that we characteristically forget the 'power' of constitutive language: 'If we concede language only its secondary [i.e. constituted] function, it is because we presuppose the first as given, because we make language depend on an awareness of truth when it is actually the vehicle of truth. In this way we put language before language.'[8] If schooling did continuously neglect the constitutive power of everyday speech, and made language depend on achieved awareness of truth rather than saw truth as emerging from the language produced in a particular situation, we should often find a sterile confrontation with the constituted language forms of subjects, and an absence of negotiations that reconstitute such language through constitutive everyday speech. Language would in this sense be 'placed before language', the constituted before the constitutive. I have suggested that such a relation to language may be pupils' experience in the work on artesian wells, that they deal with 'language placed before language', and consequently have the feeling of dealing only with words.

I have followed Merleau-Ponty in characterizing such a relation as 'formalistic'. It seems important to note the theoretical emphasis that he suggests is necessary to undercut the hold of formalism. He remarks that 'the true opposite of such formalism is a good theory of speech.'[9] Such 'speech' embraces the constitutive 'speech' of the great novel, as well as the 'everyday' kind; indeed, Merleau-Ponty appears to view them as continuous. Such language is not 'to communicate with', not technicist; it 'must be distinguished from any technique or device'. It is essentially 'a return to the speaking subject, to my contact with the language I am speaking'.[10] Such a return to an existential contact with 'my' language, which seems to be the central movement in Merleau-Ponty's phenomenology of language, might well be proposed for the pupils who have attempted to deal with the grammar of the artesian concept. They seem to be involved in a confrontation with constituted forms that denies 'my contact with the language I am speaking'.

## The grammar of 'porous': and a fourth-year lesson

What I am suggesting has happened so far, then, in relation to the artesian notion is that pupils have encountered a grammar – or, rather, fragments of a grammar – which is shorn of empirical support, and that the absence of a constitutive involvement by pupils through their own everyday language, which would necessarily draw on the empirical realities they know, has made their negotiations with language profoundly formalistic.

These theoretical distinctions do seem to sharpen the sense of what is taking place. In particular, perhaps, they help to explain why, as pupils return to the topic of porosity higher up the school, there seems to occur a variant of the same impasse. The relation between pupils' constitutive everyday language and the constituted forms seems to be the same, and difficulties with the grammar of 'porous' seem to persist. This may occur because the established habit of not (in school) continuously returning to the physical reality of porosity has slowly drained the empirical content of propositions, so that while they still look empirical, they are handled essentially as if they were merely grammatical.

One of the difficulties seems to be an incoherence in the grammar itself. In the Penguin *Dictionary of Geology*,[11] this classification is used:

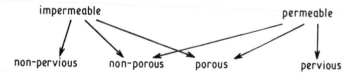

*Figure 8*

In this version of the grammar porous rock like clay can be non-permeable; water does not pass 'through' it into other strata, but is held 'in' it. 'Porous' rock can therefore be either permeable or non-permeable. In the first-year textbook 'porous' and 'non-porous' are opposed, but in the worksheet 'porous' and 'impermeable' — in that context empirically appropriate but logically misleading. And presumably, as in chalk downs scenery, which was the local type employed as illustration, the 'impermeable' strata could be 'porous' (clay, in fact, often underlies chalk, and springs occur at the point where they meet). A third-year worksheet opposes 'porous' and 'impervious'; however, a rock can be both impervious and porous, since water can be held in rock that does not possess the 'mechanical discontinuities such as bedding planes, fissures', and so on, that make it pervious. The complex relations between these words can be shown schematically. Arrows represent which linkages of attribute seem to be possible:

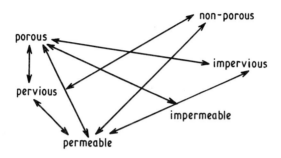

*Figure 9*

One difficulty is that while permeability appears to function as a superordinate notion, in reality it is not; it comprises all that is pervious but not all that is porous. This problem seems to be related to pupils' uncertainties about what 'in' and 'through' mean empirically.

It is also interesting that at the level of the Penguin *Dictionary of Geology* the binary nature of porous–non-porous and permeable–non-permeable can be dropped: there is a 'porosity ratio' (percentage of empty space), and a rock's permeability 'can be measured in darcies'. If one survives enough complex text, it seems that glimpses of a less simplified and more real world are restored. The essential accessibility of such withheld knowledge, and the gratuitous obscurity of the grammar, are made clear by the information that 'porosity ratios' can vary from 1 to 50 per cent and more. One might ask, why not *that*, empirically, to start with? This 'complexity' perhaps only corresponds, after all, to the notions of soakability that children have learned in 'action-knowledge', in their encounters with sand, water, clay, mud, and so on.

A problem in grammar also occurs with 'chalk' and 'limestone'. Limestone is the superordinate term; chalk is one of the limestones. The expressions 'chalk limestone' and 'limestones' (plural) are thus grammatical. Yet a looser usage is common in which 'chalk' stands for 'chalk limestone', and 'limestone' seems to be used of certain limestones only, excluding chalk. This latter 'limestone' is said to have a 'jointed' or block-like structure, to form underground caves, to be found at Ingleborough, or in Derbyshire, and so on. What is important for pupils confined to grammar is that scrupulous grammatical usages do not necessarily seem to exclude looser ones. The BBC book *On The Rocks: A Geology of Britain*, for example, has a chapter on 'Limestones' which is thus scrupulous: 'The white cliffs of Dover are made out of chalk limestone'; and there is a photograph of 'Limestone country – the chalk cliffs of The Seven Sisters, Sussex'.[12] But in this same chapter is a microscope photograph captioned: 'Chalk turning into limestone from North Sea drill core'. In school the usages limestone(s)-including-chalk and limestone-excluding chalk seem to exist side by side. And again, any caution to remember that chalk is really a limestone and that limestones are more varied than the most typical is not an appeal to pupils' experience of the empirical world, but a reminder about further complexities in a not always coherent grammar. That is difficult enough at its most coherent.

Do these matters illuminate the extracts below? The first two are from a fourth-year 'O'-level geography lesson; the third from a conversation I had with the teacher. I include the latter because my own confusion, that of someone who had taken part in several lessons on the topic and once passed 'A'-level geography, seems relevant.

T:     Another important part of the topic is the limestone scenery in Florida. Why is the limestone plateau dry?
P1:   It's porous.
T:     Why is it porous?
P1:   It's got holes in it.
P2:   There's cracks.
P3:   It's made of fossil shells.
T:     That's partly right . . . some limestone is porous . . . it's not really the answer though. . . . It's not complete. . . . Sandstone also –
P1:   Absorbs?

T:  Yes, it does – but it's not a complete answer. If you'd been to Yorkshire or Derbyshire, to the Mendips . . . that's the best kind . . . it's carboniferous rock . . . you'd see it was made of joints. That's one of the features of the drainage there . . . it goes through the limestone joints. Then it flows underground in caves. So the next sub-heading: 'Limestone Scenery' – not in too great detail because we're going to do it again next year.

Not only the pupils' uncertainty but also the teacher's air of handling knowledge to which they have not yet the right key may be related to what has been said above. In the teacher's description of limestone scenery, with its joints and caves, and so on, 'limestone' has the narrower sense. Yet his remark that 'some limestone is porous' abandons this usage for the broad one (in which chalk is a 'limestone'); the 'limestone' of 'limestone scenery' is jointed and thus 'pervious' (and so 'permeable', of course) but not 'porous'. There is no warrant for his phrase 'limestone scenery' if 'some limestone is porous'. The inconsistency seems to derive from the unexplicated inconsistency of the subject's grammar, and is perhaps tolerable only to those who have empirical instantiations for both usages, or those whose skills include the handling of such inconsistencies.

The two usages for 'limestone' make his first question ambiguous, and the pupil's answer – 'It's porous' – would be right for *some* limestone: it is grammatically right for the broad sense, the one perhaps less likely to have been employed in school (possibly in the interest of 'simplicity'). The teacher's question 'Why is it porous?' may be an attempt to check on the meaning of 'porous'; the pupil may be confusing it with 'pervious'. This suspension of judgement as to whether the answer *is* right, seems to be taken for assent to 'It's porous' and to encourage the others, who reply with answers appropriate to porous rock (holes), to pervious rock (cracks), or to both ('made of fossil shells'). The teacher is referring (though he is not using the term) to pervious limestone, but the pupils cannot be sure whether porosity or perviousness is the reason for that particular plateau's dryness. (A further confusion, which became apparent later, is that the teacher uses 'permeable'

– the seeming superordinate term in the Penguin *Dictionary* – for 'pervious' as I use it.)

The teacher's hedging – 'partly right', 'some limestone is porous', 'it's not really the answer' – reflects the dissatisfaction teachers feel when they are not getting the right answer; there seems little to do but wait, or supply it. The dialogue is flawed radically by denial of the constitutive possibilities of the pupils' replies, and here it seems related to a confusion in the subject grammar. There is the uncertainty about which sense of limestone is being employed, and the porous–pervious distinction is left unclear. The last extended teacher contribution may be read as an abandonment of the attempt at dialogue in the grammar, and a return to an exposition that deliberately buries the problems that flawed it. The question of porosity in limestones (and the meanings of both terms) is evaded by making a new distinction amongst limestones, based on value criteria not yet accessible or discussed – 'that's the best kind' – and by re-describing features of this 'best' kind of limestone scenery. Its very interestingness takes the pupils away from a real confrontation with the terms of the question as originally raised: 'Why is the limestone plateau dry?' and 'not going into it in too great detail' preserves the existing uncertainties in grammar. To avoid 'too great detail' implies keeping things simple, but the simplicity of the structure of such a content can be, as here, illusory. It might be rather an immersion in 'detail' which would help restore dialogue, the detail of more careful grammatical explication, and the detail available in the empirical world. Such an immersion would clearly 'slow down' the process of learning the content. However, it is clear that what pupils may be left with at this point is a kind of half-grasp of the arbitrarily highlighted features of limestone scenery, without a sense of either how this fits in the grammar or what it means in empirical terms. As if one remembered an incident in a story without grasping its meaning.

The next extract, which followed closely on the previous one, exhibits the same flaws in dialogue. The teacher is still talking about limestone scenery, with its jointed rocks and underground caves, as in the Mendips or Yorkshire, and here with special reference to Florida:

(1)T:  Why are there underground streams? In many rocks it percolates through. Why?

(2)P1:  It's softer.

(3)T:  Chalk's softer. That's not the . . .

(4)P2:  There's a layer of non-porous rock underneath . . . it accumulates . . .

(5)T:  I can see you've been reading, or looking at a diagram.

(6)P2:  No.

(7)T:  That's not the answer though. . . . Why are caves formed?

The question at (1) could be about either kind of permeability. The response at (2) suggests the pupil may be thinking of chalk. The response at (4) suggests the artesian notion, and the teacher seems to forget that such a response may relate to work done in a previous year. The question at (7) seems to show the teacher pre-supposing that caves are found only in jointed, pervious lime-stone, though there is no apparent reason (i.e. nothing stressed in the grammar) to argue for their non-occurrence in chalk or in artesian formations. 'Percolates' would do for chalk limestone, it might be noted, and there are underground streams there also, so his rejection of chalk at (3) is quite puzzling, unless we recall that the topic is implicitly confined to limestone scenery with caves as geography handles that notion. We could also note, then, that the 'why' questions do not invite speculation or reasoning but the recall of parts of grammatical sentences. Thus the answer to 'Why are there underground streams?' (in this limestone) is the missing half of a sentence such as 'Limestone is sometimes "jointed", and water percolates down joints, and then flows along them, forming underground streams.' In the absence of empirical observation, such a sentence, which might seem to be making causal inductive connections, really establishes only a set of verbal associations, and to ask why a 'result' is produced is really only to test the strength of these links in pupils' memory.

I had been unable to follow the logic of the lesson's questions and answers. I mentioned this to the teacher at break afterwards. I said porosity was evidently a difficult concept. He said that, apart from saying '*some* limestone was porous', he had not used the word 'porous' about the Florida limestone. His question

'Why is it porous?' thus meant, 'It isn't really, but tell me what you're getting at' – an interpretation which would only occur to those who understood the term 'pervious' and knew that there is a type of rock that water can get through or into which *is not* porous. Limestone, he said, was 'permeable', rather, using what in the Penguin *Dictionary* is the seeming superordinate term covering most of 'porous' and all of 'pervious'. (The word 'permeable' was not used in the lesson.)

Self: What is 'porous' then?
T:    That means the rock has holes in it. They're not connected, so water doesn't get through it as in permeable rocks.
      (In the third-year worksheet the holes in the diagram were connected. 'Permeable' here seems to be the 'pervious' of the Penguin *Dictionary*.)
Self: Well, how about when they use it about artesian wells in the first year?
T:    They shouldn't say 'porous' they should say 'permeable'.

I then wondered about how water got into the spaces of porous rock if they weren't connected. He said, with total frankness, though possibly (and understandably), he had had enough of my interrogation and thought to send me away content:

T:    The trouble is, I suppose, I haven't really thought it through. As you say, how does the water go through the rock to get into the holes?

I do not know if this was ironic. It came from a very enthusiastic, and seriously patient teacher, and at the time I took it as unironic. It could be that there are corners of specialist's knowledge which remain formalistic, which have not found the kind of empirical support often given at higher levels of study, through extensive fieldwork, and so on. The possibility exists that these formalisms in content are reproduced by teachers for whom they still exist as formalisms.

He then talked about the difficulty of the ideas we'd been discussing. He felt it would be valuable to put models of rock together so that pupils would understand their structure. He liked the idea of using tubes and water to demonstrate aspects of the artesian concept, and generally felt it necessary to deal with empirical embodiments of such concepts before terms were introduced. He mentioned some topics similar to porosity in that their physicality was difficult to grasp imaginatively, such as condensation, and orographic rainfall (clouds holding less rain as it cools), and the puzzling fact of temperatures dropping with increased altitude. He felt we gloss over the difficulties involved in grasping these ideas.

The teacher's reference to the need for 'empirical embodiments' and 'models', and his caution about the premature introduction of terms, are, as opinions, clearly in line with the perspectives that inform my criticism of what he was doing. They echo closely what the remedial department head later said to me at one point about writing, and what the teacher of a bottom maths set said about maths – that the most valuable resources for the development of pupils' activities in those areas lay in their own everyday world and in concrete reality. These opinions seemed to go beyond educationist rhetoric; the remedial head enthusiastically recalled a project he had been involved in only a few years previously in which pupils' writing and maths had come out of practical activities in an everyday context, albeit at camp.

Nell Keddie remarks that, 'while some educational aims may be formulated by teachers as *educationists*, it will not be surprising if "doctrine" is contradicted by "commitments" which arise in the situation in which they must act as *teachers*.'[13] The classroom situation of these teachers did reflect this contradiction between 'doctrine' and 'commitment', but it would not be true to say further of them, at least, that it 'reveals how teachers can hold discrepant views without normally having to take cognisance of the contradictions which may arise', for the discrepancy was adverted too explicitly. That is not to say that similar contradictions do not go unrecognized (particularly with reference to notions like 'their own experience' and 'the real world'), but to suggest that this 'educationist' insight into the formalism of much of what they may be doing as teachers, in so far as it notes such a contradiction, counts as a revealing and potentially useful 'penetration' of their routine world, to use Willis's term (in *Learning to Labour*).[14] Their immersion in the routine of courses and timetables may well cause many teachers to suppress a certain scepticism about the value of what they are doing.

## Returning to the real world

In schools attempts are continuously made – often courageous and zealous attempts – to breathe life into abstract subject notions. The enormous efforts that go into organizing visits, camps, expeditions and fieldwork of all kinds are the committed expression of a faith in the importance attached to children having 'their own experience', making their own observations, seeing for themselves, in being stimulated or even moved by what they see. It might well be assumed that getting out of the class-room to confront the real physical world will alter the relation between the learner and what he learns, and will necessarily begin to find for the pupil real-world empirical support for the abstract conceptual language. On the other hand, perhaps, there may be no necessity at all in these things; it seems possible that a mere change of milieu will not of itself dissolve the propensity to handle language and knowledge in certain ways, and in particular that the formalizing tendencies I have noted may survive such a move.

Fieldwork is an accepted feature of the work of the research school, and during my time there all the first years made visits to a Roman palace, the nearby downs, and a well-known pond rich in bird life, and they all did work in the town on a town trail. In this way science, history, geography, art and English all offered children the chance of seeing things for themselves, and so on. Similar, perhaps less active, programmes were organized for second and third years and older pupils. For example, two weeks or so after the lesson recounted at the end of the last chapter, the class went on a few days' visit to the West country, from which they returned very enthusiastic and knowledgeable. Ironically, though, this access of commitment seemed undercut by the need to cast some of their observations of the river valley they had studied in the form of an 'hypothesis': this was a course-work essay for 'O'-level. As the pupils pointed out, they had been taught *in situ* about what *had* happened, so what was the point of writing a long essay that was supposedly about their own theory of what *might* have happened?

A glance at some aspects of the first-year fieldwork indicates the extent to which routine classroom procedures for organizing learning can persist despite the advantage of contact with the 'real' world. On the Roman palace visit, a certain nervousness about how the children might behave in public places might have contributed to their being given very specific written tasks. They were given a worksheet, for which 60 per cent of the marks were for short-answer questions; and of these several related not to visible objects – mosaic floors, fragments of column, and so on – but to the photographs and accompanying text in the foyer of the exhibition. 'How were the baths heated?' was a comprehension question answered by reading the foyer account and studying the photographs of the hypocaust. It seemed as if the experience of encountering the building was thrust aside by some of the questions, which related not to what was visibly present, but to knowledge about the building and its inhabitants; these were book questions taken out of doors: 'What was the site used for after the Romans left?'; 'Where are there two Roman palaces of a similar size?'; and so on. These accompanied (potentially) empirical questions such as 'What is the wall in the west wing made of?'

Most of the questions could, in fact, be dealt with by interpreting pictures and text in the foyer. The worksheet stated: 'The following questions (all but two) have the same numbers as the museum displays'. The rest of the project offered a range of optional tasks called 'suggestions': 'Do some of the following'; 'These are only suggestions, try to think of your own ideas to make the project as interesting as possible'.

One girl's later classroom work covered a number of subtopics, including Roman roads and clothes; she also invented 'her own idea', a diary of the local king who collaborates: 'I talked to my wife about our son. She told me it would be better if he went to live somewhere else, he hates the Romans. She agrees with what I am doing but is upset about our son.' This delineation of the personal situation of an historical figure seemed persuasive. Her next entry reads, 'Talked again to Vespasian, this time in his camp. I was served with Italian wine, such as I've never tasted before. Vespasian was very pleasant. But in gaining a friend I have also gained many enemies.' Yet this sure touch seemed to spring from a felt response not evident elsewhere in the project writing, most of which is perfunctory: 'Quite a few of the Roman roads exist today roads such as Staine Street, part of Fosse Way and a few others.' Only one personal note is heard in a plain recital of what Romans wear: 'The outdoor dress for well-to-do Romans was the toga. This was made out of wool and was usually white. Uncomfortable!' These project accounts were assembled from books later.

She wrote rather little during the visit, given the time available. There was 'too much to do. If you could just go and have a really good look, I'd prefer that. What happens is you go round, you just want to get the worksheet done – I suppose a lot of kids just wouldn't look.' The project had bored her. She thought of doing a diary of King C 'to bring it back to reality. There's so much done in school, in school work – you don't think it's real.'

Writing done after an 'integrated' visit (geography and history) to a pre-Roman encampment on the chalk downs suggested similar problems. Written in the same girl's exercise-book prior to the visit there was a dictated piece on 'How chalk is formed'. This was a tonally neutral, informative paragraph about 'tiny sea creatures falling to the sea bottom 135 million years ago'; one result of having this is presumably to make on-the-spot speculation about how chalk is formed unnecessary.

Her writing about this trip, afterwards, consisted of two pieces of about 150 words each on the journey and the encampment. There was also a paragraph on 'dry valleys' which recapitulated the earlier 'How chalk is formed' piece. Next in the note-book comes a dictated piece on 'porous v. impervious rock'. It thus seems that the focus of the fieldwork was the cluster of notions 'dry valley', 'sedimentary rock' and 'chalk and flint'. Yet the relation of this content to the fieldwork is not clear. The empirical observations are handled as taken-for-granted examples of the concepts 'dry valley', and so on. There is no sense in her writing that the concepts that were the core of the work were partially constructed or even enriched by speculative talking and thinking about what lay in front of them amongst the hills. The experience itself, in its intellectual character, is missing, and there seems to be a split between being there and thinking about what surrounded them there. This does seem to entail a neglect of even the geological nature of the downs. The flints, the chalk, the absence of water, lose any mystery they might have. The geological process is placed before them as already inhering in objects. What they encounter is not the object as they naively meet it, but a group of ideas which tends to push it aside.

A further way of formalistically subverting the empirical while seeming to relocate it is apparent in work done by the same girl on a science trip to a local lake. The worksheet consistently asks for names: 'Name the rocks', 'List the names of birds', 'Name the plants', and so on. Some names might well have been provided on the spot or gathered from *Observer* books, but the bias towards naming is, of course, a bias away from observation, except such observation as comes through identification, itself often possible only after repeated observation. This not only affects what happens at the time, it also socializes pupils into a confusion of things with their names, a kind of magic nominalism. Most of the worksheet tasks could be accomplished at a glance by those who already knew the names, so that they need not, strictly, observe at all. On the other hand, those who did not know the names had little or nothing to do – 'Try to name some of the plants growing in or on the lake'. No alternative describing or drawing is asked for. The empirical content of the visit, then, in so far as these items are concerned, is slight. The tasks are done without observation, properly speaking, or cannot be done.

A more detailed account of one particular field trip might be useful at this point to fill out the sketch I have attempted. This was a third-year visit to a nearby beach. As seems conventional, pupils were provided with a worksheet. The first page was two sections from OS maps; the second began with a definition of terms, the first of which was 'shore':

The shore – the area from low water to the highest point reached by storm waves (i.e. the storm beach). The shore is divided into two parts which are:
(a) Foreshore – extending from the lowest low water mark to the average high water line.

(b) Backshore – extending from the average high water line to the highest points reached by storm waves, which is the *storm beach* or *coast line*.

'Shore' and 'coastline', and perhaps 'foreshore', belong to pupils' ordinary language – locally, 'foreshore' is part of one well-known name. But the words are redefined here to fit into a grammatical complex that includes 'storm waves', 'lowest low water line', 'average high water line', and so on. The grammatical recasting of the meanings of everyday words takes place in this one reading, and precedes empirical exploration. The first of thirty-four tasks on the worksheet diagram was to 'indicate the types of beach material on various parts of the shore (sand, small pebbles, etc.), and label the point reached by the last high tide'. Thus, the grammatical recasting of meanings for 'shore' terms, and then the process of recognizing marks and signs on the beach, are taken-for-granted achievements needed for the first task, neither reading nor recognition being acknowledged as a problem.

Almost symbolically, the work of the group of about twelve that I was attached to began with a communal examination of the worksheet. And it was that, as much as the beach, which remained the focus of attention. Many of the questions themselves, though, suggested that the empirical appearance of the fieldwork had an illusory side. Many questions required no engagement with the empirical: 'High tide today is at _____', 'Tides are caused by the _____ pull of the _____ and _____'. The second question was done while the group was assembled, and 'gravitational' was given to them as answer. Pupils could say nothing from observation about the tide, unless they saw it turn, and they did not; nor, obviously, is 'gravitational pull' visible on the beach. Other questions in this section referred to spring and neap tides, and asked pupils the size of the moon last night, and so on.

The section on waves began with a diagram and a request for what 'caused' them – a question that observation does not resolve. 'Wave' was redefined orally by the teacher in a way that, again, shifted the pupils' everyday meaning for 'wave' without drawing on constitutive speech: 'The broad ups and downs are the real waves.' The grammar of 'breaker', 'swash', 'backwash', 'undertow' and wave 'height' was introduced by the worksheet, and was required for such questions as 'Which is more powerful today, the swash or the backwash?' This was a question that did require observation, but the new bits of grammar are required to do the observing with. Similarly with 'constructive' waves, which 'build up the beach', and their 'destructive' opposite: a grasp of that new grammar is required for attempting 'Are today's waves CONSTRUCTIVE?'

Some questions foreclose or peripheralize both observation and any interpretive speculation arising from it: 'Oblique waves move beach material sideways along the beach and this is called _____. To stop this movement of beach material _____ are built.' Both the movement of beach material which could be observed, and the hypothesis which could be constructed through observation, are given in the reading, while the term requires to be re-presented. Again, this is a clear example of the way in which the relation between formalistic language and the real world – or, rather, the absence of a relation – survives transplantation into a context thought likely, presumably, to re-align it. The physical world is very oddly ignored, in consequence, through questions that draw pupils *away from* observation.

There were 'identification' questions, requiring the names of birds, plants, and so on: 'List some of the birds seen on the shore'. There were *Observer* and other books available for this task, but the request merely to name or identify tended to divert both those who did and those who did not recognize certain species from close observation of them; those who did not tended to skip these questions and go on to those they could answer. Small groups were none the less totally absorbed in identification, looking through books, caught up in deciding what species they had found.

There were questions about the sand dunes which drew on ideas deriving from prior knowledge: 'The four conditions for the formation of dunes are _____'; 'Why have the dunes suffered severe erosion in recent years?'; 'What measures are being taken to preserve the dunes?'. At one point, when pupils had gathered for another examination of the worksheet, the missing word in the phrase 'suitable vegetation like _____ grass to hold or fix the sand in position' was discussed. The teacher pointed out that this word was 'a special name', and she would spell it for them. In contrast, answering 'Why have the dunes suffered severe erosion in recent years?' a pupil muttered 'Vandals like us', a value-conscious constitutive ordinary-language reply that he none the less half-concealed as rather frivolous.

On the final page there was more scope for observation: pupils were asked to identify various features of the riverside scene as they came into the town, and to mark them on the map. Again, most categories were given, and their handling pre-empted at least some kinds of observation and reflection: pupils were told that one category was a 'yacht club-house', another 'caravans to let'; these functions were not derived from observation. Similarly, the various 'Industries and Businesses' were pre-categorized as 'Timber Merchants', another as 'Roadstone Sea-Dredged Aggregate'.

The worksheet as a whole, though, produced for a context of direct observation, inhibited observation in various ways, deflecting pupils' attention to the predefined geographical entities and language-centred tasks which the classroom deals in, and foregrounds. Essentially, it is the classroom *en plein air*, and it is language which is being observed, against a backcloth of things. Reading the worksheet involves pupils in the same formalistic negotiation with foregrounded terms 'placed before language' that goes on in the classroom, but it is perhaps made more puzzling by the presumption that it *is* about what surrounds the pupils as physical reality. It seems not to be, and their non-empirical absorption in the worksheet was a recognition of that. The work was the sheet, the beach was (otherwise) for fun and 'larking about'. One boy said, 'After we've finished our work can we muck about a bit, Miss?' Others drew large words in the sand, or romped about. A boy said, with the air of someone who had made a discovery, 'I'm gonna come back here at the weekend.' It was a good place, even though you had to fill in a worksheet.

Given there was a good deal to do (34 tasks) in the time available (about 2 hours, during which about 2 miles of terrain was covered), the observation that did take place was constrained by the need for it to be translated into written answers. This also meant, it seemed, that pupils did not raise their own issues, or that these were not developed when they arose. One pupil, for example, asked if the sea ever came over the foreshore onto the low-lying land behind. Some interesting guesses and comment might have come from noting that there was vegetational cover on the foreshore itself, and that the ends of breakwaters were overgrown. However, the answer – 'Sometimes' – was promptly given, and the work continued. Another pupil who had found broken glass in the dunes similarly did not connect his perception to either a set question or a discussion.

In another respect the beach was less than empirical, in that it was seen through the filter of a single-subject discipline. The classification of knowledge about the beach was tightly geographical within the visit, even if it was not envisaged in advance as being. Though birds were mentioned on the worksheet, and gulls and oystercatchers could be seen all morning, it was as if they were edited out of consciousness. The beach was defined by the work to include 'gravitational pull' and 'conditions for the formation of dunes' and so on, but did not include other obvious features. There are huge concrete anti-invasion blocks from the second world war, and a road which stops abruptly that once led to a hamlet. It is the only stretch of open, undeveloped coast for about 30 miles, and in the distance were visible that morning other towns and features of the coast. There is also a huge shallow crescent of sandy beach which is unique in the area.

The suggestion is not that all such matters could have been broached, and certainly not that the teachers were imperceptive. It is rather that their perceptions, and real perceptiveness, seemed to operate within the frame of a routine and given notion of what a beach in geography is, so that while pupils talked about going for a swim, and the light in the waves, the teacher was 'helping' them by saying, 'If you write "neap" you'll be nearer than if you write "spring"' – for the question 'It is a _____ tide today'. An almost dramatic cleavage seemed to exist between the technical language that there, one might say, represented the 'life of the mind', and the pupils' casual talk about broken glass, birds, the

view, mucking about in the dunes, coming back at the weekend
– all the things they took note of which were none the less
excluded from the grammatical version of the beach.


## References

1 D. Barnes, *From Communication to Curriculum* (Harmondsworth,
   Penguin, 1976), p. 79.
2 M. J. Bradshaw, *A New Geology* (London, English University
   Press, 1972), p. 236.
3 E. K. Specht, *The Foundations of Wittgenstein's Late Philosophy*, trans.
   D. E. Walford (Manchester, Manchester University Press, 1969),
   p. 150.
4 M. Merleau-Ponty, *The Prose of the World*, trans. J. O'Neill and ed.
   C. Lefort (London, Heinemann, 1974), p. 14.
5 ibid., p. 117.
6 ibid., p. 13.
7 M. Merleau-Ponty, *Themes from the Lectures at the College de France*,
   trans. J. O'Neill (Evanston, Ill., Northwestern University Press,
   1970), p. 12.
8 Merleau-Ponty, *Prose of the World*, p. 14.
9 ibid., p. 89.
10 M. Merleau-Ponty, 'On the phenomenology of language', in J.
   O'Neill (ed.), *Phenomenology, Language and Sociology* (London,
   Heinemann, 1974), p. 82.
11 D. G. A. Whitten and J. R. V. Brooks, *A Dictionary of Geology*
   (Harmondsworth, Penguin, 1972), p. 344.
12 R. M. Wood, *On the Rocks: A Geology of Britain* (London, BBC
   Publications, 1978), p. 77.
13 N. Keddie, 'Classroom knowledge', in M. F. D. Young (ed.),
   *Knowledge and Control* (London, Collier-Macmillan, 1971), p. 136.
14 P. Willis, *Learning to Labour* (London, Saxon House, 1977), p. 126.

# 3
# CORRECT LANGUAGES

## 'Maths is a precise language'

I have suggested that an obstacle to pupils' genuine involvement
in learning – through the constitutive features of their own everyday language – seems to be the way in which concepts like
artesian wells, porosity, tides, dry valleys, beaches, and so on
come to be embodied in a kind of minimal grammar, a selection of
language forms which is handled as if it were the concept itself.
The attempt to return to the 'real' empirical world, moreover,
doesn't necessarily free learning from this formalistic impasse,
since the belief that subject knowledge is expressed through such
minimal grammars often survives the move from classroom to
beach, Roman palace, chalk downs, and so on. I should like to call
such a conception of knowledge 'objectivistic' because it seems to
define knowledge as an object and so equates knowing, and
coming to know, with its possession; it effaces the crucial distinction between the learner's subjective experience of moving

towards knowledge and the objectifying of a knowledge finally achieved. In his influential 'Teaching and learning as the organization of knowledge' (1971), Esland suggests that such a view arises when objects of knowledge 'can be considered to have meaning other than in the minds of the individuals in which they are constituted, irrespective of their human realization.'[1] Opposed to this is the conception which stresses the constitutive involvement of the learner: 'objective reality as an agglomeration of phenomena external to the body has to be subjectively realized before it has any meaning.'

Those who hold to an objectivistic view of knowledge will therefore be particularly disposed to look for the production of appropriate language – the correct language 'of' the subject. It might be said that objectivistic habits of thinking amongst teachers make the conflation of knowledge with minimal grammars appear to be a routine, 'disguised' feature of school life; one tends to accept without too much question the claim of the maths teacher who says 'Maths is a precise language', or of the science teacher who says that science is objective, dispassionate and so on. And yet, if a conception of knowledge opposed to objectivistic views is to be entertained at all, it needs to confront any claim that an intellectual capacity resides in a language *per se*, considered apart from its use.

Clearly, like any assumption about the correct language of a subject, the belief that there is a mathematically correct language can overlook what is being done by learners in and through 'correct' or 'incorrect' language. In an article in *Mathematics Teaching* (1972), Dagnall writes, 'I have found that the language used in mathematical activities has frequently been a compromise between what is mathematically correct and what conforms to normal English usage.'[2] He stresses the need for 'precise and correct language in the infant school', and would like 'to reserve the use of "big" and "small" for volume relations', and not use it for area. Apart from the odd denial of children's usage involved in proscribing 'big' for area, this raises a logical problem: while the notion of 'a mathematically correct language' implies an existing set of linguistic prescriptions, the suggestion that 'big' should be used in a particular fashion implies negotiation. In theory, correctness can be absolute; in actuality, it is situated in a particular social context, it seems. Thus, though the article enjoins teachers to be 'precise', and though it is undogmatic in its acceptance of some 'compromises' (such as 'group' for 'set' from infants), the basic problem remains, namely the tendency to look at decontextualized bits of language and label them 'precise', rather than to examine what lies behind a particular usage to see if precision has been brought to it.

A similar kind of confusion – or contradiction – seemed to arise at a maths meeting that had been organized to discuss some of the observations I had made – as a 'stranger' to maths – about first years' and fourth years' difficulties with certain basic mathematical terms. There were nine staff present, and myself. The following discussion, which is slightly abridged, arose from noting pupils' uncertainty with 'divide'. (A is a deputy head from the upper school; B is head of the lower school; and C and D are other members of the department.)

A:   Maths has a conciseness of speech, each word has a precise meaning . . . whereas when kids communicate with each other there's . . . you know . . . they say a few words and they get the drift and don't bother to complete the sentence. . . . Perhaps we in maths departments are working against current trends in communication amongst young people . . . and we should learn maths language in the same way we learn French language.
     (Then, a few seconds later)
A:   We tend to be precise in our terminology, the term 'subtraction' for instance . . .
     (And in the same passage)
A:   It's a very precise and concise form of communication.

I asked if 'take away' was any less 'precise' than 'subtract'; a few moments later an argument started about 'divide' and 'share':

C:   There are lots of traditions from primary school that they keep. . . . As soon as they get here I say, 'No more are you writing down remainders; I want fractions after whole numbers.'

B:     But that is a valid notion of one aspect of division . . . with a remainder . . .

C:     That's the sharing aspect, isn't it, though – we share out 11 things between 3 of us and we get 3 each; you can't do anything with 'remainder 2'.

B:     When you share, things are by definition equal, you mean grouping.

C:     It depends whether . . .

D:     No, no, it's different again, sometimes you need your remainders, however advanced, and sometimes you need it fractionally done . . .
       (B interjected that there are two aspects of division)

B:     One where you're sharing into equal portions which implies fractional things and some method of grouping where you may have a remainder.

C:     But 'share' and 'division' are similar but not precisely the same.

It seems unwise, then, to say that 'maths is a precise language', and so imply that language itself makes precise meanings, rather than makes them possible. Whatever precision maths language has, its situated use by maths teachers reveals imprecision, ambiguity and conflict. Moreover, five minutes of concentrated talk did not resolve such problems – whether you can 'share' unequally, how 'sharing' and 'dividing' are related and so on, remained to be sorted out.

## The word 'divide'

Do pupils have more precise meanings for 'divide' than their teachers? It emerged from a questionnaire that first-year pupils felt they knew what 'divide' meant, unsurprisingly, since it is a word in constant use. One might assume from the number who said they knew what it meant (100 per cent) that it represents a familiar term and a familiar operation. In fact, the explanatory 'descriptions' the pupils gave of the word in operation (and of the sign ÷ ) suggested great uncertainty. Before looking at some of these descriptions, a comment or two about the word 'divide' might be in order.

One problem is the range of its usages. To become linguistically competent with 'divide' means learning to handle both active–passive transformations, and transpositions of word order. There is the curious feature also of words like 'divide' and 'split', that their active and passive forms often express similar meanings. Thus, 'the ship split in two' and 'the ship was split in two' seem to have the same sense.

The range of possible sentence-types for 'divide' is daunting, even with 'into' alone. If S is a subject who does the dividing, and O is an object (like a cake) or an amount, and D is the number representing the divisor, there are six types at least that seem to be idiomatic – two commands and four statements:

Divide O into D (e.g. divide the cake into two)
Divide D into O (e.g. divide 2 into 6)
S divides O into D
S divides D into O
O divides into D
O is divided into D

This could also be heard: D is divided into O.

There are also a number of terms used as synonyms of 'divide' – 'share', 'go into', 'into' (as in '2 into 4'), 'how many . . . in', and 'partition'. All these have different usages, particularly with regard to the prepositions they need; and it is worth noting how frequently 'into' is a carrier of the passive–active ambiguity noted above.

A few examples of their 'descriptions' show children's difficulties with a term they believe they understand. (It will be noted that they sometimes devise separate problems for describing the word and the sign.)

(a) Six divide twelve is two.
(b) Six share two is three.

Neither of these is grammatical. More interestingly, since they are non-colloquial, they may be derived from doing maths, and not from usages outside it.

(c) Divide is share. 5 ÷ 20 = 4. Five divide by twenty is four.
(d) 2 ÷ 4 = 2. Two share four is two.
(e) 2 ÷ 4 = 2. Ten shared by five is two.
(f) 3 ÷ 6 = 2. Five shared between fifteen is three.
(g) How many times can it go into? 6 ÷ 12 = 2.

(b) and (d) may be compared; unlike 'divide', 'share' does not produce both passive and active forms meaning the same. (g) is interesting in that it seems that ÷ is a straight translation of 'go into'; one sees, apparently, where the failure in formulation is, at what point in the working process. Here it is in the shift from language sentence to maths sentence. I shall call such a shift 'translation', and distinguish it from 'transformations' (involving voice) and 'transpositions' (involving word order); thus one can say that (g) involves a translation, but does not produce the necessary transposition. With (h) (below) there is a similar failure, this time in the opposite direction, going from maths language to words:

$$2\overline{|4}$$

(h) $2\overline{|4}$ . Two shared by four is two.

In (i) and (j) there is a similar problem:

(i) 12 ÷ 2 = 6. It means share 2 by 12 which is 6.
(j) 3 divided by 9 is 3.

It is curious that the nonsensical flavour of the words in (h), (i) and (j) is apparently not noticed. It is as if the words bore no relation to their colloquial meaning. It seems unlikely that they *believe* that 'sharing by' a whole number increases what is being shared; it is again as if the language comes out of maths, not the everyday world.

If something of this sort happens, then 'two shared by four is two' may be a kind of back-formation from '2 $\lfloor 4$ '. That is, an
$$2$$
ungrammatical language sentence may be formed on the model of a grammatical maths sentence. The fact that 12 ÷ 2 = 6 becomes '2 shared by 12 is 6' lends support to this, in that the order of 2

and 12 has been transposed but without unseating the same language 'error'. *If* the child's use of 'share' in maths stemmed from situations in which the sign ⌐ were used, the subsequent learning of ÷ might not disturb it. So (i) is consistent with (h), but the maths sentence is a more complex operation. The child comes then to retain a meaning of 'share' which is synonymous with 'into' when teachers say '2 into 4'. (It may also be that teachers themselves sometimes use 'share' for ⌐ and/or ÷ , which would further complicate the problem.)

The possibility then exists that some children have two quite distinct meanings for 'share' – a colloquial one from everyday use, and one from maths. The children in the examples noted may, scrupulously and logically, be keeping their maths meaning for 'share' quite distinct – because they have to. (As they have to with, for instance, 'volume', 'oil' and others which have everyday meanings and school meanings.) If teachers do not notice such scrupulousness where it occurs, because it is either not produced in words or is confused with looseness of expression, there is a problem with dialogue, in that teacher and pupils are unaware of using the same word in radically different senses. The pupils' meaning ('share', ⌐), though consistent, becomes idiosyncratic and privatized; that is a conjectural, but perhaps not fanciful comment on: '12 ÷ 2 = 6. It means share 2 by 12 which is 6.'

In the same way, it seems that any of the phrases used to describe this mathematical operation, in either its passive or active (mathematical) form, may be used to describe the active form only. As the answer '2 share by 12' might mean '2 (people) share 12 (apples)' or '2⌐12', so other pupils use a broad range of inappropriate expressions to describe what are, apparently, successful active operations. Thus from 'divide': '2 divide by 6 is 12'; 'four divided into the 12 is 3'. From 'share': '2 share 4 is 2'; '5 shared into 10 is 2' (set 1); '3 shared by 24 is 8'; '5 shared between 15 is 3'.

These various shifts of order and mood, and the oscillation from language to maths, make clear how precarious the handling of 'divide' is. Thus a common reversal of order like 3 ÷ 6 = 2 can be produced in four ways – which means there are four ways of going wrong at this point.

(1)      3 goes into 6, 2 ⟶ $3 \div 6 = 2$
(2) or: 6 divided by 3 is 2 ⟶ $3 \div 6 = 2$
(3) or: $6 \div 3 = 2$ ⟶ $3 \div 6 = 2$
(4) or: $3\overline{)6}^{\,2}$ ⟶ $3 \div 6 = 2$

(1) and (4) seem likely, (2) less likely and (3) somewhat improbable, as perhaps self-evidently contradictory.

Another common misformulation, this time in language, is exemplified by 'two shared by four is two'. This could be produced thus:

(1) $2\overline{)4}^{\,2}$ ⟶ 2 shared by 4 is 2
(2) $4 \div 2 = 2$ ⟶ 2 shared by 4 is 2
(3) Divide 4 by 2 ⟶ 2 shared by 4 is 2
(4) 2 goes into 4, 2 ⟶ 2 shared by 4 is 2

Given the complexity of the operations and the possibility of confusion, it would not be surprising if some pupils settle for a routine where 'divide' and 'share', with a preposition if necessary, are merely the language equivalents of ÷ . This pupil's solution is draconian, but compels sympathy:

(1) $2 + 3 = 5$        two added to three is five
(2) $2 - 1 = 1$        two taken by one is one
(3) $2\overline{)4}^{\,2}$        two shared by four is two
(4) $2 \times 3 = 6$        two times three is six
(5) $\frac{1}{2} + \frac{1}{4} = \underline{2 + 1} = 3$   half added to a quarter is three

All her translations preserve sentence order, all but one use the passive (language) voice, and all assume the verbs are the exact counterparts of the maths symbols. Is there evidence here for the existence of the kind of privatized language referred to above? The maths sentences (her own productions) are − except the last − correctly formulated: (3) is the type in which 'shared by' seems a translation of ⌊_ ; in (2) it is interesting that she does not say 'taken *from*', the usual preposition; she might sense that 'from as in '2 from 4', is active.

Reversals of the correct order of mathematical sentences with ÷ were common (as in 2 ÷ 4 = 2). I have suggested that the commonest cause of this might be the problem of translating an 'active' maths sentence ($2\overline{)4}^{\,2}$) or an active language sentence (2 goes into 4 two times) without transposing. Thirty-seven children made this kind of error with terms in the wrong order (n = 100). The three sets tested were one of the all-ability blocks into which the first years were divided.

The difficulties children have with 'divide' have several sources, it seems. First, maths contexts – the constituted forms of maths – demand that it be used in frequent transformations, transpositions and translations by children who do not yet handle the passive with real assurance. Second, its grammar – the way it functions in relation to other words, and (here particularly) in relation to subjects, objects, prepositions and adverbs – is complex. Third, children often appear to confront 'divide' in the context of dependence on 'share', a term only roughly synonymous, and with a different grammar.

### Division in two popular textbooks

With this in mind, I shall look at two pages from *Beta 3*, a book in common use in local primary schools, which was in its eighteenth impression in 1975.[3] (A revised edition was published in 1979.) When asked 'Which maths book did you use in junior school?', 52 out of 92 first- and second-year pupils named this series, and 5 out of 8 local primary schools used it. The pages reproduced as Figures 10 and 11 could be encountered between the ages of 8 and 10 years. The previous book in the series also deals with division. Figure 10 shows the first page of the section on division.

The text is very complex. Starting at F, the first sentence 'Divide each of these numbers by 2' is in the order: verb, object, adverb phrase. The splitting-up on each side of the object of 'divide' and 'by' is likely to be difficult for children who haven't yet grasped the sign ÷ . It seems ambiguously to suggest an active sentence through the command 'divide' (which $\lceil$ would translate) and a passive through 'by 2' (which ÷ 2 would translate).

# Number   multiplication and division

Multiplying and adding   Write answers only

| **A** | **B** | **C** | **D** |
|---|---|---|---|
| 1 (4 × 4) + 3 | (4 × 8) + 7 | (7 × 7) + 4 | (4 × 9) + 5 |
| 2 (9 × 8) + 5 | (6 × 5) + 3 | (6 × 8) + 7 | (8 × 7) + 6 |
| 3 (0 × 7) + 2 | (9 × 10) + 7 | (3 × 9) + 4 | (9 × 9) + 7 |
| 4 (1 × 5) + 4 | (0 × 9) + 5 | (6 × 3) + 2 | (1 × 8) + 6 |
| 5 (3 × 7) + 6 | (1 × 6) + 4 | (8 × 8) + 7 | (4 × 7) + 3 |
| 6 (8 × 5) + 3 | (5 × 5) + 4 | (9 × 2) + 2 | (5 × 9) + 8 |

**E** Factors
A number which will divide exactly into another
number is called a FACTOR of that number.
e.g. 12 ÷ 3 = 4. Therefore 3 is a factor of 12.

1 There are more factors of 12. Find them.
2 Write all the numbers up to 30 which have 3 as
  a factor.
3 Write all the numbers up to 70 which have 7 as
  a factor.
4 Write all the numbers up to 40 which have
  a 5 as a factor  b 6 as a factor  c 8 as a factor.
5 Write all the factors of each of these numbers
  a 20      b 24      c 36.

**F**  Dividing and subtracting
Divide each of these numbers by 2 and show the
remainder. The first is done for you.

1 a 2)9  4 rem. 1      b 13      c 17      d 21

Now continue with the following

|  | a | b | c | d | e | f |
|---|---|---|---|---|---|---|
| 2 Divide by 3 | 7 | 8 | 11 | 17 | 20 | 29 |
| 3 Divide by 4 | 19 | 23 | 29 | 34 | 39 | 42 |
| 4 Divide by 5 | 4 | 11 | 29 | 34 | 42 | 51 |
| 5 Divide by 6 | 10 | 19 | 35 | 44 | 49 | 58 |
| 6 Divide by 7 | 2 | 20 | 48 | 55 | 60 | 69 |
| 7 Divide by 8 | 13 | 25 | 39 | 54 | 61 | 86 |
| 8 Divide by 9 | 6 | 19 | 26 | 43 | 68 | 75 |
| 9 Divide by 10 | 11 | 36 | 55 | 79 | 88 | 104 |

**G** Write the answers only

1 (8 × 3) ÷ 6      2 (4 × 9) ÷ 3      3 (12 × 3) ÷ 9

Find the missing numbers
4 45 = 9 × □        5 63 = □ × 7      6 □ × 10 = 100
7 8 × □ = 72        8 3 = □ ÷ 9      9 7 = 56 ÷ □
10 □ ÷ 7 = 7        11 □ ÷ 9 = 1      12 90 ÷ □ = 10

Find the number $x$ stands for
13 72 ÷ 9 = 4 × $x$   14 $x$ × 3 = 36 ÷ 4   15 2 × $x$ = 100 ÷ 10
16 7 × $x$ = 2 × 0    17 0 ÷ 8 = 4 × $x$    18 6 × 6 × $x$ = 0
19 5 × $x$ = 7 + 8    20 42 ÷ 7 = $x$ × 3   21 2$x$ + 7 = 21
22 72 ÷ 9 = $x$ × 2   23 5$x$ − 8 = 32      24 7 × $x$ = 70 − 7

*Figure 10*

# Multiplication and division

## A

1 136 children in a school are formed into 4 equal teams.
How many children are there in each team?

2 For the school concert 35 chairs were placed in each of 8 rows.
a How many seats were there?
b How many people attended the concert if there were 19 chairs empty?

3 96, 121, 78, 65
a Find the total of these numbers.
b Divide this total by 4 to find the average.

4 27 × 4 = 108   Write 108 ÷ 4 = □.

5 126 ÷ 7 = 18   Write 18 × 7 = □.

6 Find the missing numbers
a □ × 6 = 162       b □ ÷ 9 = 22
c □ × 8 = 312       d □ ÷ 7 = 57.

7 When a number is divided by 5 the answer is 47 rem. 4.  Find the number.

Write the answers only to the following.
Check each answer by division.
First work Group **B**.
Mark the answers and correct any mistakes.
Then go on to Group **C** and so on to Group **F**.

| **B** | **C** | **D** | **E** | **F** |
|---|---|---|---|---|
| 1 14 × 2 | 58 × 5 | 24 × 5 | 46 × 7 | 58 × 9 |
| 2 23 × 3 | 47 × 8 | 86 × 9 | 57 × 10 | 43 × 7 |
| 3 51 × 7 | 73 × 9 | 36 × 8 | 75 × 4 | 28 × 4 |
| 4 40 × 6 | 96 × 4 | 15 × 10 | 19 × 6 | 64 × 8 |

**G**  Write the answers only

| 1  $37\frac{1}{2}$p | 2  $19\frac{1}{2}$p | 3  $12\frac{1}{2}$p | 4  $18\frac{1}{2}$p | 5  $9\frac{1}{2}$p |
|---|---|---|---|---|
| ×2 | ×4 | ×3 | ×5 | ×9 |

| 6  $11\frac{1}{2}$p | 7  $10\frac{1}{2}$p | 8  $14\frac{1}{2}$p | 9  $5\frac{1}{2}$p | 10  $15\frac{1}{2}$p |
|---|---|---|---|---|
| ×7 | ×8 | ×6 | ×10 | ×5 |

In the following there are no remainders. Work to $\frac{1}{2}$p.

11 2)49p   12 4)34p   13 6)57p   14 5)$27\frac{1}{2}$p   15 9)$76\frac{1}{2}$p

16 3)$58\frac{1}{2}$p   17 7)$94\frac{1}{2}$p   18 10)65p   19 8)76p   20 5)$87\frac{1}{2}$p

**H**
1 Mary had 74p. She spent $\frac{1}{4}$ of it on a book. Find
a the cost of the book
b how much she had left.

2 James saved three times as much as his sister who has $26\frac{1}{2}$p.  How much has James?

3 David has 65p which he changes for FIVES.
How many FIVES does he receive?

4 7 metres of ribbon costs $80\frac{1}{2}$p.  Find the cost of
a 1 metre       b 3 metres       c 8 metres.

*Figure 11*

The next sentence (1a) changes the order, then b–d have to be read as elliptical versions of a, using the clue 'these' from the first line.

With Question 2 a further variant occurs. The objects 7, 8, 11, and so on are transposed to the end of the sentence. Not divide 7 by 3, but divide by 3, 7. This is so archaic as to be ungrammatical.

With G the first use of ÷ is in the sentence $(8 \times 3) \div 6$. Then $\square$ is re-introduced, which though common in the book needs interpreting, and finally a light algebraic note: an adapted multiplication sign become a 'number', as in $72 \div 9 = x \times 2$.

Figure 11 appears two pages later. A1 employs a new phrase for the operation – 'are formed'. Further changes also occur. In 7, the Ls is a translation from the maths sentence Ms type on previous pages (cf. $\square \div 5 = 47$ rem. 4). Though fractions are dealt with later in the book, $\frac{1}{2}$ is introduced to $\ulcorner$ questions, and H1 does not explicitly say that '$\frac{1}{4}$ of it' means 'divide'. H3 and 4 use further different ways of *implying* pupils should divide. In 3, recognition of the dividing implicit in 'changes for FIVES' depends also on reading 'FIVES' as '5p pieces'. In 4 the command 'divide' is implicit in 'find the cost', but b and c are different from a so that they require division, then multiplication.

Figure 12 shows a page from the first edition of a more recent, similarly popular series, Fletcher's *Mathematics for Schools*. Level II, Book O was meant for 5- to 7-year-olds. A second edition, which clears up some of the ambiguities described below, was published in 1982.[4] An analyst commented on the first edition that some pages seem 'to sacrifice clarity to brevity' and that 'the absence of subsidiary clauses does not always facilitate understanding'.[5] The page on 'partitioning', an activity that functions as a prelude to sharing and dividing, it seems, is almost as complex as *Beta 3* is with division – thus, 'Jill partitions', but then the drawing suggests the *set* partitions. In between are the words 'a picture of her partitioning', which ambiguously is either of her as she does it, or of the doing of it. Neither is it immediately clear that 'Jill's set' is the one on the left. Question 2 seems to mean 'Draw the two sub-sets ''wearing glasses'' and ''not wearing glasses''', but could also mean put the male and female sub-sets into the further sub-sets wearing glasses and not wearing glasses. It demands

## RELATIONS

Peter draws, then colours a set of vehicles. He draws black arrows for the relation "has the same colour".

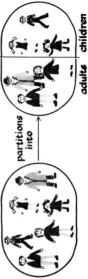

has the same colour as

**1**
a] Draw a picture of Peter's set.
b] Draw black arrows for the relation "is the same type".
c] Draw red arrows for the relation "has the same number of wheels".

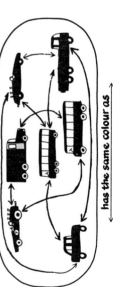

**2**
a] Draw, then colour a picture of this set of toys.
b] Draw black arrows for the relation "has the same colour".
c] Draw blue arrows for the relation "is like".

*Figure 12*

---

## PARTITIONING INTO SUBSETS

Jill partitions a set into subsets. She draws this picture of her partitioning.

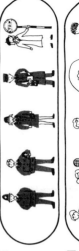

partitions into

adults | children

**1**
a] Copy Jill's set.
**2**
b] Partition the set into the subsets "male" and "female".

Repeat Exercise 1 for the subsets "wearing glasses" and "not wearing glasses".

**3** Copy, then partition each set. Label each of the subsets.

a]

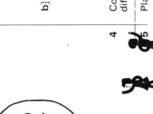

b]

**4** Copy, then partition each set in Exercise 3 in as many different ways as you can. Label each of the subsets.

**5** Play the Partitioning Game.

sophisticated reading of quotation marks and a grasp of the whole phrase to avoid misinterpretation. In Question 3 'copy' has no object. The analyst's comment seems appropriate. The difficulty of the instructions seems to be produced by a brevity which aims to be precise but which sacrifices clarity.

The contention that 'in maths each word has a precise meaning' is exposed by such contexts as a thoroughly objectivistic conception which neglects to take account of the fact that precision is a human accomplishment situated in social contexts.

Perhaps it would not be wise to see division as representative of the level of difficulty of first-year maths generally. If it is intrinsically a more difficult concept than artesian, porosity, and so on, or simply a different kind of concept, it becomes harder to suggest that some formalizing denial of the constitutive features of children's everyday language is implicated in their difficulties. And yet children appear to struggle also with other notions: for instance, and in a not dissimilar way, with subtraction. The following 'descriptions' for the − sign come from sets 1 and 2 in the first-year block already referred to. The first column uses the sign itself; the second gives an example of its use in words.

1 (a) $5 - 6 = 1$    2 take one is one

(b) $\begin{cases} 1 - 6 = 5 \\ 2 - 4 = 2 \end{cases}$    3 from 6
    six minus 12 = six

(c) $\begin{cases} 3 - 2 = 1 \\ 4 - 1 = 3 \end{cases}$    three taken from two is one
    four taken from one is three

(d) $1 - \frac{1}{2} = \frac{1}{2}$    take one from a $\frac{1}{2}$ is $\frac{1}{2}$

(e)    subtract 4 and 2 is 2

2 (a) $2 - 1 = 1$    two taken by one is one

(b) $2 - 8 = 6$    take the first from the second

(c)    5 subtracted to one is six

As with divide, there are difficulties with passive–active transformations and so with word order, with the relation between maths sign and language, and with the relation between 'correct mathematical' words and everyday language. In particular, in both situations the everyday sense of words like 'take' and 'share' seem for some children to have been affected by the prevailing uncertainty, so that they are no longer being used as means of bridging the gap between the empirical situations they ultimately derive from and the maths contexts they are now used in. In that their own natural forms of expression are affected, this in itself might suggest a deeply formalistic contamination of the language they do maths in.

The outcome of another test with the words 'parallel', 'right angle' and 'triangle' seems to bring this out clearly, and to hint again at the need for continuous dialogue between this kind of first-year 'maths' and the empirical world as it is expressed in the constitutive features of pupils' every day language.

The test I used was adapted from one described by D. Kerslake in *Mathematics in Schools*, vol. 8, no. 2.[6] Figure 13 shows it as I gave it to three sets of first years in one vertical block.

In the earlier test referred to above (p. 52), 'triangle' was confidently defined by most pupils; the explanations for 'parallel' were on the whole convincing. And yet in the present context there was a good deal of error in recognizing less common examples of those shapes. Table 1 indicates the extent of this.

*Table 1*  Number of errors in 3 sets picking out 6 triangles, 6 right angles and 6 pairs of parallel lines from 3 displays of 8 shapes

|  | Set 1 (30) | Set 2 (29) | Set 3 (22) | Total errors excluding blanks | n |
|---|---|---|---|---|---|
| Triangle | 18 (0 blanks) | 35 (8 blanks) | 36 (48 blanks) | 89 | 81 |
| Right-angle | 75 (0 blanks) | 56 (8 blanks) | 48 (48 blanks) | 179 | 81 |
| Parallel lines | 31 (0 blanks) | 63 (16 blanks) | 34 (40 blanks) | 128 | 81 |
| Total errors for set excluding blanks | 124 | 154 | 118 | 396 | |

Perhaps one answer to why they make so many errors lies in the fact that first-year pupils meet a relatively small number of (labelled) referents, while the teacher's own experience with these terms is the wider one of his training and his work as a whole.

Decide for yourself whether the shapes drawn below are triangles or not. In the column on the right put *'triangle'* or *'not a triangle'* opposite the letter referring to the shape.

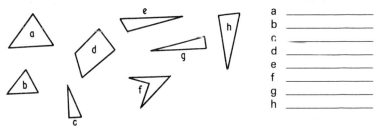

Decide for yourself whether the pairs of lines drawn below are *pairs of parallel lines*, or not. In the column on the right put *'parallel'*, or *'not parallel'*, opposite the letters referring to the pairs of lines.

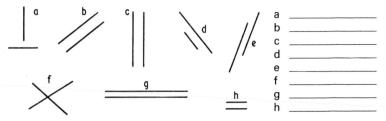

Decide for yourself whether the angles drawn below are *right angles*, or not. In the column on the right put *'right angle'*, or *'not right angle'*, opposite the letters referring to the angles.

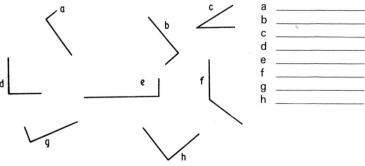

*Figure 13*

The referents for 'triangle' or 'parallel' are more numerous and varied for the teacher than they will be for first years handling the same terms. This is inevitable up to a point, but, just as the mother hearing her baby say 'shoe' realizes the child refers to an initially very limited range of footwear (one kind only to start with), so the teacher needs to bear in mind the pupils' analogous limitations. If he does not, if he assumes that a pupil's 'triangles are 3-sided figures' necessarily refers to the full range he, as teacher, is aware of, then dialogue becomes precarious through lack of feedback. When the small child makes 'mistakes' with 'shoe' – by, say, calling a Wellington boot one – the mother is aware of the break in communication because the object is clearly inappropriate as a referent. In other words, the empirical world provides the feedback to renew contact. If there is no similar continuous return to the empirical world, described in pupils' own language, the potential flaw in the classroom dialogue may stay hidden.

One problem seems to be that textbooks, worksheets and so on seem to work with only a selection of possible shapes, so that pupils' predictive capacities – working from definitions they have been given in the context of only a few shapes, for example – are over-taxed, and they fail to recognize some 'strange'-looking triangles as triangles. This might help to explain why, in the set 1 mistakes on parallel lines, 25 of the 31 mistakes occurred with two shapes, d and e. It may be that the range of experienced shapes for 'parallel' did not include lines that were not the same length and exactly opposite each other.

The danger of relying on a limited range of referents is also that pupils' descriptions are likely to generalize from insufficient evidence, and to assimilate non-essential and essential features of particular shapes or groups of shapes. Thus there were many references to parallel lines being the same length. Out of 103 attempts to explain 'parallel', 13 referred explicitly to lines being the same length. Many pupils also said parallel lines were 'opposite each other'. Thus: 'It's two lines like this ======, not like this ———=——. The 'same length' notion and the 'opposite' notion might reinforce each other. One set 1 pupil said 'two lines the same measurement and opposite each other'. Lines that 'run alongside each other', as pupils put it, perhaps *have* to be the same length. The analogy many pupils used, that of railway lines, also implies 'same length'.

With right-angles, some pupils consistently rejected shapes

that did not include a vertical line. (One pupil asked which was right, and which left, then chose turns to the right from the vertical.)

Without continuously returning to referents so as to make sense of language, there may be an over-dependence on language. Hence, perhaps, the curious growth into prominence of 'oppositeness' and 'same'. Small, even accidental, variations in verbal formulation are likely in such a situation to contribute to the construction of a concept. Thus the word 'always' in 'always the same distance apart' could by extension imply 'same length'. The test itself, as a teacher pointed out, unconsciously helped to distort in this way by talking about 'pairs of lines'. In our culture pairs are symmetries – shoes, ear-rings, fish, and so on. Bransford and McCarrell's demonstration of how subjects will construct by inference from actually heard sentences other sentences they believe they have also heard is interesting in this context.[7] A pupil who hears 'opposite' might, by this kind of creative inference, construct a mental sentence with 'continuously opposite' in it, or 'the same length', so that verbalization, unaccompanied by a return to examples, may work the pupil well away from the appropriate conceptualization. 'Lines that do not meet' (for 'parallel') was in one pupil's paper accompanied by:|_____|. This is, seemingly, the process noted earlier, where pupils made similarly inappropriate projections for the artesian idea. The very privateness of such structures may account for their not being revealed to teachers and friends in the classroom.

A comment that Keddie makes, discussing Gladwin's *Culture and Logical Processes*, seems to illuminate these pupils' difficulties with words like 'parallel' and 'divide'. She is suggesting that the dichotomization of 'abstract' and 'concrete' is untenable in the form in which it commonly occurs in discussions of thinking.

> So-called concrete thinking can be meaningful only because of the abstractions or constructs that provide for its sense. Equally the abstraction or construct only has meaning within specific 'concrete' socially located situations.[8]

In the same spirit, Jenks remarks that knowledge 'emerges from a context, and remains essentially inextricable from that context'.[9] To assume that 'maths is a precise language' seems to involve not acknowledging that pupils' notions of 'parallel' derive from a particular context, or socially located situation, in which the word has been handled in ways specific to that context – in respect of matters like the range of examples that have been offered and the language used to describe or 'define' them. There is thus an intimate relation between the abstract and the concrete, a kind of dialogue or interplay, the possibilities of which the teacher needs to be aware of. What seems to be discernible in children's handling of maths language is a rather too frequent struggle with the grammar, the constituted forms, carried on with less support than might be conscripted from the kind of constitutive everyday language they employ in situations familiar to them; in fact, there are even signs – as with 'share' and 'take' – of such everyday language being used formalistically.

Such a situation – the kind I referred to as a formalistic impasse – is, of course, only likely to be sustained by objectivistic conceptions which think of knowledge as somehow pre-existing and apart from actual attempts to know. A conception which stresses the unchanging thing-like character of knowledge – which reifies it, in sociological terms – to the point where it forgets that teachers and pupils have in partnership to re-awaken such knowledge (in the interests of children, moreover), will be likely to take 'the language of maths' so much for granted as to assume, or behave as if, it were in itself the source of meaning for children handling it. This seems to me not essentially different from the way in which the concepts artesian well, porosity and the other matters were handled earlier. If meaning is thought of as residing in the constituted language forms of a subject, even a regimen of continuous 'curriculum reform' will be unlikely to do anything to alter the ingrained formalistic character of much learning, since new contents will tend to be thought of in the old objectivistic way. What Bruner says of school maths has wider applicability. He perceives in the teaching of maths an 'end-product formalism, which makes it seem that maths is something new rather than something the child already knows. By interposing formalism, we prevent the child from realising that he has been thinking mathematics all along.'[10] Unless what 'the child already knows' is in part the content of subject contents, 'reform' changes little of the relation between the learners and what they learn, and children will be deprived of the realization that they think mathematically, historically, scientifically and poetically.

It may be that teachers are often aware of the pressure of this impasse without discerning anything of its true nature; they can hardly do so, indeed, if they think objectivistically. They are certainly made aware of the failure of children with school knowledge, and there are continuous attempts to remedy what is seen as the frequent difficulty of school work. Again, though, if learning is conceived objectivistically, it seems likely that 'difficulty' will be thought to inhere in the subject itself, as this is expressed or objectified in a grammar, and to be most susceptible of remedy by a process of 'simplification' of content – that is, of the language that embodies content. This need not necessarily, any more than field trips that issue in formalistic negotiations with grammar, directly confront the problems sketched out so far.

## References

1 G. M. Esland, 'Teaching and learning as the organization of knowledge', in M. F. D. Young (ed.), *Knowledge and Control* (London, Collier-Macmillan, 1971), p. 75.

2 W. Dagnall, 'The use of language – correctness and compromise', in *Mathematics Teaching*, no. 60 (September 1972), p. 12.

3 T. R. Goddard and A. W. Grattridge, *Beta Mathematics 3* (Huddersfield, Schofield & Sims, 1969), pp. 9 and 11.

4 H. Fletcher and A. Howell, *Mathematics for Schools, Level II, Book O*, First Edition (London, Addison Wesley, 1975), pp. 2–3; A. Howell, R. Walker and H. Fletcher, *Mathematics for Schools, Level II, Book O*, Second Edition (London, Addison Wesley, 1982).[Publisher's note: In the 1982 edition of *Mathematics for Schools*, the authors specifically redressed the criticisms made of the language level and readability in the first edition.]

5 *Sussex University Textbook Analysis Project*, '*Mathematics for Schools*' (1979, in draft), p. 15.

6 D. Kerslake 'Visual mathematics', in *Mathematics in Schools*, vol. 8, no. 2 (March 1979), pp. 38–40.

7 J. D. Bransford and N. S. McCarrell, 'A cognitive approach to

comprehension', in P. N. Johnson-Laird and P. C. Wason (eds), *Thinking: Readings in Cognitive Science* (Cambridge, Cambridge University Press, 1977), p. 390.

8 N. Keddie, quoted in C. Jenks, 'Powers of knowledge and forms of the mind', in C. Jenks (ed.), *Rationality, Education and the Social Organisation of Knowledge* (London, Routledge & Kegan Paul, 1977), p. 18.

9 C. Jenks, in Jenks, ibid., p. 25.

10 J. S. Bruner, *On Knowing* (Cambridge, Mass., Belknap Press, 1979), p. 104.

# 4
# MAKING THINGS EASIER

## Elizabeth's problems simplified

I suggested earlier that in their work on the Great Artesian Basin pupils confronted a highly selective version of the artesian idea, and that in the absence of any physical realities to study it was essentially a minimal grammar of 'artesian' that was encountered. It sufficed for that grammar if 'non-porous' and 'porous' were merely opposed, though such either/or-ness is not a clear indication of how rocks behave in reality, where there is a continuum of degrees of porosity. Since pupils' dealings, though, are with the verbo-logical oppositeness of porous and non-porous, the empirical grounds of that either/or-ness are not part of the subject. One teacher of geography I spoke to argued that first-year pupils needed the 'clarity' of 'porous' v. 'non-porous'; degrees of porosity would 'confuse' them, 'complexity can come later'. It seems that what might also be objectionable in a move towards

'complexity' would be the implied threat to the idea that manage-
able conciseness makes for accessibility. Perhaps this is generalizable. Confronted by the possibility that pupils do not understand,
it may be that teachers tend to move towards further précis of
content, in the belief that such 'simplifying' renders accessible
what has proved difficult.

I had observed a second-year class working with a recently
qualified mature teacher on the 'difficulties that Elizabeth I faced'
on her accession. We had talked at some length about the difficulty of the language of the textbook she was using, and children's problems generally in understanding history. After a day or
two she initiated a second conversation, remarking that 'she'd
thought a lot over the weekend about what we'd said'. She had
decided that 'a rethink was needed . . . you have to think about
what you're doing.' The simplifying that she had decided on
involved a kind of précis, turning the continuous 'difficult text'
into a number of discrete 'main points' that could be 'put over
visually'. Thus, the group of problems faced by Elizabeth was
translated by means of a metaphoric model into a group of *boulders*
on the *road* to the future. She had asked pupils to fill in the spaces
(represented by the boulders) 'with their own ideas' about the
topics. She had wondered about the value of their writing
'modern expressions' in the spaces – 'Job Centre' in the unemployment space, 'Right, get him' in the Catholic *v*. Protestant
space, and so on. The textbook phrase 'The country was poor,
there was no money in the Treasury' becomes 'shortage of
money' in the model. The accessibility of the notion of a whole
country being poor remained unexamined. What it means to say a
country is 'poor' is, of course, an exploration in itself. Equally
compressed notions like 'vast unemployment', 'the threat from
France and Spain', and 'the religious problem' have to be handled
as well.

Interestingly, the teacher agreed that a phrase like 'the country
was poor' would mean little to a 12-year-old. She guessed that a
phrase like that would conjure up an image of 'everyone in rags'.
Yet, rather than work from this perception of how children
might see this idea, she proceeded with her 'simplification'. This
could be seen as a fining-down of the grammar, as leading yet

further away from the complexities of 'interesting' detail; but it seems 'easier', in that there is less language to handle.

At the same time, for later use with the same class, she decided to photostat copies of inventories of possessions and so on, to see what children might make of those. This is a quite different

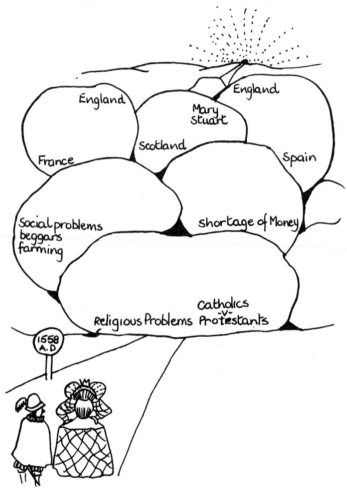

Some Obstacles in the Path of Elizabeth I

Figure 14

response to the problem of drawing children into history, in that its redefining of content is a shift from the satellite picture 'clarity' of textbook categories towards the particularity of daily life in history. She was moving towards a conception of history of the kind Cobb endorses here:

> Most collectivities are textbook creations imposed on unknowing groups a century or more later. In order to carry conviction, the historian must be alert to minutiae – to the texture of stone, the coldness of metal, the cadence and local accent behind reported speech. Such attention to detail is designed not only to carry conviction, but also to produce enjoyment, which is as much the function of history as of romance.[1]

The approach the teacher was contemplating for later use with the class would not only offer this kind of empathizing and enjoyable immersion in persuasive 'minutiae', it would also relax the definitional grip, as if to say 'this point will do as well as any to start from', and so imply an openness which does not, unlike the model as précis, exclude other starting points.

If there is a struggle in the teacher's mind here, it is also part of a struggle to define for herself what teaching history is, and what history itself is; it is likely that a probationary teacher feels a need to find her own pedagogic style, but perhaps less likely that, at the same time, she will redefine for herself what school history is in ways that break sharply from accepted versions. This perhaps explains what seemed to be her way of handling the problem, which was broadly to accept history-as-given, but to venture into novel modes of handling given content. (It was in this light that I also saw her occasional lessons using role-play and small-group talk. Very few other humanities or English lessons I observed included small-group talk; in this, she was being somewhat revolutionary.)

What of the 'simplification' itself? Has it, for the pupils, resulted in an easier handling of the ideas? Perhaps not. The apparent simplicity of the visual model may be more deceptive than I have suggested, and might be seen rather as a heightened arbitrariness. Below is a set of questions I devised for that part of the year-group who worked with this teacher. It comprised one vertical band of about ninety pupils of all abilities, in three setted groups. The questions were meant to be not just routine questions but also to be reflexive: they attempt to reveal problems that may lie hidden in the grammar of routine questions. Thus Question 3 – 'Was this a real path?' – is unlikely to be asked by the teacher who thought up this metaphor, or piece of grammar, as a means of making the content more accessible. This recapitulates the suggestion made earlier, that routine questions themselves are part of the grammar of history, are themselves a selection of possible questions. Given the initial constraint that they be grammatical, and relate to the version of content that pupils are offered, they will tend to recapitulate features of the grammar, so that departures from routine questioning may raise problems which cannot be confidently answered. This consideration may also go some way to explaining why here, as in the artesian well example, such knowledge can become oddly precarious, and easily be unseated.

*Questions on a simplified visual model of 'Elizabeth's Problems at Her Accession' (second years)*

1 If you were Elizabeth ruling over England, an '*obstacle*' would be one of these things to you. Which one?
(A) A big boulder.
(B) Something very difficult.
(C) A sign-post.
(D) An explanation.
(Just write down A, or B, or C or D.)
2 Do you think the little circle with '1558 AD' in it is meant to be an obstacle?
3 Was this a real path that you could actually have walked along? If it was, where do you think it could have been?
4 It says 'Catholics *v*. Protestants'. What do you think the '*v*.' means?
5 Guess how many queens of England were called Elizabeth before this one: was it 3, or 2, or 1, or 0?
6 Was Mary Queen of Scots a bit of a nuisance to Elizabeth?

7 Was there any trouble between Catholics and Protestants in Elizabeth's time?

8 Was Mary Queen of Scots an obstacle?

9 The '1558' refers to one of these things. Which one?
   (A) The height in feet above sea-level.
   (B) The distance from the end of the path.
   (C) The year she became queen.
   (D) The number of miles to Spain.

10 Which of these are called 'social problems' – shortage of money, religious problems, beggars, England, farming, 1558, Spain, Mary Queen of Scots?

The responses generally seem to illustrate the extent to which pupils' negotiations with this piece of 'simplified' history are formalistic.

*Question 1 answers*

The responses were:

(A) 21 ⎫
(B) 48 ⎪ 85
(C)  3 ⎪
(D) 13 ⎭

The (A) answers, a quarter of the group, might suggest that the boulders model is not seen as a metaphor at all. Though it did not occur to me at the time, the (D) answers could be seen as appropriate, in the sense that the phrases on the boulders do explain, in rudimentary fashion, what she was up against. Some pupils saw the connection – rather, made a connection – that I did not. My assumption was that 'shortage of money', and so on, were not full-blown 'explanations'.

*Question 2 answers*

There are 9 'yes' answers here (n = 85). Possibly the circle only was seen, perhaps as a 'beyond this point' sign, marking where things begin to get difficult: 1558 was an obstacle, in that the accession itself raised problems.

*Question 3 answers*

There were 17 'yes' answers. 'Real' and 'actually' invite them to contemplate the metaphor and answer from a literal viewpoint. The metaphor is in some way not seen.

*Question 4 answers*

Only one child was unsure of the '*v.*' abbreviation. Perhaps sporting contexts make this familiar.

*Question 5 answers*

3–  6 pupils
2–12 pupils
1–10 pupils
0–57 pupils

This seems an example of the question that might create misinformative new possibilities. If pupils see it as a trick question they are confident that 'called Elizabeth' means called on the throne, as queen. For those who do not, the additional idea that a woman might have a name Elizabeth but not be 'called' by it is created by the question.

The responses to Questions 6 and 8 are placed together for comparison.

*Question 6 answers*

|     | Set 1 (34) | Set 2 (27) | Set 3 (26) |
|-----|-----------|-----------|-----------|
| Yes | 34        | 27        | 25        |
| No  | —         | —         | 1         |

*Question 8 answers*

|     | Set 1 (34) | Set 2 (27) | Set 3 (26) |
|-----|-----------|-----------|-----------|
| Yes | 34        | 20        | 19        |
| No  | —         | 7         | 7         |

Though Question 8 omits 'for Elizabeth' after 'obstacle', it might be thought a fair question – given the diagram, even an unnecessary one, because that 'tells them the answer'. Yet it evidently does not. Fourteen pupils (17 per cent) contradict its message. On the other hand, only one pupil denies she was 'a bit of a nuisance'. It may be that pupils are making a distinction between Mary as a severe problem and Mary as a less severe one, deliberately contradicting, or qualifying, the model.

I shall refer briefly to some of the other questions.

*Question 7 answers*

All the pupils who answered this said 'yes'.

*Question 9 answers*

(A)   1
(B)   6
(C)  75
(D)   3

The literal interpretations of (B) and (D) seem similar to literal answers earlier.

*Question 10 answers*

The central notion, 'social problems', was taken to include, with varying degrees of justification, Mary (21), 1558 (3), England (3) and 'all of them' (5).

One final point about the diagram. Unless the metaphor is explicated, it may be that pupils have the notion of *im*movable objects in their heads. Their *in*surmountability may be what is learnt: Elizabeth did not solve her problems.

Teachers tend to distinguish between history and the language used to do history with. For teachers, if the personal reality of history is rich, and comprises empirical knowledge – anecdotes, people, objects – then the usage is to some extent acceptable. It is less so for pupils if history is realized merely as language. For pupils here it does seem the case that there is language but little sense of the realities pointed to by language. If there is little beyond language, pupils are at its mercy. The simplification I have looked at may be seen, then, not as offering a greater accessibility but, in so far as it slenderizes the grammar of 'Elizabeth's accession', as making it more elusive and arbitrary.

The 'rethink' that led to the simplification had been just this sense that phrases of the kind she was using would not be meaningful or would misleadingly summon up pictures of 'everyone in rags'. This perception seems fundamentally at odds with what, nevertheless, she proceeded with. When Young says that 'teachers have theories of knowledge, teaching and curriculum which . . . are crucially important for the possibilities of change',[2] it seems necessary to look for the constituents of theories in that kind of passing perception or comment which she offered here. Just as routine practice – represented by her original attempt at Elizabeth's problems and by the simplification – may imply objectivistic ways of conceiving knowledge, her remarks about how children might try to make sense of these phrases are fragments of 'theory' implicit with a view opposed to those objectivistic conceptions. What Young sees as a need for 'enabling pupils and teachers to theorize' may well proceed from similar starting points.

That she was thinking at this time in a quite different way about the learner's ability to 'make sense' of 'knowledge' was made clear by her decision also to photostat copies of inventories of family possessions and see 'what could be got out of them'. Perhaps a real but less conscious shift of attitude is taking place (under the apparent shift she calls a rethink) which, unlike the rethink, is implicitly non-objectivistic. There seems little point in speculating about why she chose, of the two ways of making history more accessible she had decided were possible, to opt for slenderizing the grammar. But it is worth noting that the way she chose seems to go with the grain of what has been noted so far about school learning, in that it was objectivistic, and represented a further turn away from the pupils' constitutive involvement through their own ways of speaking.

It also seems unlikely that a shift towards the kind of open complexity represented by personal documents, inventories and similar minutiae – which lack in themselves a general conceptual dimension – could be for long sustained by one teacher alone in a context where the emphasis is on the kind of accessibility represented by compression and generality. In itself, this programme already seems to have been simplified, in that the notions, models and schemes in the first-year exercise books seem to have gone through stages of distillation. This then makes possible, or is caused by, the pace and compression of the course. First-year history began with pre-history: 'The British Isles before man . . . many thousand years ago . . . when coal was formed . . . and we were joined to Europe.' There followed the Bronze Age (October), the Romans (October–November), the Anglo-Saxons (December), the Vikings (January–February), Alfred (February), the Normans (March), the Feudal System (March), the Medieval Church (April), King John (May), Henry III (June), Crécy, Agincourt and Joan of Arc (June–July). The bulk of the work written in the exercise books is dictation, short answers to questions, reference work done in single sentences, and short paragraphs. One simplifying model deals with political relationships:

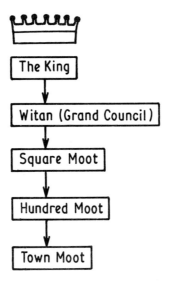

*Figure 15*

The high degree of compression that marks this programme allows only for elementary treatment. A collection of topics on Hastings, William the Conqueror, the Domesday Book and the

Feudal System takes up four sides only, covering three weeks (six lessons), and two and a half sides were diagrams and models. One of these was about William's achievements:

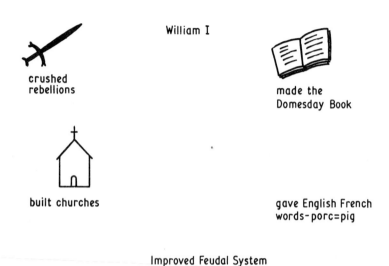

William I

crushed
rebellions

made the
Domesday Book

built churches

gave English French
words-porc=pig

Improved Feudal System

*Figure 16*

One can only speculate about the diverse meanings pupils will ascribe to these highly elliptical statements. A sword is hardly an adequate image for 'rebellions', and 'made the Domesday Book' implicitly hides the scale of the enterprise. The usage 'William did x' is extremely common though, and it is worth pausing to examine this 'simplifying convention of written history'. Literally, all five diagram propositions are untrue. *William* couldn't 'crush rebellions', build a church, 'give' words to English, and so on. The shorthand form 'William did x' is a synecdoche so conventional that one tends to forget it is a synecdoche. If it is agreed to say the King did things, we mean in literal terms something of this kind: that it might have been his decision, after discussion amongst the Council – if any – to ride or send letters and ask or tell or beg certain others to do something unknown about building a church, say. It is agreed to say 'William built churches', and this is acceptable provided we recall that he didn't

– if one may so put it. Otherwise, this formalism enacts a drastic telescoping of events, and hence a destruction of them, in that the particulars of history are excluded.

J. L. Austin raises this issue in *How To Do Things With Words*, but his treatment of it, in passing, is illuminatingly unsatisfactory. Observing that 'France is hexagonal' is suitable for, and 'true' in certain contexts, 'as when generals discuss strategy', he compares such a 'roughly true' statement with a 'rough' but 'true' statement in a school book:[3] 'What is judged true in a school book may not be so judged in a work of historical research.' The statement 'Lord Raglan won the Battle of Alma' – 'a soldiers' battle if ever there was one' – is 'justifiable in some contexts', and 'perhaps in a school book'.

But there is an important difference between the 'roughness' of 'France is hexagonal' said amongst generals, and the roughness of 'Lord Raglan won the Battle of Alma' said to school pupils. For the generals, 'France is hexagonal' is (one trusts) a simplification of the more complex information they also have access to, and it is taken up as simpli*fied* for a purpose. If they saw, knowing the more complex information, that a choice of strategy turned on the assumption that 'hexagonal' was literally true, and so *un*simplified as description (that AB = CD, and time and transport costs for AB equalled those for CD exactly, and so on), the strategy could be discarded as leaning too heavily on the model. It would be recognized as a negotiation with the mere terms of the model, rather than with the terms as they related to other more complex awarenesses.

This is not true of 'roughly true' statements when taken up by pupils who have no means of filling out the simplification, and no means, therefore, of recognizing that Lord Raglan's contribution is conventionally reformulated as simplification, for historians who recognize it as such and read beyond it to see what it means. It is only acceptable as 'roughly true' for those who have access to the (implicit) complex model, and can de-simplify it to see the simplification. The knowledge needed properly to read 'Lord Raglan' etc. in that way is considerable. If pupils confront highly compressed, simplified statements without being able to appeal beyond them, they then normally have access only to statements

that they cannot make meaningful. This seems to raise the philosophical problem that children making statements (in exams, for
instance) such as 'Lord Raglan won the Battle of Alma' or
'William made the Domesday Book' are saying things that are
not even, for them, 'roughly true'. Austin's stress at the end of
his book, though, is on the notion that not only clearly 'per-
formative' sentences, such as 'I promise', show speakers 'doing'
things with words, but that merely expository statements –
assertions such as 'There are forty people in the next room' – also
have a performatory element, so that 'stating is . . . performing
an act', in a particular situation.[4] And one of the rules for 'stating'
or making an assertion, he suggests, is that one should have good
grounds for doing so. The pupils repeating 'William made the
Domesday Book' without attributing even a 'roughly true'
meaning to it are hardly making an assertion or statement. It is
interesting to speculate about what, in terms of the notion of the
speech act, they are doing with words.

## Curriculum problems simplified

The existence of such a simplifying language convention so frequently and obviously woven into the fabric of school history
might itself suggest the way in which pedagogic or curricular shifts
towards minutiae and complexity – in the interests of access –
are likely to be undercut by the basic drift of established history
towards generality and simplification – in the interests of access.
This tension might well generate a regular kind of fruitful dialogue or oscillation between the two. If the shift towards
minutiae lacks conviction, however, because the relation between
that and the role of generality is not clearly perceived – owing to
the embedded prestige of the latter – one might expect to find
offers of the former open kind reneging on their promises, and
generally over-insuring themselves in various ways against
'failure', which will tend of course to be defined as a loss of the
general–conceptual or satellite picture version of history. This
would happen at any level of interpretation, presumably, so that
one might see shifts toward satellite picture simplification occurring at any time.

I shall look briefly at signs of this in the school's implementation of the Schools Council History, 13–16 Project. Interestingly, it seems to me that this kind of initial retreat towards simplification is implicit not just in teachers' handling of the Project concerns but earlier, at certain points in the Project's own articulation of its basic concerns. These seem essentially intended to divert history study from the fact-dominated content of traditional chronological history to the arousal in students of an awareness of what doing history is. Rather than see history as 'a coherent body of knowledge' it might be preferable to see it as 'a heap of materials which survives from the past'.[5] History in this sense involves a perpetual act of resurrection in which teachers and pupils reconstruct the past and so make it become near and 'present' to them. It implies active enquiry of pupils into the various kinds of 'primary' and 'secondary' sources which make up the raw material of history: 'Since the outcomes hoped for are attitudes and abilities rather than facts, classroom methods should be favoured which create an active learning situation for the pupil rather than those which cast the teacher in the role of a transmitter of information.'[6]

The point I wish to focus on is the way in which the basic concern to have pupils encounter pieces of 'evidence' and interpret them is filtered through the notions 'primary' and 'secondary'. The materials in use in lessons I observed included a booklet on evidence.[7] The 'work done so far' is described as 'detective work' (the work is in sections, on a mysterious murder, Tollund Man, the Aesborg ship, Richard III, and Emily Davison). 'The historian' uses evidence, which he 'divides' into two kinds: '(1) Evidence which comes from the actual time of the people and events. These are called primary sources because they are first-hand evidence.' Then examples are given: a flint-tool, a coin, a vase, a castle, a newspaper, Samuel Pepys' diaries, a film. Then, on the next page: '(2) Evidence which comes from historians who are writing about people and events at a later date. These are called secondary sources, because they are second-hand evidence, though often they are based on primary sources.' Examples are: a textbook, an essay, an historical novel.

This classification seems to be done on the basis of an intrinsic criterion as much as on the kind of relation they have to whatever they are evidence *of*. Clearly, a textbook can be 'primary' source evidence of how textbook writers see things. 'Second-hand' seems to hint at the relational point about distance and reliability, but to say only that 'these are secondary sources' without specifying for whom, and in respect of what, is to use a simplifying, merely intrinsic criterion. The slightly more explicit term 'second-hand' is thereafter neglected and the term 'secondary' used throughout.

The Tollund Man material that was used in one lesson reflects clearly at one point the same tension between open course aims and the simplifying tendency of the course materials. Although the 'detective's' question, to which the unit gradually builds up, is 'Why did Tollund Man die?', there is a phrase in the introduction preceding the 'scientists' account' which refers to the 'air of gentle peace about the man'. The photographs perhaps were not enough; to help pupils satisfactorily to 'sacrificial murder' the sign-post 'peaceful' would be needed. The openness and complexity of 'active enquiry' is undercut by simplification. One way is to provide a narrow multiple choice of possible answers: 'Which of the following was the most likely cause of death – old age, disease, suicide, murder?' Another is by underscoring certain facts which are (literally) underlined, like 'seeds connected only with the spring'.

A similar retreat towards simplification seemed apparent at a department meeting held to discuss the half-year exam results, and review the working of the new course. At one point exam questions were discussed. One question listed ten items and asked, 'Are the following sources primary or secondary?', without specifying what each source was meant to be evidence of. Some pupils challenged the answer for 'Bayeux Tapestry' afterwards in class, suggesting it was secondary but not writing it down. One teacher suggested that perhaps 'this sort of question was not exact'. He might have been referring to the underspecified nature of the question, so pointing to the simplification which the exam paper, following the course booklet, enacts. If so, his pertinent remark was not sharply enough focused to raise the question explicitly, and other later remarks suggested that their handling of the primary–secondary distinction had become non-problematic. 'Primary and secondary is easy – once you have slipped into it – you give them a definition and a list – it's easy to translate, it's a right and wrong thing.' Other teachers tended to endorse the 'clearly right or wrong' judgement. (It might be noted that the same usage is found in the project's official exam in 1979, as administered by the SREB for the CSE examination. After a cartoon about cholera, drawn in 1852, this question: 'The cartoon, Evidence A, is a primary source. Does this mean it is necessarily more reliable?')

The discussion moved on to the suitability of different project materials (A is head of department).

A:   Is it feasible?
C:   They do not like that one.
A:   They are sufficiently mature to grasp the interpretation approach . . . evaluation suggests that circles 3 (bottom set taught by C) can cope with it . . . with abstract ideas. Though it probably is not 'work' to them.
C:   It is frustrating for me . . . they are not grasping it.
A:   Were they earlier?
C:   Yes.
E:   Perhaps the burial ship could be left out . . . it is too vague.
B:   There are some bad questions on it . . .
C:   They did not know what is expected of them.
A:   There is the teacher's guide, of course . . . working through it is the point, not the answer . . .
E:   There is too high a degree of craft needed.

E criticizes the material for demanding 'too high a degree of craft', C says the lower groups are not 'grasping it', and even as A says they can or should, he suggests the work is 'abstract'. There is thus a three-pronged scepticism available to help accomplish any return to a narrower, more 'accessible' kind of work than the project stands for. In particular, E's suggestion that 'craft' is required turns on its head the Project's attempt to hold open to pupils a dimension of the historian's traditional 'detective' skill. The Project suggests, in effect, that part of what the historian does is handle a merely human 'action knowledge'; E argues that using 'action-knowledge' of this kind is a craft.

In a written comment on the Project, C (the only contributor here) described the project as an attempt 'to get pupils to think logically for themselves rather than receive all the analysis "pre-digested" by the teacher.' It was

> a very valid aim, but rather unrealistic with the less intelligent, [for] many kids find it impossible to grasp logical solutions. Kids need precise answers, at least to some exercises – they are too open-ended (which is like real life, but kids find it difficult to appreciate this).

This seems like an argument for withholding from pupils just that kind of thinking the Project aimed to offer, and is put forward by a teacher aware of the dangers of pupils' receiving an analysis 'pre-digested' by the teacher. It is interesting that it is the notion of 'logical thinking' that justifies this line of thought. It is likely that a view of bottom-set pupils as 'unable to grasp logical solutions' is derived from judging their encounters with the kind of linguistic formalism I have been trying to describe. Their need for 'precise answers' is likely to be acute in such circumstances, and, of course, is a need generated in them by the school's endorsement of 'precise answers'. It seemed strange that basic issues came so near to the surface of the meeting yet did not threaten to emerge into full view. Part of the reason for this might be that, like many such meetings, it was dominated by the need for a kind of social consensus to be kept up, to keep being a department working together in solidarity despite a threat of schismatic issues. What becomes essential *vis-à-vis* the issues is to appear to confront them. One has to appear to confront them to be professionals; one has to avoid them to be a group.

It was also C who contributed the section called 'Questions on knowledge of CONTENT', a missing-word exercise. I interposed a question on this section when 'wrong answers' were being discussed. 'A Norman castle would be a _____ source of evidence'. The 'right' answer was 'primary'.

Self: What if someone says 'interesting' in that question, so they say, rightly, that a Norman castle would be an interesting source of evidence?

C: No, he is wrong. The right answer is 'primary'.

Self: But he is right in a way, surely? What is the difference between your rightness and his?

C: Well, the difference is he has been primed. All the teaching has sort of been around that.

A: He did not get what I wanted so he did not get the mark.

What makes it less obvious that 'primary' or 'secondary' is wanted is the fact that the other missing-word answers are mostly unrelated to those terms: thus, 'Henry the _____ was an important English king who had _____ wives'. The grammar of primary–secondary is here thinned down further, in that other grammars (relating to Henry, knights, and so on) compete with it on the page. If 'priming' means that the mention of 'source of evidence' itself triggers 'primary' or 'secondary', when the other missing terms are quite miscellaneous, the formalistic narrowing of the grammar has proceeded to the point where only stimulus–response priming produces answers.

It seems that Project aims are in these ways interpreted in the direction of a formalizing simplification and compression. A's assumption that the work is 'abstract' may be seen in this light. It is only 'abstract' once certain formalistic interpretations have taken place, such as the loss of the 'in respect of what' things are primary and secondary source-evidence for. Had the work, though, been more to do with the concrete, with the handling and interpretation of objects themselves, it might have clarified for the teachers not only this formalism, but a further problem with 'primary', which is what, other than itself, a primary source can be taken as evidence of without in some sense no longer being primary. A Victorian cartoon is, at its most primary, evidence of the fact that the Victorians made cartoons, just as the Stone Age tool is evidence of the fact that they made tools. Beyond this immediate signification, or tautology, it is hard to see how one talks about one thing being evidence for another without inter-posing some degree of spatio-temporal distance (or 'secondari-ness') between objects and what they 'say'. As with the binary porous–non-porous distinction, an empirical involvement might have dissolved the dichotomy, and pupils' problems with it.

In such a context it is not surprising that a pull away from openness and minutiae is exercised by pupils themselves, of the kind that influences any teacher who wishes to be innovative. Thus a traditional bias was evident in comments of four bright A stream pupils on the relative 'reliability' as sources of truth about the Edwardian Age of 'an expert in Edwardian history' and 'an old lady who had been young then'. I asked if perhaps the old lady would be more reliable, 'a better source', not generally but just for her particular milieu. It was 'hard to say', it 'depends on her memory'; she 'probably wouldn't remember things'; she 'might be biased'. 'Supposing the historian's own primary sources were dicey, like the old lady?' (We agreed 'flawed' was a better term.) The lecturer was more reliable: 'He'd probably have talked to four or five', been able 'to compare them', and so on. It was not just the fact of the preference for the overall general view but also the unequivocal mode of its expression that suggested a reluctance to enter the Project's categories. Similarly, their comments when I asked about replying 'interesting' to the Norman castle question showed a preference for the more primed reply, and the whole context as not concerned with enquiry so much as what's 'in the book'.

P1:  It's not really relative to what we've been doing.
P2:  You should know from what you've learnt that you're not meant to put your opinion – we haven't done opinions yet. (This was corroborated enthusiastically.)
P3:  Yes, you should know.
P2:  He should mark it wrong . . . because it's not in the book.
P1:  It doesn't ask for your opinion.

A third-year top-set lesson on evidence conveys a sense of having come full circle, through simplification after simplification, back from open enquiry and the interpretation of particulars to a formalistic confrontation with generalities – the minimal grammar of 'Greece', complicated by the admixture of the minimal grammar drawn from the primary–secondary idea.

T:  If I was on an archaeological dig . . . and I was at Camelot . . .

P1: Who?

T:  If I was at Camelot and came up with a chalice or a drinking cup . . . (interruption–silence) which . . . came from King Arthur's court . . . I'll start again. (He repeated the above.) What kind of evidence would it be?
(Pause. Silence.)

T:  What's the special name for it?
(Several hands go up.)

P2: Primary.

T:  Primary, good lad. Now, if I decided to find out who used it . . . and looked it up in a book . . . what kind of evidence . . .

P3: Secondary source.

After this, exercise books were given out. There was then a session that lasted ten minutes or so on seeing pupils with work not done, and going over some simple language errors, particularly spelling: 'Another thing is your poor spelling. . . . When you're copying down from the board quite simply in your exercise books . . . you're lazy some of you and make mistakes. So the next five minutes I want you to correct your spellings.'

Then the booklets were given out by number (each pupil had a particular numbered booklet).

T:  Right I'd like you to look at page 5, classical Greece.

PP: Ugh, Argh.

T:  Less groaning please. Now this is one of the places from which we're going to get a lot of sources. . . . The map gives the well-known . . .

P4: Why is it called classical Greece?

T:  It's prior to the Romans . . . it's about [indistinct] years before . . . now, who knows anything about Athens?
(One boy had been there. I think another said it was the capital of Greece.)

T:  Does anyone know the name of the famous building on top of the hill?

P5: Sir, is it an Athenian temple?

T:    Yes, but it has a special name . . . The Parthenon . . . and it's on top of a large hill. . . . Has anyone heard of Sparta?

P6:    Yes.

P7:    Yes, Spartacus.

T:    Spartacus was a Roman slave. . . . I wasn't asking about Spartacus . . . Sparta.

P8:    That's where Helen went.

T:    No, she didn't, she . . .

P8:    I seen the film . . .

T:    Be quiet. I don't care if you have seen the film. . . . Anyway Sparta were the main opponents of Athens. . . . They had completely different ideas to Athens. . . . There wasn't much art or poetry . . . but they were very strong and very good at games and races. . . . Does anyone know what happens at Olympia?
(Brief comments on Olympic Games followed.)

T:    Does anyone know about Delphi – at Delphi there was an oracle, like a prophetess . . . she used to sit in the temple . . . all the important people used to come along to ask the prophetess . . . strange incantations . . . used to sacrifice the odd animal . . . she said strange things, because people on both sides in war asked . . . RIGHT . . . The other important thing is Mount Olympus. Has anyone heard of any of the Olympians?
(Four hands up.)

P3:    Zeus . . . leader.

P4:    Aphrodite . . . goddess.

P9:    Hermes.

P10:    Hera.

T:    Right, if we turn to page 5, we see a photograph of the Parthenon . . . a very big piece of evidence . . . what kind?

P10:    Primary.

T:    Right. How would you describe . . .

P10:    Temple.

P11:    The pillars at the front?

T:    I think they're Doric.

P4:    Are those seats or something . . . at the front? (Referring to fallen columns.)

T:    No . . . what happened was the Greeks and Turks had a war . . . and they stored the ammunition there . . . and it blew up. . . . Now at the top . . . are two angles . . . triangles . . . and inside it were all manner of sculptures . . . called the Elgin Marbles . . . they were taken from here by an Englishman called Lord Elgin . . . let's describe it more. . . . It's got a bit of a frieze, hasn't it . . . what would you be able to say by looking at the temple?

P7:   They were good craftsmen.

T:    Yes.

P2:   Strong.

T:    Not necessarily, but they had the means . . .

P4:   They were clever.

T:    Right . . . anything else? What is the building . . .

P10:  Temple.

T:    So they worshipped.

P10:  God would have [indistinct] them.

T:    It tells us they had religion. If we knew it belonged to Athena we know who they worship . . .

P8:   How big is it . . .?

T:    Quite large – if you take the fourth column from the left and go up to the line [indistinct explanation of height]. NOW, in your books, put the title 'Classical Greece'.

P3:   They wouldn't half have a lot of trouble getting up there . . .

T:    Then . . . on page 5 . . . then put 'Primary Sources'. Then put 'The Parthenon'.

The question written on the board was:

(1) Describe the Parthenon.
(2) What can you tell about the ancient Greeks from this building?

The pupils wrote answers to this question for the rest of the lesson.

This is, to use Douglas Barnes' term, essentially a traditional 'transmission' lesson,[8] in which the idea of sources of evidence of different kinds functions as a content added to the content relating to Greece. The complex, open encounters with minutiae and particularity envisaged in the course aims, and by some of the teachers at times, have been refined to opaque generalities about Sparta and anecdotes about the Delphic oracle and the Parthenon, and the 'enquiry' into the kind of building the Parthenon seems to be comes to the 'temple' conclusion without there being, apparently, any inference made from the photograph. Moreover, the pupils' speculations, that the Greeks were good craftsmen, and strong and clever, and their musings about what 'classical' means, and whether those are seats at the front, and about its size, and how difficult it would be to get up there, are handled as peripheral to this slenderized interpretation of the question of how historians handle evidence. But this lesson, I think, ought to be seen primarily not just as a not very good lesson taught towards the end of an exhausting week, but as the expression of a series of redefinitions of an initially openly conceived content, all of which – at the level of course materials, or department meetings, or pupils' views and expectations, or lessons themselves – gradually reduce and simplify in a quite purposeful way, in the interests of making the work 'easier to understand'.

## Remedies

If this kind of choice, away from the minutiae and the particulars of subjects, is a routine response to the routine dilemma that teachers find themselves in, it seems likely that it has consequences for the relation between pupil and teacher. In particular it will mean that there is less opportunity to construct a relation within and through the essential, central concern with knowledge, for the attenuation of grammar makes genuine dialogue about that increasingly difficult. If subject knowledge which is initially formalistic is slenderized towards an extremer formalism in the interests of access, and it then becomes taken for granted that this is the comprehensive school's most efficient way of equalizing opportunities of entry to subject knowledge, the chances are greatly reduced of redefining the teacher–pupil relation so that dialogue flows through the knowledge that school handles, rather than amongst its other concerns, such as assessment, sociability, discipline and pastoral affairs generally.

Remedial work is an area where it might be thought that the more informally human relationship that often exists between teacher and pupil, the relative freedom from subject constraints, and the basic rationale of the work, would make it unlikely that pupils would be engaged in formalistic encounters with language. Remedial work is based, after all, on the assumption that it proceeds from a special awareness of pupils' problems with school learning, a genuine understanding of what they find difficult, and so on. A circular from the head of the remedial department to all staff dealing with matters of written 'presentation' demonstrated this sense of concerned awareness; it reminded staff how generally 'less able pupils become confused', and made useful comment of this kind: 'Many pupils are not aware that when we tell them to use capital letters we do not mean that a word or group of words is to be written with printed or block capital throughout, but only the first letter should be a capital.'

The remedial work in the lower school was meticulously organized on an 'individualized' basis, in the sense that programmes were individually designed in such detail that pupils coming in at the beginning of each lesson either knew what to do or were able to look up in their personal folder what they should start on. The implication of such an approach that pupils' individual needs are catered for might also be expected to mean that their encounters with language would be richer and less formalistic than those I have looked at so far.

I shall analyse some talks I had with B, a first-year boy who was withdrawn weekly from twelve of his lessons (in geography, history, religious education, science and classical studies) to receive remedial help with reading and writing. In both remedial work and normal lessons he had great difficulty. I first saw him at work in a third-set English class, where I helped him with the task described later in this chapter. This first example of his difficulties is drawn from a later visit to look at his work in the remedial context. The problem is one that would not be thought to represent something new or difficult; it was an encounter with 'or' sentences.

B was doing a comprehension test and seemed to stick on the question 'Is it morning or afternoon?' – he evidently read 'morning' as 'money'. The next question was 'Are you polite or rude?' He wrote, 'I am polite and rude'. As I watched him working on the 'or' questions I began to wonder if his loss of the question was not in some way a loss of 'or'. Thus 'Do you like oranges, apples or pears best?' was again answered with 'yes', though he had by then read out the question aloud to me without error. I then read it aloud to him, and he replied 'yes' again. This short conversation then took place.

(1) Self: Do you like apples or oranges?
(2) B:    Both.
(3) Self: Do you like apples or oranges best?
(4) B:    Yes.
(5) Self: If you had to choose between apples and oranges which would be best, then?
(6) B:    Apples.

Clearly, 'or' questions do not always imply 'pick one'. (For instance, the old joke, 'Do you intend to work for the overthrow of the United States by propaganda, subversion or violence?'.) The question at (1) could be of this type; (3) seems to imply choice, though it is only when an explicit 'choose' is introduced that B is willing to relinquish one of the fruits.

What is happening? I registered acceptance of his reading of (1) by proceeding with the conversation after his answer (2), then asked the same question again, with 'best' added to imply that he had to make a choice. But I had accepted he need not make a choice, so that 'best' in (3) may have sounded as if it meant simply 'a lot', or did he like those things best, as compared with other things. The phrase 'if you had to choose' may then have recalled choice situations, catalysing – or coercing – an actual choice, whereas the other 'or' questions do not. The forms of words 'Do you like x or y?' and 'Do you like x or y best?' seem for B to resemble the kind of 'do you' questions that need yes/no answers, rather than to be seen as the surface structure of something in deep grammar that suggests 'compare your liking for x with your liking for y and state a preference'. Most 11-year-old readers will read 'Do you like x or y?' (even without help from distinct voice tones) as frequently involving that kind of transformation, but for B, presumably, no such transformation is accomplished through these words. They lie then, in a sense, on the surface, and he negotiates with that surface, not with the transformation where meaning might be said to lie. So 'or' in these sentences for B is like a word shorn of that meaning which at times it would presumably have – in situations of choice; as in meals, for example, where a question like 'Do you want tea or coffee?' uses 'or' to hold up two real alternatives in a typical social situation. This third 'or' is perhaps situated in his biography in a way that the earlier 'or' is not. Until B is as familiar with the linguistic–formal conventions of that other situation as he is with what might be thought of as the conventions of mealtime he may hardly see the make-a-choice 'or' as he reads.

There seems to be a shadowy resemblance to the situation often reported in cross-cultural studies where 'primitive' groups fail to handle problems involving 'simple' syllogistic reasoning because they are somehow unable to accept, or enter into, the unfamiliar conventions of such reasoning – such as that the conclusion is reached from the stated premises, not from outside knowledge, that its logical validity is different from its possible truth as a statement, and so on.

For instance Luria presented to Uzbekistan peasants who had no schooling this incomplete syllogism:

In the far north all bears are white.
Nova Zemlya is in the far north.
What colour are the bears there?

Very commonly, replies took the form, 'I do not know. I have not been there', or, 'Ask the people who've been there'.[9]

Cole et al. found a similar 'empirical bias' in their thorough study of the Kpelle in Liberia,[10] when they presented subjects with logical problems. Thus:

E:  Flumo and Yakpalo always drink cane juice together. Flumo is drinking cane juice. Is Yakpalo drinking cane juice?

One response, quoted for its typicality, was:

> Flumo and Yakpalo drink cane juice together, but the time Flumo was drinking the first one Yakpalo was not there that day.

Just as a willingness to suspend what is known and accept the conventions of such hypothetical thinking are necessary to perform such reasoning tasks, so there has to be for these 'or' questions a willingness to suspend the pressing knowledge that one likes both, and to accept the convention that one makes a hypothetical, non-empirical 'choice'. That choosing in this way involves rejecting is also interesting. B was reluctant to make hypothetical choices, as if he saw them as actual choices and rejections. He was also reluctant to choose, and displayed the same anti-hypothetical 'empirical bias', when I asked him what his favourite TV programme was. He had given me three titles and I said, 'Do you like "Blake's 7", "Bionic Woman" or "Wonderwoman" best?' He said it was hard to tell because he liked all of them a lot. He could see here that he *was* asked to make a choice, but was not willing to do so without further pressure. Had he merely read the question, or been asked it earlier in our conversation, he might have said 'yes'. Perhaps he had learnt something of that conventional manner of eliciting non-practical choices and responding to it during the course of our extended conversation. That this is not such a far-fetched notion is, for me, suggested by other uncertainties he displayed, such as one relating to the names of months:

Self:   What is a month, do you think?
        (Pause)
Self:   Could you name one?
B:      (After short pause) Eh, Saturday?

The previous week I had seen B at an English lesson. Five pupils had been given a special task because they were finding normal work too demanding (Figure 17[11]). B could not start. He could not complete. 'The air inside the crown . . .'; nor did he know what 'brim' meant. An examination of the page makes clear why he found it hard.

# 12 More Than Just a Hat

A man named Stetson made a special kind of felt hat for cowboys. That is why cowboys' hats are often called Stetsons.

The pictures show you some of the many uses of a Stetson hat. Write about them by finishing the sentences.

| | |
|---|---|
| campfire | head |
| cool | horse |
| drinking | keeps |
| ears | pillow |
| eyes | pulled |
| fan | tied |
| water | |

A cowboy's hat is often called a Stetson.

The air inside the high crown ....

The wide brim keeps the sun ....

On rainy days ....

In cold weather ....

The brim can also ....

The whole hat ....

He can use it ....

Rolled up it ....

Figure 17

Though they are not necessarily available to the pupil, a number of assumptions are made by the writer about how the page will be read. The words in the box are used to complete the sentences. They need to be combined to do so (keeps . . . cool). The pictures describe sentences; so, they are clues. The order of the pictures is the order of the sentences; so, the pictures have to be read down the left then down the right. One could also quibble and say 'finish the *sentence*' refers to phrases like 'the whole hat'. And a natural ending 'keeps the sun off' is not offered. The obscurity of the pictures' meanings is such that text is necessary to interpret them; pupils need the answer to understand the clue. Thus, the quaint picture of what looks like an old lady's hat (bottom left) needs 'in cold weather' for it to be understood. The first picture is so neutral as to make it hard to juxtapose specifically with 'high crown', just as 'the whole hat . . .' could be completed with reference to any of the eight pictures.

Had B been working on a cowboy project, reading a western, or writing a story, some of the puzzle-page language might have had a nearer history, a sharper context. He might have seen the rolled-up hat or the shaded face and shoulders in terms of knowledge drawn from that context. As it is, he starts, as it were *ab initio*, with the dictionary, and its meanings. This starting afresh on a different subject with each new page or lesson is a way of ensuring that attributions of meaning made in reading or writing do not normally include those that have gathered over time, or those that are already in place because they are personal. Such a discreteness seems likely to cut off the pupil from his own language and its constitutive elements, and from the sense that what he uses is his own language. B's role seems restricted, almost, to merely reactive responses to fresh sets of instructions about what to do. In a profound sense, he cannot gather *his* thoughts, or *his* language.

Two days later, in his remedial work, B was reading on the 'Language Master' with the remedial teacher. (The Language Master plays back taped sentences that accompany written cards. The tape is played before, then after, the pupil's attempt to read aloud what is on the card.) The same discreteness – here pursued through phonics – is evident in both the commercially prepared cards and in those the teacher prepared.

Mother will gather the apples.
Ruth lost a tooth.
I see a moth in my bath.
I like chops and chips.

In another remedial lesson:

> In the woods in spring
> The . . . are collecting . . . in their beaks.
> They are going to build a . . .
>     nest – bird – twigs

That exercises of this kind can impede the attributions of personal meaning and *prevent* language seems clear from a lesson ten days later. It was a missing-word exercise. Its subject, which B could discover only through reading, was 'Making a cake for tea'. Some of B's false starts are attributable to the discreteness of the new task; thus he read 'flour' as 'floor', then (after I had said 'flour' – or 'flower') read 'She flowers . . .'. Neither 'error' would have occurred if the context had given him the sound 'flour'/'flower', with the meaning 'flour', before he had started on the exercise.

The revealing sentence was the second – 'She puts the . . . in a big . . .'. He had four words to use up in the two sentences – flour, makes, cake, bowl – and had already used 'cake' in 'She makes a cake for tea'. He read, 'She puts the flour in a big . . .', and paused, then said 'cake', then said 'no'. With some prodding – and with reluctance on his part – we arrived at 'She puts flour in a big BOWL'. Then he said with real astonishment, 'I don't get it. You put CAKE in a big bowl!' I explained we had already used 'cake'. I then said did he know what a bowl was. 'Yea, but you put cake *in a oven* in a bowl.'

His resistance, then, was due to his narrowing of the contexts of 'bowl' to something in an oven. There could be cake in a bowl-in-an-oven (pulled out of an oven?) but not flour in a bowl on a table. Perhaps he only sees cakes coming out of the oven, not being made. At any rate, the inclusion of 'bowl' in the list prevented him from reading the sentence.

On the same day as the remedial lesson I observed a maths lesson with B. His experience here strongly suggested that the language, the symbols, the algorithms of maths were profoundly unfamiliar, in the sense that he did not appear to use them, or think with them; rather, they were the puzzles in a primary sense. Handling them in combination, which is what maths is, means not only that 'he hasn't the faintest idea of what he is doing', but that his basic bewilderments go unacknowledged. To be given $2\overline{)2034}$, and to start 'doing it', was for B already to pass over profound difficulty.

He was 'making a sum', as he put it. On the board was $2\overline{)2034}$, which he copied thus, complete with answer, from his friend:
$12\overline{)1012}$
    2034.

$$1010$$
Next, $4\overline{)2416}$, copied as $5\overline{)2416}$, and his (own) answer: $5\overline{)2416}$. He had divided 2 into 5, 4 into 5, and so on. I wondered if he had been employing a binary idea, saying 'goes' (1) and 'does not go' (0), but got '4 into 5' wrong. He then proceeded by adding 7, 9, 6 and 11, as answers to the same process. His reversed way of 'doing it' on the first attempt was perhaps an echo of $5 \div 2$, $5 \div 4$ and so on; the transposition confusion noted in the previous chapter might have occurred here.

I resorted to 'ordinary language' to try to talk about division. Some of the problems arising in this conversation show how difficult it is, it seems to me, to find a way of talking about division that does not continually obtrude what are formalisms for the pupil, deriving from one's own settled notions of division.

Self: How much ice-cream could you eat in one go?
B:    About this much. (Hands describing amount.)
Self: All right, suppose I gave you four times that amount, four lots of it, how much would you be able to eat?
B:    I could eat it all.
Self: I thought you said you could only eat *that* amount. What about the rest?
B:    I could eat it later.

Either he is having me on, or it is a genuine intrusion of the empirical into my formal hypothetical question; he perhaps does not hear it as a maths question, about relations between amounts, but as a practical empirical question: what can be done with this huge amount of ice-cream?

Self: All right, let's imagine you've got one empty milk bottle over here.

B:    Yeah.

Self:  And over here you've got four full milk bottles. How many times could you get the milk that's in the four bottles into the empty one?

B:    Once.

My silly question (meant to translate $4\overline{)1}$) produces what is empirically appropriate, but not helpful with $4\overline{)1}$. Clearly you could fill the bottle once only.

Despite all this – including his temporary teacher's obtuse questions – he can, providing the hypotheticality offered him looks enactable, and providing the language is 'his', reason mathematically:

Self:  All right, supposing . . . how many times could you run round the school field, do you think?

B:    About twice.

Self:  Supposing there was a field that was twice as far round as the school field, how many times do you think you could run round that?

B:    Once.

Self:  If there was a field that was four times as far round as the school field, how many times do you think you could run round that?

B:    Half-way round.

I attempted to translate this (it seemed akin at the time) into $2\overline{)1}$. This was too much of a shift; he said first 'once', then 'it didn't', then 'twice'. I went further back then to the 16 squares I had drawn on his paper just before resorting to the example of ice-cream. He counted the squares. 16. He counted again the number in each group marked off with a heavy line. 4. Thus:

*Figure 18*

Then, 'How many fours are there in 16?' 'One.' After a recount it was 5; finally it was 4.

I take it that most of my questions, apart from the running-track ones, somehow brought him up against a way of speaking that did not elicit or accommodate the reasoning demonstrated in his answers about the running-track. In some way those modes of questioning became formalistic obstacles to understanding. He tended to treat various modes of questioning 'arbitrarily'. Thus all these written questions produced the answer 6:

What is 2 into 4?
2 add 4
4 divide by 2
4 ÷ 2

Even when it seems one has found a reality and mode of speaking which does accommodate his thinking, communication is still precarious.

Self: How much pocket money do you get?
B: 50p.
Self: Every week?
B: Yeah – once a week.
Self: How many weeks in a month?
B: Two – no ten.
Self: What is a month do you think?
(Long pause.)
Self: Could you name one?
B: Er – Saturday.
(A little further clarifying talk about months.)
Self: If you had your pocket money every week for four weeks and then added it up how much would you have?
B: £2. (Very prompt – in answer to a syntactically complex sentence, moreover – though the context which has begun to be established renders it, apparently, immediately apprehendable.)
Self: How much would you have if you had 30p a week for six weeks?
B: (After a pause of several seconds.) About £2.
Self: If you had 30p a week and not 50p, how much would there be if you put two weeks' money all together?

B:     (After about ten seconds.) Er . . . 60p.
Self:  If you had three weeks?
B:     (No reply . . . but counting on fingers uncertainly.)

The way that hypotheticalities might be rejected, and the empirical world become intrusive, is hinted at in the next interchange, which was meant to deal further with amounts of 30p pocket money.

Self:  Suppose I borrowed 90p off you last week.
B:     Yeah.
Self:  Then I asked you to lend me another 30p.
B:     I wouldn't give it yer.

After he was 'sure he would get it back' he answered my question. Perhaps it was merely humorous. Or perhaps the humour is prompted by not immediately recognizing my question as a mathematical one. He was in a real social situation and was telling me exactly what he would do.

I have suggested that B's experience in the classroom in varying contexts over a few days is of a similar character. That similarity seems to lie in the relation of the learner to what he attempts to learn. I should describe it as essentially formalistic. B does not seem to be using his own language or thinking to gain a purchase on subject knowledge. Rather, subject knowledge is simplified and packaged in such a way – not least in my own questions – as to render it inaccessible; the offer of help-to-understand in this remedial context is made in terms which themselves need help-to-understand.

My own interrogations, starting from the formalisms encountered, seemed to me not to escape that relation except briefly, but repeated reading of his and my own words gives me a strong sense of an occasional breaking-out of this formalistic circle into a kind of dialogue, followed by a lapse into the initial sterility. Some of the oscillation between dialogue and its absence might be usefully recapitulated. He handled 'or' with 'choices' that explicitly recalled social choice situations, but not with those where the choice was hypothetical and implicit. He handled division with an explicit running-round-the-field context, but not with the ice-cream context, where presumably answering in terms of the supposition I offered meant ignoring what to do with the rest. He handled the addition of sums of pocket money, until he refused to join in the game and gave the empirical reply: 'I wouldn't give it yer.' His 'sense of humour' is not unambiguously the reason of his opting out, the converse is just as possible: opting out makes him seem funny.

Even a cursory look at B's attempts to handle these problems reveals the source of his thinking in the autobiographical, in the personal way he interprets and handles language. His failures here stem from attempts to use formalistic fragments of language that he has not employed personally and socially. Moreover, it seems that the 'easier' language of remedial work remains relatively inaccessible and formalistic despite – or because of – the attempts made to simplify it. These attempts often seemed, in their discreteness and arbitrariness, to take him away from that more complex but recognizable everyday world, the social situations of which, with the language he possesses to articulate them, appeared to be his only means of access to this school knowledge. Even then, it was only by searching that we discovered workable terrain; the problematic guise in which particulars of this everyday social world were placed released him only intermittently to deploy his own thought and language.

There is perhaps a resemblance here between B's experience and what Valéry says about the way one can lose the sense of meaning that comes from 'rapid passage over words'. He describes the loss in this way:

> You have surely noticed the curious fact that a certain word, which is perfectly clear when you hear or use it in everyday speech, becomes mysteriously cumbersome the moment you withdraw it from circulation and try to find its meaning after taking away its temporary function. . . . We understand each other, and ourselves, only thanks to our rapid passage over words.[12]

And for Merleau-Ponty 'expression has failed' when 'I have the feeling of dealing only with words.' In this way, 'we begin to reflect on language instead of living it' and language can thus become 'an object of thought rather than "mine"'. Hence his project of a return from the notion of language as a 'technique or device', an 'instrument of communication', to 'the speaking subject, to my contact with the language I am speaking'.[13] The relevance of this existential stress for B, and not only for children like B, seems clearly suggested by the manner in which what looks like B's return to intermittent contact with the language he speaks draws him back into a relation with his temporary teacher in which there seems to be genuine 'dialogic' talk.

I should like to deal briefly with a final example from B's work, particularly in the light of the notion that some of what he might have deployed is closed off by an encounter in which 'expression has failed', and words have become 'cumbersome', withdrawn from circulation. B was working on a comprehension exercise in which single, discrete sentences, bearing no content relation to each other, were followed by questions. I joined him at the point where he was silently reading 'Conifers, or cone-bearing trees, have shallow roots'. (Note that reading this involves his translating 'or' to mean 'another description of which, is'; a usage which, in the light especially of his other 'or' problems, he may not have known.) Reading aloud to me, 'conifers' became, hesitantly, 'cauliflowers'; 'shallow' became 'small', and 'roots' became 'roads'. His second attempt was 'Cauliflowers are called being . . .'. This, in a way, shows that 'he cannot read'. And yet what is noticeable is how near he comes – although he 'cannot read' – to accurately deciphering 'conifers' and 'roots'. If it is true to say 'B cannot read', it is true here only with two important qualifications: reading is implicitly defined as deciphering print, with no contextual help for predicting what the print is likely to be about; and the things that B 'cannot read' are these kinds of sentence; there would be no warrant for assuming from this failure that he could not read other kinds of language than this specially discrete, decontextualized type.

Wittgenstein remarks that 'we are strongly inclined to use the metaphor of something being in a particular state for saying that something can behave in a particular way. And this way of representation, or this metaphor, is embodied in the expressions, "He is capable of . . .".'[14] The verb, he also points out, is in the present tense. 'B cannot read' means rather that B does not (or has not) 'read' such sentences in such situations. The sentences B does not read, in the sense that he cannot decipher them, are sentences he cannot decipher because he cannot 'read' them, in the broader sense. He cannot here successfully employ that predictive skill which uses minimal visual typographic clues to fill out expectancies derived from awareness of context. He cannot attribute meaning to this print because there is for him no meaning which is anterior to, and forms a context for, print. B is left 'dealing only with words' in the form of print, though it is only by reducing the discrete autonomy of print, by in some way employing it as means to meaning, rather than substituting it for meaning, that B could use print to read with.

This emphasis, which is also a psycho-linguistic truism perhaps, is developed at length in Frank Smith's *Comprehension and Learning*.[15] Comprehension is a matter of sampling surface structure – the 'visual information' of written language – in order to test predictions and resolve uncertainty about underlying meaning. His emphasis, which is implicitly phenomenological, is on the learner as maker of meanings. 'How does the reader get meaning from the surface structure of language? He does not. The listener does not extract meaning from the surface structure because there is no meaning there. He must supply it himself.' B had words and meanings to supply – 'cauliflower', 'roads', and 'small'. If he had known that the subject of the writing was vegetables or food then 'cauliflowers' would be an accurate guess (which Smith suggests is what the deciphering component of fluent reading consists of, since visual cues that do not confirm expectations tend not to be seen), and might well have been read, showing that B 'can read'. It seems then as if the programme designed to help him to read may have the effect of closing off access to essential components of his developing capacity to make sense of print.

If this can be called closure, it is clear that a tendency to present knowledge formalistically can become accentuated exactly as teachers attempt some kind of reflexivity, in trying to see what is difficult about routine work. The decontextualized discreteness of remedial work, and the abstract schemata of simplifying models like the 'Elizabeth's problems' model or the artesian concept as presented, or the notion of primary and secondary kinds of evidence, are then alike in that they define absence of difficulty, ease of access for beginners, in terms of a succinct essentiality of the sort that belongs rather to the finished skill or the settled view of things, an essentiality that is post-complexity, and is properly called formal. It is the genuinely formal character of the achieved knowledge of a notion that is absent for anyone starting to learn anything, and yet it is ironically the absence of that very deciphering skill necessary to decode decontextualized discrete sentences that qualifies B, it seems, for remedial work consisting largely of such language.

## References

1 Richard Cobb, 'The tempting threshold', *The Listener* (6 April, 1978).
2 M. Young, 'Curriculum change, limits and possibilities', in M. Young and A. Whitty (eds), *Society, State and Schooling* (Ringmer, Falmer Press, 1977), p. 242.
3 J. L. Austin, *How To Do Things With Words*, J. O. Urmson (ed.) (Oxford, Oxford University Press, 1963), pp. 142–3.
4 ibid., p. 138.
5 D. Sylvester *et al. A New Look at History*, Schools Council History Project 13–16 (Edinburgh, Holmes MacDougall, 1976), p. 36.
6 ibid., p. 38.
7 Schools Council History Project, *Looking at Evidence*.
8 D. Barnes, *From Communication to Curriculum* (Harmondsworth, Penguin, 1975), p. 140.
9 A. Luria, quoted in S. Scribner, 'Modes of thinking and ways of speaking: culture and logic reconsidered', in P. N. Johnson-Laird and P. C. Wason (eds), *Thinking: Readings in Cognitive Science* (Cambridge, Cambridge University Press, 1977), p. 484.
10 M. Cole, J. Gay, J. Glick and D. Sharp, *The Cultural Context of Learning and Thinking* (London, Methuen, 1972), pp. 187–8.
11 C. V. Burgess, *Burgess Composition, Book 2* (University of London Press, London, 1967), p. 17.
12 P. Valéry, 'Poetry and abstract thought', in J. Mathews (ed.) *P. Valéry – An Anthology* (London, Routledge & Kegan Paul, 1977), pp. 138–9.
13 M. Merleau-Ponty, 'On the phenomenology of language' in

J. O'Neill (ed.) *Phenomenology, Language and Sociology* (London, Heinemann, 1974), p. 82.

14 L. Wittgenstein, *The Blue and Brown Books* (Oxford, Basil Blackwell, 1964), p. 117.

15 F. Smith, *Comprehension and Learning* (New York, Holt, Rinehart & Winston, 1975), pp. 98–106.

# 5
# CLOSURE

## Unused knowledge

Using the term 'closure' in the way I have just done implies that children may in some way be denied the use of their own capacities – their language, the things they already know and can do – in the learning that takes place in school. Clearly, it is important to ask how one recognizes that this is happening, how one becomes aware of what a particular closure consists in, and how it comes about. In B's case something seemed to emerge from talking to him while he was engaged in work he had been given; one of these conversations lasted about three-quarters of an hour. Other un-conscripted knowledge may lie much nearer to the surface. A brief talk may uncover what took some considerable time with B; or pupils may display in lessons bits of relevant knowledge which, because they are not taken up into the fabric of the lesson in some way, could be said to encounter closure.

But, of course, it is very difficult for a teacher, who ultimately orchestrates what takes place in the classroom, to be so continuously alert to the often apparently digressive relevances of children as to sense the closures implicit in many a decision not to go along with the seemingly frivolous question or the seemingly vague comment, but resolutely to stay with the matter in hand, the topic of the lesson, the structure of the course. And yet it is equally arguable that, despite the daunting idea of having to listen for the resonances for learning barely audible in the idiosyncratic tones of twenty-odd voices, this kind of listening may be a primary concern for the teacher if continuous closure is not to take place. The observations made so far might give one reason to wonder whether closure is not likely to be a routine feature of pupils' encounters with subjects that are conceived objectivistically and so conduce to formalistic negotiations with the language that represents them.

The following short account of a talk with M, another first-year boy doing remedial work, illustrates how accessible, for the teacher who is willing to suspect its existence, may be some of the relevant unconscripted knowledge that pupils have. In an English lesson M was working on a vocabulary exercise (Figure 19[1]). The initial instruction was: 'first learn the meanings of all the words in the list' (this might have meant using a dictionary, but M did not); and then 'use as many of them as possible in your description' of 'six to ten sentences'. M's description omitted the following words: ostler, tankards, ale, balconies, crowded, landlord, luggage, stake, unharnessed. I sat down with him and pointed to parts of the picture, asking questions. 'What's that?' 'A balcony.' 'What's happening to the front horses?' 'They're being unharnessed.' And so on. In this way it became clear that seven of the nine unused words – ale, balconies, crowded, landlord, luggage, stage and unharnessed – were in fact part of his vocabulary; they were not used, but were known.

The teacher had interpreted M's exercise as revealing something about the extent of his vocabulary; this seemed clear from her surprise when I showed her that M had not used a number of words which he none the less knew. Her view that such work provided help with vocabulary may have originated in the judgement that 'his vocabulary is weak' made on him the year before in

# 23 *A Scene to Describe*

The picture shows a coaching station about 150 years ago. The station was really an inn, and here the horses were changed and the passengers had a quick meal. Describe the scene in six to ten sentences.

But first learn the meanings of all the words in the list. Use as many of them as possible in your description.

*Remember to begin sentences with capital letters and to end them with full stops.*

| ale | crowded | ladder | ostler | stable | tired |
|-----|---------|--------|--------|--------|-------|
| balconies | fresh | landlord | passengers | stage-coach | unharnessed |
| coachmen | horses | luggage | | tankards | whip |

*Figure 19*

his last year of junior school; she perhaps expected the exercise not only to 'improve his vocabulary' but also to show that it needed improving. (Interestingly, the judgement that 'his vocabulary is weak' was followed by the remark in his junior school reports that 'he could talk for a long time, given an audience', as if 'vocabulary' related only to written contexts. Other judgements included statements like 'untidy nonsense after the first few words'.)

M's remedial programme was constructed from such judgements. Omitting several words in a list in this kind of exercise showed that he 'does not know' them, which in turn showed that he has a poor vocabulary. With other judgements, mainly of a psychometric kind from verbal reasoning scores, reading tests and so on, such opinions helped to demonstrate that he should be on a particular programme. Hence the twelve lessons weekly of remedial work, when he was withdrawn from ordinary lessons, and hence the kind of extra remedial work that he did in normal English.

There may be many situations in school where a pupil's knowledge is hidden in those very tasks that are meant to elicit it. M might use his linguistic knowledge in a fuller way 'talking for a long time, given an audience'. Why this particular closure has taken place I shall not speculate about; it is the existence of relevant, unconscripted knowledge that seems important. Perhaps M 'could not be bothered' to do this exercise thoroughly; but perhaps not being bothered is a result of doing work more suitable for someone with a genuinely weak vocabulary – he said he found the work 'very easy', and was working hard to get out of his 12-lesson remedial timetable. Later in the year he did.

Though M's unused knowledge was soon discovered, it was sought for behind what was going on. For whatever reason, it was hidden. Often pupils' knowledge and awareness are made openly available to teachers but for some reason still remain unused. It may be that the relevance of what children say is not fully grasped. (With structures of knowledge defined objectivistically, this may be only too likely.) I made a habit of noting down pupil questions and comments that seemed voluntary or spontaneous and to bear some relation to the task in hand. Once I had started to look for them, it was striking how infrequent they were. The focus here, however, is only on what happens to these intrusions of interest.

I shall comment briefly on some of the apparently spontaneous contributions that occurred over a period of ten days or so. In a classical studies lesson, the teacher was recounting the story of the origins of the Trojan War. This elicited from pupils a number of voluntary questions, four in the space of about six or seven minutes, the only ones in the lesson. These questions sometimes came in groups, with several bunched together. One boy said: 'Sir, I saw this programme on telly . . . was it anything to do with it?' He then described a programme which clearly could have had some relation to Troy and the war. The response was: 'I don't know. . . . I didn't see it, it doesn't sound like it – anyway let's get on.' A minute or so later, referring to something that had been said about Agamemnon and Menelaus a boy asked: 'If they were kings in the same area, why didn't they live together?' The reply: 'Now we're getting a bit short of time, so we'll get on – and not have so many questions.' Immediately after, from a third pupil, 'Why didn't Agamemnon have a wife?', responded to by, 'I'm not sure', and no discussion, though the teacher did add, 'An interesting thought'. Something of a flurry of questions had been produced – the cliché perhaps appropriately suggests the implied disturbance – with two final ones, 'Did she know that she hadn't dipped his heel in?' and 'How could you get killed by not having your heel covered?' These provoked answers from other pupils, and for a very brief space pupils asked and answered each other, and the convention of teacher being in charge of both questions and answers was suspended. It was not for long, however; the task for the latter part of the lesson, writing names in a 'Who's Who' at the end of the exercise book, was introduced in the middle of this, and the questions stopped – or were stopped.

There was evidently here, for a brief space, an intrusion into the lesson of priorities from the knowledge world of pupils, with its own curiosities and fascinations with Greek myth, accented differently from those which the lesson consisted of. The manner in which the questions were handled stressed the peripherality of at least some of the authentic interests they carried. Thus there were two references to 'getting on' or 'getting short of time'. However interesting to speculate why Agamemnon had no wife, the question was treated as a form of not getting on. The pupils were thus also learning what kinds of activity belong to 'getting on with' classical studies. Filling in the 'Who's Who' belonged, talking to others about 'how she knew she hadn't dipped his heel in' at this point did not. In particular, they were learning that mentioning what simply interested them was not necessarily an appropriate way of being interested since certain other things were intrinsically (i.e. objectivistically) of particular interest.

A first-year geography lesson on cattle-raising in Australia produced a few voluntary questions and a similar reluctance or inability on the teacher's part to weave the interests that the questions represented into the central fabric of the lesson. One pupil asked, 'Do they go on horses, like on telly?' It might be worth commenting on the seemingly high proportion of these initiations that were related to television and seemed to amount to attempts to make explicit the connections with school knowledge that televised knowledge makes possible. Such knowledge also seems useful because it gives pupils the opportunity of telling the teacher something about 'his' subject that he does not know, and the contradictions of this kind of closure seem particularly noticeable. The reply was: 'They do, we'll discuss it in a minute', but it was not discussed. Not only was the minute already allocated, the topic was not recalled. A similar thing happened a moment or two later when the teacher referred to three methods of taking cattle to the slaughter-houses. A pupil interjected, 'There's trains . . .', and the teacher said, 'We'll talk about that in a minute', but did not so much 'talk about' it as handle the new item in his lesson the way the lesson, not the pupil's interjection, demanded: 'The advantage of using road trains is that they get to the slaughter-houses quickly, so that cattle do not lose weight or farmers lose money.' This is a somewhat academic gloss of a routine kind, hardly a 'talking about' trains.

A minute or two later, referring to cross-breeding, a pupil asked, 'When you cross-breed, what do you call it [the new breed]? There must be different names for them'. The teacher replied: 'I'm not sure, I suppose . . . at this time all you need to know is that they're cross-breeds.' It is interesting that references to time were used to handle all three questions. The clear import of the last comment is that items of knowledge belong in slots of school time. Focusing on an item of knowledge at the right time is part of learning it. One other pupil produced a little later a long account of a sheep-dip operation in answer to the teacher's question. This fascinating, transient redefinition of content and the temporal distribution of content seemed to exist somewhat on its own; it was heard with interest, but it started nothing, produced no developed responses. The class went quickly on to copy notes from the board into jotters, though it had felt the most vital bit of that lesson. It seemed to suspend the lesson in time, but did not divert it, as if it were acceptable for a lesson to *wait*, but not for the temporal distribution of its contents to be further tampered with.

## One Anglo-Saxon village

This issue might be seen in clearer focus by presenting a much longer extract from a first-year history lesson about Anglo-Saxon village life. Announcing there would be no test that day, the teacher asked pupils to open their history note-books, and began a question-and-answer session: 'Were the Anglo-Saxons interested in the remains the Romans had left behind?', 'What attracted them to Britain?', and so on. Then she asked the question, 'What *is* a village?' She spoke briefly about building huts and fences to keep out invaders, then referred to a dictated note-book paragraph about the village's 'self-supporting' character. She began a line of questioning which related to building and building materials, and the topic of thatch cropped up.

T: How many people have seen a lot of thatched houses? (About one-third to one-half of the class put their hands up.)
T: *Have you?* (sceptical-sounding tone). Rows and rows?
P1: We have a thatched roof.

This was not an 'answer' to the question, of course, but the boy described the roof of his home for thirty seconds or so. (I forgot to write what he actually said, because it was engrossing.) Then the teacher commented on the 'interestingness' of the boy's contribution, but in leaving it at that, it seemed she judged it, but did not really respond to it. The judgemental sense of her comment signalled, perhaps, the end of that particular sub-topic. It seemed from her next comment that she was concerned to correct the erroneous impression the class might have that 'a *lot* of' thatched houses can be seen in a village somewhere.

T: Well, you may have seen quite a few, but if you think carefully for a moment I wonder if you'd still say you'd seen a *lot*?

P2: At F_____ there are thatched houses round the square; but they've got black stuff on them.

This suffices for an answer, but avoids the manner and shape of an answer, as if the knowledge the boy possessed shaped his contribution, made it less of an answer and more of an initiating move done by means of answering. The teacher responded to this by asking a question to which she seemed not to know the answer herself – an a-typical utterance.

T: What – a covering to stop fire perhaps?
P2: Yeah, it was poured on, perhaps to do with fire.
P3: There was a fire once, at a thatched house near us.
P4: There was a fire near our house, a spark got on the roof.

A number of other 'there was a fire near us' contributions might have followed, but the teacher perhaps felt things were fraying a little – or not progressing – and attempted to staunch this interest in burning houses: 'All right!' (loudly). However, one pupil's curiosity had gained too much momentum to be stopped: 'If you kicked a ball, would it go through the thatch?' The whole class chorused 'No' to this, taking the teacher's answering function from her. Though such rare moments are threatening, because they are not only noisy but because the teacher's control of the interaction has gone from her hands, albeit briefly, they seem particularly valuable, because to see talk between pupils about content arc across in that startling manner is a glimpse of a relation that could be a commoner feature of classroom learning.

T: I don't think so, thatch is very thick really. All right, now . . . yes, Alison.
(It seems she wishes to leave the subject of thatch altogether.)
P6: Miss, there was a fire . . .

T:    All right, now look back and notice in the picture how one
      of the houses is larger than the other.

This led on to comments from the teacher about 'The thane's
house' and the other 'special houses'. It was evidently the social
structure implied by the buildings and how they were arranged
that the teacher wished to focus on. Her first question about
thatch had sent pupils off towards the material structure of the
buildings – a kind of action-knowledge stress deriving from their
own world – whereas she had, it seemed, been keen to talk about
the concept of 'thatcher' as a social entity.

Then there were questions about beehives: why were they
important?

T:    All right, what do bees produce?
P7:   Honey – to eat.
P8:   And you can use it for wounds.
T:    How do you know? (surprised tone)
P8:   Well, I cut my finger on a walk in S_____ woods, and I
      put honey on it.

The teacher then talked about mead, the importance of the bee-
keeper, the serfs' huts, and the main gate, somewhat rapidly, for
she evidently wished not only to rescue the topic of social structure but to get to the worksheet. This was about the buildings of
the village as a reflection of social structure. Even then, after work
had started on the worksheet, one pupil suddenly asked, without
being answered by anyone: 'How did they keep bundles of hay
together?'

One could speak here of a pressure of pupil interest building up
behind the ideas of thatch and fire. As sometimes happens, one
boy had specialized knowledge, living in a house with a thatched
roof; his thirty-second lecture was handled by the teacher not as a
realizing of what the discourse was about, as an uncovering of the
subject of the lesson, but as a possibly quite interesting but essentially extraneous private comment. Why? One answer might be
that the theoretical stress on the importance of acknowledging
'their interests' and so on may function in a merely rhetorical way
because it is not accompanied by a parallel theoretical recasting of

the notion of history itself. It seems to invite contradiction to suggest that for children at school – who might comprise the majority of doers of history – doing history is now different, while real 'history itself' ultimately stays as it is. If, in practice, historical knowledge is still conceived objectivistically, the implicit contradiction may be muted to an awkward but quiet compromise in which 'their interests' help the subject in some vague way, as a kind of emotional lubricant, without being thought of as in any way constituting it. So that pupils' concerns with thatch and so on, however they may be enthusiastically welcomed in social terms (or not) are likely also to be seen as peripheral to history itself. So it is unsurprising that sooner or later teachers are puzzled by what to do about 'their interests', since they are welcomed in their rhetoric and implicitly rejected in their epistemology. My reading of this teacher's unresponsiveness was not that she was insensitive, but that she had no theoretical means of taking hold of it. Evidently, moreover, she was pre-occupied with the original question of how many thatched roofs pupils might have seen and with the need to correct an untidily erroneous impression. And yet it seemed that the knowledge and experience of those pupils were available for conscription as the driving force of the lesson. Had it been conscripted, the lesson would have had a different subject, and would have had to go in a different direction, at a different pace.

Perhaps the obvious is worth underlining: this would have amounted also to a reworking of a piece of historical content; the topic Anglo-Saxon village would have been redefined in this enacted version, with its idiosyncratic bias towards fire and thatch, by the presence of matters like the games they played, the tools they used, the availability of thatch, their fire-fighting techniques, and so on. One could then say that at least some aspects of this content had been produced not reproduced; created, not given. There might then have been established, to use Esland's terms, a dialogic relation between pupils' 'consciousness' and the socially distributed 'knowledge' of 'Anglo-Saxon village' that already existed.[2] And in Heidegger's terms, it need not have amounted to 'perverting the act of disclosing into an act of closing off'.[3]

Perhaps expressions like '*the* Anglo-Saxon village', in referring not to a concrete empirical village but to an 'abstract' topic, in themselves push the notion towards the frozen conceptual immobility that sociologists term 'reification'. 'The' and 'village' signify in such contexts not a particular, or a constant, but the variable sums of imagined experience of villages in the past, as these varying summed experiences exist in the minds of communities (like single classes) studying 'the village'. A question like 'How did they keep bundles of hay together?' adds constitutively to that class's encounter with 'the Anglo-Saxon village' a curious notion unlikely to have been drawn to that topic in preceding incarnations of the idea. And it could have added more, had it been developed. For that class it was not an encounter with a quasi-platonic 'Anglo-Saxon village' that was available, but the experience of considering that transient collection of ideas gathered in that place at that time when they were talking about 'the Anglo-Saxon village', including the questioning awareness, here meeting closure, about what they did use to keep bundles of hay together. In this sense, then, '*the*' Anglo-Saxon village does not exist, and the closure here is a consequence of forgetting that the unchanging name is a label used for a succession of unique experiences. There can hardly be knowledge without knowing, and each act of knowing has its own accent. Which is why I suggest that 'How did they tie bundles of hay together?' and 'If you kicked a ball, would it go through the thatch?' are important questions. They reveal the central constitutive relevances of some pupils in that performance (if I can use the term) of 'the Anglo-Saxon village'; it is because those questions are asked that those subjects are part of a non-reified, unplatonic, 'Anglo-Saxon village'.

Why did this particular closure take place? I talked to the teacher in the staffroom at break to find out what was passing through her mind as she brought the discussion back to the thane's house, and finally to the worksheet. My question was: 'What was going through your mind when they were pressing the anecdotes about fire on you?' I explained, before she answered, that I was interested in the possibility of a tension in her mind during the lesson between the claims of a predefined terminus (the

worksheet) and the claims of what I saw as an interesting in-
cursion of pupils' interest into a routine lesson.

She said that she felt she could have spent more time on the
thatch, but that it was getting 'gossipy and repetitive' and had
rather 'worked itself out'. She also felt that she had to 'get on,
otherwise you spend too much time on one thing'. I also wondered
what she felt had been learnt and had been valuable in the lesson.
She wasn't sure, but felt that the thatch episode was 'a tangent'.

The teacher's explanation is couched in language which is
thoroughly time-conscious: 'gossipy', 'repetitive', 'get on',
'worked itself out'. It seems as if the pupils' speech came to her
through a particular filter; its temporal features are more salient
than its other features. What seems to be perceived by the teacher
seeing 'gossip' is a set of social relations not normally associated
with learning; what might perhaps be called her hyper-chronic
sense filters out the learning that occurred during the 'gossip' and
receives only those parts of the signal that 'show' the kinds of
social relation ('gossip' round a table, and so on) where learning is
thought not to take place. Her perceptive apparatus is perhaps
interpreting the surface of an interchange in terms of teacher
expectancies about what pupils are bound to do with casual talk.
It is then a failure in interpretive perception.

It is also interesting that judgements about 'spending too much
time on one thing' not only suggest that such 'things' have an
intrinsic temporal value, but in so doing support teachers' control
over subject knowledge particularly effectively, since the temporal
value of a content is not visible. Even if pupils can find out about
Anglo-Saxon thatch, they cannot find out, except from teachers,
how much time ought to be spent on it. Pupils necessarily take
definitions of what constitutes 'getting on' from teachers,
because the time-value of every piece of work is hidden, and in the
teacher's hands.

I wish to say much more about time in the next chapter, but
here one other comment is perhaps worth making. The teacher
said she felt 'trapped by the forty-minutes deadline'; understandably so in this lesson, where she had on four occasions either to
give out or collect things (textbooks, exercise books and a worksheet). Some hyper-awareness of time is induced in teachers by the

forty-minute lesson and the bells they wait for, but if her aim for that lesson was, as she put it, to enable pupils to appreciate something of the close organic interdependence of Anglo-Saxon village life, it seems possible that it is her own temporal horizon rather than the temporal unit *per se* that to some extent creates the pressure of time she feels. She wished to 'get something across' in the one lesson; her feeling of being trapped perhaps comes partly from treating the lesson end as a deadline.

## Atoms and time

The teacher snipped off burgeoning shoots of talk about thatch so that she could 'get across' the idea of the organic community before the end of the lesson. In the following extract from a fourth-year physics lesson with the top 'O'-level set, the relation between closure and the objectivistic tendency to see a lesson entirely in terms of its allotted place in a predefined course – which means that topics have the time-value apportioned to them by the course – seems even clearer. It could even be said to be apparent to the students themselves, who become aware that the exercise of close control over the distribution of knowledge, and the denial of access to topics raised prematurely, is here integral to 'teaching'.

The first part of the lesson which had been devoted to reworking an equation done for homework was quiet; the second was less so, and the teacher's discomposure when discipline wilted seemed to energize his flight to rigorous definitions of content explicitly apportioned to units of time.

T:   We're going to start today doing radioactivity.
     (This was announced amidst noise and talk.)
P1:  Have you got my book, sir?
P2:  What's the date?
P3:  Have you got my book, sir?
     And there were other questions as the teacher wrote on the board: '*Introduction–radioactivity*'.
P4:  Is radioactivity all one word?
     (It was evidently to be a note-dictating session.)

T:      Now I'm going to start by talking a minute about the atom.

P5:     Radioactivity's hyphenated.

P2:     S'not!

T:      Now, who knows anything about the atom?

P6:     Molecule.
        (Indistinct; the only reply.)

T:      Who knows anything about the structure of the atom?
        (No reply.)

T:      No? (Pause.) Well, an atom is made up of a nucleus with a positive charge, and around it it has a field of negative charge. . . . the nucleus is very small . . . you could compare it with the size of a pea on the centre spot of Wembley Stadium. . . . So an atom is mostly . . .? (Pause.) What's in between?

P7:     Air.

T:      Air is made up of atoms. . . . What's in [indistinct]?

P5:     How do you split them?

T:      We're interested in . . .

P5:     How did they find out about the nucleus and [indistinct]?

T:      It would take too long to tell . . . it would take half a term in the sixth form. (Noise.) All right, then . . . there was this chap called Rutherford . . . he produced a sheet of atoms of [indistinct].

P5:     How?

T:      . . . and bombarded it with particles.

P5:     *Where* did he [bombard them?]

T:      Well, it would take a long time.

PP:     Half a term in the sixth form!
        (Small chorus.)

Some of what was said in this discussion was indistinct, but the dramatic shape of the passage, the urgency of the questions, and the continuous, rather grudging, redefinition of content as it reflects the teacher's priorities (in particular his need to cope), seem clear.

P2:     How did he get the atoms off it?

T:      He knocked them . . .

P2:  (interrupting) *HOW?!!* How did he get them . . .
T:  Well . . .
P2:  I want to KNOW!
     (Voice rising in exasperation.)
T:  Jane!

After this small explosion his exposition went on for a short while uninterrupted by questions, or anything else.

T:  They thought an atom was just solid, but because . . . [indistinct] they found that 99 per cent went straight through, 0.9 per cent got deflected, but 0.1 per cent got bounced straight back.
PP:  Cor!
T:  They couldn't explain it . . . they thought the only reason could be . . . the mass was concentrated at one particular point . . . if all the rest went through [indistinct] . . . RIGHT, so we have . . .
P8:  (interrupting) Is that splitting the atom?
T:  No, we'll get on to that later.

The teacher then rather abruptly started his dictation of notes.

T:  . . . small heavy particle, positively charged. It was found that if you shot particles at a nucleus, it would break up. It was found that there were two types of particles, neutrons and protons . . .
P8:  So the nucleus [indistinct]?
T:  Well, yes, we'll see . . .

The note-taking was completed two minutes or so later with the words: 'surrounding this are electrons in constant motion'. Immediately, a pupil spoke:

P9:  Do they go round?
T:  Yes, but it's not as simple as that, because they behave both as particles and as waves – it's a very complex part of chemistry.
PP:  Half a term in the sixth form?
     (Small chorus.)
P5:  University.

The bell went, appropriately enough, at exactly this point.

It is worth recapitulating the questions pupils asked:

1 How do you split atoms?
2 How did they find out about the nucleus and . . .?
3 Where did he (bombard it with particles)?
4 How did he get the atoms (?) off it? HOW?
5 Is 'bombarding', etc. 'splitting the atom?'
6 Do electrons go round?

Questions 1, 3, 4 and 5 go unanswered. The questions about split-ting the atom seem to be met by the suggestion that it will be done later, presumably in the sixth form. This deferral is not accompanied by any provisional enlightenment, only the reminder that (at the moment) 'we're interested in' the structure of the atom. Question 2 is 'answered' – almost as a favour – with 'All right, then'. Its appropriate slot is the sixth form, but in the circumstances they could have some of the knowledge now. Question 6, 'Do electrons go round?' also meets the closure of 'it's very complex', presumably implying something like 'too much so for you at the moment'.

It is an obvious point that these pressing questions – at least 1, 3, 4 and 5 – seem related to the lay person's everyday curiosity about atoms and how they function. What is interesting also is that the questions seem to imply an awareness that language like 'splitting atoms' of itself means very little. Their questions are questions about the language of science. They could be seen as asking, what does it mean to say 'split the atom'? 'bombard with particles'? and so on. The teacher's attempts to 'simplify', using words like 'knock' (presumably for 'bombard') and metaphors like the pea in Wembley Stadium, leave untouched this particular dimension of the pupils' curiosity. In this respect they resemble earlier 'simplifications' noted in maths, the humanities and remedial work in leaving the students stranded in a formalistic impasse.

It may well be that what lies behind the vibrant urgency of some of these questions – P2's 'How?' was almost screamed out – may be an awareness that the kind of language being used tells them little about the experiential particulars of 'finding out about the nucleus', for instance. P2's saying 'How did he get them off . . .?' I should see as expressing my own confusion, as an ignorant listener, as to what *happens*: I wanted to be told – and I think that the pupil did too – what kind of machine is used, how it works, how you know when a particle gets 'knocked off', and so on. Clearly, language like this is necessarily abstract in the sense that its referents cannot be apprehended by the senses or their technological extensions; it is hypothetical also in that it projects – 'nucleus' has fitted the facts so far and may go on doing so. However, although science students clearly have to accept such abstract-ness, they do not have to accept – in the sense of take for granted without enquiry – the empirical basis of that necessary abstractness. So they will ask, exactly what kind of thing is constructed to 'bombard' atoms with, and what does it do, and what kind of object is it that's 'bombarded', and how do you know that particles 'go through' and so on.

Without this dimension the language becomes formalistic, a series of vague metaphors ('go though', 'deflect', 'bounced back', 'knock', 'sheet') comparable with the metaphors I have examined in other work – 'basin' in the artesian context, for instance. It may be necessarily vague, but again it seems appropriate and necessary for pupils to have precise notions about why language becomes seemingly vague, or rather at what level it cannot encompass a particular reality with any adequacy. The simplifying in this situation seems to be formalistic in the sense in which it was in the other contexts described earlier. The closures that take place – the questions not taken up – also involve decisions about time, and about discrete contents apportioned to bits of time. A Freirean kind of fragmentation is again essentially what is produced, more nakedly under the stress of a threat to the teacher's personal control.[4]

The lesson produces a situation in which pupils see what is normally hidden. They 'penetrate' the closure inflicted on them by seeing it (twice) as a 'fragmentation' of content in the interests of control over the pacing of knowledge: 'Half a term in the sixth.' The pupil saying 'University' had clearly grasped the essential arbitrariness of the distribution process. In my own innocence of the topic, I saw the lesson as an ignorant interested pupil: I wanted the answers to the other pupils' questions, and I felt strongly that the simplifications I was being offered were no help. To say that a nucleus was like a 'pea in the middle of Wembley Stadium' said nothing; and I presume that other pupils, judging from their responses to 'Who knows anything about the atom?', were no more privileged.

The dramatic structure of the situation made it clear that the knowledge the pupils were given in response to their questions was not really intended for them yet, and was somehow the 'wrong' knowledge. It was clear to them that their questions about atoms could only be answered by the teacher's putting the 'right' knowledge to one side. And it seemed clear that the arbitrariness of this control over what knowledge to dispense became evident to the pupils only when discipline to some extent broke down. As a result there was perhaps less closure of the pupils' opportunity of realizing the topic of radioactivity in 'subjective consciousness' than there might have been in a well-disciplined lesson such as that on the Anglo-Saxon village, where the teacher was firm enough to be able to bring the class back to the subject as she wished to define it.

Perhaps such closures take place as a matter of course in routine, well-run lessons, and in any subject at any age. But this sugges-tion seems to conflict with much of our well-expressed concern these days for working with the grain of the pupils' experience, using their interests, and so on. One speculative comment as to how it is that such a conflict can continue not merely unresolved but for the most part unconfronted has already been offered – that our notions of what subjects essentially are does not yet embrace the idea of their being in some sense constructed through pupils' awarenesses. It was Esland's view that there was beginning to emerge, by the beginning of the 1970s, a conception of teaching (which he called 'phenomenological') which stressed the part in learning played by 'subjective experience and its composition', and which saw that it was necessary for 'objective reality' to be subjectively realized before it has any 'meaning'.[5] But if the objec-tive reality of the Anglo-Saxon village or the atom is still routinely thought by teachers to possess 'meaning' before and apart from the pupils' subjective encounters with such knowledge and apart from their imagined experience of problems about thatch and fission, then Esland's account is not descriptive of actual practice. There are areas of school work which are particularly interesting in this regard, those that are most explicitly devoted to working through the requisitioning of pupils' creativity and their subjective awareness and knowledge. These areas will be examined later. For the moment it seems appropriate to look further at how considerations relating to time may enter lessons.

## References

1 C. V. Burgess, *Burgess Composition, Book 2* (London, London University Press, 1967), p. 28.
2 G. M. Esland, 'Teaching and learning as the organisation of knowledge', in M. F. D. Young (ed.), *Knowledge and Control* (London, Collier-Macmillan, 1971), p. 94.
3 M. Heidegger, *Being and Time*, trans. J. Macquarrie and E. Robinson (London, SCM Press, 1962), p. 213.
4 P. Freire, *Education: The Practice of Freedom* (London, Writers and Readers Publishing Co-operative, 1973), pp. 105–7.
5 Esland, op. cit., p. 75.

# 6
# APPORTIONING TIME

## Getting on in first-year science

I have already suggested, commenting on a lesson about the Anglo Saxon village, that 'closure' has a temporal aspect, in that the teacher's view of what happened is shaped by considerations relating explicitly to time. The talk about thatch catching fire was a 'tangent'; the pupils were 'gossipy'; the 'forty-minute deadline' was 'a kind of trap'; she felt she had to 'get on'.

The generalized need 'to get on' that can cut across the specific 'need to get on with' a particular piece of work might be seen as laying a diffuse anxiety about the future over a more task-related apprehension of time. There is, arguably, a time scheme or temporal structure intrinsic to the task itself; 'this is taking too long' can be a recognition that the time needed by particular children for a particular task is being squandered. And there is a less persuasive, perhaps less human way of saying 'this is taking too long', when we become aware not of the sagging rhythms of the task, but of the looming presence of a pre-ordained time-scheme. I should like to term this diffuse awareness of an urgency that is related not to the particular task but to a nebulous, if no less demanding future, 'directionality'.

The comments I offered earlier about time were prompted by lessons where pupils themselves felt this directionality like a rein bringing them back on course – so strongly in one case (the fourth-form science lesson) that the process became clear to the pupils themselves, and enabled them to understand something of what they were missing in the process of 'getting on'. What I should like to suggest now is that lessons will often show, on examination, a kind of directionality which is perhaps less evident on the surface but in certain ways is more radical and continuous than in the examples offered above. Clearly, this is not to imply that lessons should not move forward purposefully, only to make a distinction between kinds of movement.

The lesson I shall comment on first was about the effects of heating on various substances. One of its purposes was to introduce the notion of 'subliming', the vaporizing of substances when heated without their passing through a 'melting' stage. I shall discuss parts of the lesson first, and later look at the overall structure, with particular regard to its temporal aspects.

The teacher performed the demonstration experiments at his bench, while pupils watched. The first extract is from very early in the lesson. The teacher had just heated the first substance.

T:   Tell me how you'd describe that.
P1:  A green powder.
T:   Green, is it?
P2:  It's lime.
T:   Yes, it's lime in colour. Anything else about the powder?
P2:  It's in lumps.
T:   Yes, but what about *most* of the powder?
P3:  It's fine? (questioning intonation).
T:   So we can say that 'sulphur is a pale-yellow fine powder'.

First 'we' need to 'say' what 'sulphur' is. This 'we' is not earned through the interchange, for P1 wanted 'green' and P2 'lumps'. 'Green' has been edited out, with 'lumps'; and 'pale-yellow' is the teacher's. Likewise, 'so' is illicit. A situated conclusion here would be multiple; A says sulphur is x, B says y, the rest are silent, and I say it's pale-yellow.

As a piece of conversation, also, the interchange is curious, being made up of *non sequiturs*. It is as if it had to be in order that the appropriate description of sulphur be formulated. The de-situated 'conclusion' was presumably already 'there' in science. The directionality that produced this also has consequences for the meaning of producing 'green' and 'lumps'. That they are not used seems to mean that their truth is not acknowledged. It might seem more puzzling to be involved in a collective formulation where one's observations are lost than merely to receive authoritative formulations.

The existence of a predefined conclusion in a particular formulation also renders the questions 'trivial', in the technical sense in logic of a question the questioner knows the answer to. The pupils' 'participation' perhaps creates an impression that these questions are, unlike many other school questions, not 'trivial'; the answers look as if they might determine the direction of discourse, and themselves produce the conclusion. It might even be suggested that this 'trivial' mode annexes the whole of this brief dialogue and 'trivializes' it. Thus, P3's revealing questioning intonation – 'It's fine?' – suggests at that point a search for the 'right' term in the midst of what is apparently open dialogue.

One other fragment of dialogue from early in the lesson might be related to this. A minute or so later, this interchange occurred:

T:   What *didn't* happen to the iodine?
P1:  It didn't form fumes.
T:   Oh, yes, I think it formed fumes. What happened to the naphthalene?
     (Two 'wrong' answers I couldn't hear followed this.)
T:   Then what happened to the iodine?
P2:  It melted.
T:   No, it didn't melt.
P3:  Sir, smoke's coming up in the neck!
T:   We'll come to that. Yes, so it's turned straight from the

solid to a vapour. And it does this at quite low temperatures.

Here, what happened – twice – when pupils 'reported' observations was a denial, rather than a check with other views, or a re-
run of those parts of the experiment alluded to. The terminal
point of this series was evidently to be 'so it's turned straight from
the solid into a vapour'. The two denials, 'yes, I think it formed
fumes' and 'it didn't melt', may therefore be seen as pre-echoing
the conclusion, as a negative counterpart to it 'brought forward'
by some twenty seconds and so closing the intervening piece of
talk. While the talk is carried on as if it were about what pupils do
in fact observe, it functions as a short search for the conclusion and
is thus really preliminary to that. The denials look crude. Yet to
see this kind of thing as simply inept and imperceptive would be
wrong. It is arguable – and the discussion of the rest of the lesson
is meant to exemplify this point – that the need to say not only 'x
is on the syllabus' but (which is here the same thing) that 'it will
be finished by t' often makes the kind of interchange reproduced
above extremely probable, and especially so if we are also arguing
for pupils' participation through their observations and through
discussion. The decision to arrive at x by t of itself creates the
possibility that the temporal rhythms that engage the pupil will
not be those of his own learning but the imposed pace of the
objectivistically defined 'course', in which 'knowledge' means a
predefined set of items of content each with its own time-value.

I should now put these fragments back into context. The lesson
began with a résumé by the teacher of the previous week's work
on heating metals. It sounded like an attempt to recall the final
summarizing that the teacher often closed the lesson with. Thus,
'We also found . . . that it burst into flames. . . . We also found
. . .'. His manner was easy, the tone colloquial: 'I've got three
more things to show you today, and they're all a bit different.' It
is worth underlining here some of the ways this teacher displayed
sensitivity to his audience. His tone was one way; another was the
manner in which the newness of a term was explicitly signalled:
'If something is crystal, we call it crystalline'; 'a substance called
sulphur'; 'a substance called naphthalene'; 'what we call a flask'.

Thus, drawing attention to an act of naming alerts the pupils to
the newness of what they are handling.

Today, then, they were to heat 'a substance called sulphur'.
(The move from heating metals last week to this lesson was of
course pre-planned.) There was some apparently spontaneous
note-taking, then:

T: Tell me how you'd describe that.
P1: Green powder.
T: Green, is it?
P2: It's lime.
T: Yes, it's lime in colour. Anything else about the powder?
P3: It's in lumps.
T: Yes, but what about *most* of the powder?
P4: It's fine.
T: So we can say that 'sulphur is a pale-yellow fine powder'.

This was written on the board. Next the sulphur was heated.
'Jot down what you notice happening.' The pupils called out
words like 'orangey', 'red round the edges', 'treacly', 'it's melting', and these were written down by the pupils.

The interchange down to 'sulphur is . . .' is thus a prelude to
something a bit livelier, the heating itself, and the teacher suggested
they jot down all the terms that were offered, making a note of them
on the board too. Some statement about sulphur was needed, he
perhaps felt, prior to the heating demonstration, and so the heavy
editing of pupil responses initially might seem, when contrasted
with the suspension of that manner a minute later, to be temporally provoked, a consequence of the interchange's functioning
as a prelude, to be dealt with quickly.

There was then a brief oral résumé, led by the teacher, using the
kind of terms the pupils offered, of the heating of sulphur. Then:

T: Right, having melted, it doesn't boil . . . does anyone
   know what we call that yellow smoke?
P1: Vapour.
T: Anyone tell me what vapour?
   (No response.)
T: Well, what have we got in the glass?

P2: Water.
T: Where from? (Pause, no response.) What's in the glass?
P3: Sulphur?
T: Right.

The teacher immediately wrote on the board: 'When the sulphur is heated, it is seen to melt and form an amber liquid.' I had not heard a pupil say 'amber', but could have missed it.

To comment first at the surface, so to speak. There is a routine briskness about these interchanges. For instance, 'Tell me what vapour' is followed by a pause without an answer, then 'Well, what have we got in the glass?' This is making a causal connection, not just recasting more intelligibly; it amounts to deciding that an answer to that question will not come, or not quickly enough. The pupil who thought it was water may have been left holding that belief. A little later, a single-word answer, 'Sulphur' was sufficient to prompt the written résumé.

To probe a little more deeply, the résumé sentences seemed a sensitive and helpful way of allowing pupils to record and gather together what they had done. The problem is that they seem less an objective record of what has been seen and said than a version of an event which is edited to anticipate what might be appropriate as a formulation in 'real' science. The written record omits, for instance, certain constitutive features of the pupils' speech, their idiosyncratic expressions for what they see ('treacly', 'orangey', 'dry liquid'). It omits mention of mistakes, like 'water', and hesitations. In this way, it is already abstracted from its historical context in this particular lesson. It is desituated speech, language which is already – to use a phrase of Merleau-Ponty's – 'torn out of history'. It is directional, then, in the sense that what purports to be the record of a particular event is distorted to conform with the paradigmatic account of such events in general. Young makes the same point in broad terms, commenting on the way 'school science as a conception of "knowledge to be transmitted" underpins the teacher's talk and his way of listening to pupils' questions and responses.'[1]

This editorial distortion may be seen happening in other ways. For instance, there are interesting linguistic shifts between dialogue and résumé. Rather than employ forms which would 'normally' be used in describing an experience that has occurred in the immediate past – 'We heated the chocolate . . . we saw it melt' – the appropriate universal-sounding form is used: 'The sulphur is heated . . . it is seen to melt.' And: 'If the flask is allowed to cool, the sulphur vapour condenses and forms sulphur powder on the sides of the flask.' It is not merely a matter of 'forms' in the sense of conventions. The shifts represent by implication alternative statements about what this community of science-doers now knows. The present tense is the present of universally-valid truths. 'Always' is implied; but the truth in this sense of saying that sulphur when heated melts, forms vapour, condenses and forms sulphur powder, is not yet known by these participants in science. The pupils have not arrived at that point. It might be thought inferrable, but the problem of such inference is not raised; only one instance is observed. The single operation is summarized as if it even offered a truth inductively arrived at. Its truth resembles a fictive truth, in functioning as a particular which fixes or establishes something general.

In this connection it is worth noting that the teacher scrupulously referred to *the* sulphur (though it makes logical nonsense of the résumé sentence about all sulphur), as if resisting the pressure to state or clearly imply that all sulphur behaves like this sulphur. I take this to be an example of the sensitivity I noted above. Even he, however, omitted the article before 'naphthalene' and 'iodine' later. There is no attempt to combat these ambiguities by explicit use of terms like 'this', 'some' and 'all'. Is it the directional urge to handle an objectivistically 'real' or 'exact' science that is responsible for not using such aids to situated clarity, and so not confronting this basic philosophic problem of science while doing science? And is there perhaps also present 'the concealed presupposition' of natural science 'that a universal inductivity might prevail . . . an inductivity which suggests itself in everyday experience but remains concealed in its infinity'?[2] Here 'inductivity' does not seem to be present for pupils even in the 'everyday experience' of the experiment, but the strength of the teacher's presupposition may help to conceal the fact.

The use of the passive, which is related to the use of the present (one cannot say 'we heat sulphur' half an hour later without strain), seems a necessary preparation for teaching pupils the notion of a neutral, objective science. The subjective performer of science is removed in a syntactical gesture. The filtering-out of mistaken interpretations which then, of course, becomes necessary, works to the same end. Not saying who did it or when, or with what degree of success, thus also contributes to sustaining the idea that science is not a purposive, historically-situated human activity. Each of these shifts away from the pupils' accounts is directional, in that each is made in order to make room for the articulation of experimental knowledge in the constituted forms of a science which for them still lies in the future.

There are also signs that directionality works against understanding. For instance, in the lesson the notion of subliming is in danger of being lost, partly because there is a conservation problem implicit in observing the transformations. Pupils do not reply when asked what the vapour is; but one said 'water', in response to 'What's in the glass?' They are given in words the very notion that the empirical demonstration was intended to allow them to 'see', namely that the vapour is 'still' sulphur. It is 'green powder stuff' that is left, for one pupil, and 'dry liquid' for another. Only after this, and the explicit analogy of water, does one ask, 'Is it sulphur?' It seems as if the matter of seeing the conservation of sulphur behind the apparent changes is difficult even for the pupils who speak. For those who do not, it may be more so. This comment may be compared with the conclusion Hardy reaches in an account of pupils doing a very similar experiment. She suggests that, despite having worked carefully through the experiment, it is precisely 'the knowledge that the "gummy substance" formed is sulphur that is not directly available to the students'.[3] If that is so, there may be more to do initially with familiar examples of such conservation – or more pondering by pupils on what goes on in the flask – before any verbalization led by the teacher using such words as 'forms' which imply conservation.

Naphthalene was the next substance to be heated.

T:   Right, now for the second . . . a substance called naphthalene. . . . What does it smell like?

P1:    Apples.
P2:    Mothballs . . .
T:     *YES!*

They went on to describe its structure and appearance, and the teacher wrote: 'Naphthalene is a soft white crystalline solid', adding orally, 'If something is a crystal, we call it crystalline.' (A pupil had produced the word 'crystal'.) Note that 'smelling like mothballs' is already edited out from what naphthalene 'is'. Then it was heated.

T:    What was the first thing that happened?
P1:   It turned red.
T:    Did it? If it did, it must have been the bunsen.
P2:   It melted.
T:    If it turns to a liquid, how would you describe it?
P3:   Transparent.
T:    What colour? Has it got a colour?
P4:   No.
T:    What would you *say* it is? (his emphasis).
P5:   Colourless.
T:    Right, colourless.

And he wrote: 'When naphthalene is heated, it turns to a colourless liquid.'

It was heated further, and it was noted on the board that 'it began to boil' and that 'white fumes of naphthalene vapour were formed', and finally that 'when the glass was allowed to cool naphthalene crystals are seen to form on the cooler parts of the glass'. (The regularity of those summaries makes them function as temporal boundaries.)

Here again we see the form of the pupils' observations shaped by the retroactive effect of the résumé-to-be. The redness that one pupil observed 'must have been the bunsen', 'transparent' becomes 'colourless'. Of three contributions, one goes into the description, one is dropped and another modified.

The third substance to be heated was iodine. First, the description:

P1:   Small lumps.

T:  Let's describe it more scientifically than that.

P2:  Small crystals.

T:  What colour?

P3:  Shiny.

T:  Iodine is a shiny black . . . (pause to wait for the next word) crystalline solid.

    (Normally during the résumé the teacher didn't wait for pupils to offer terms.)

Heating produced dense purple fumes, and one pupil asked, 'What colour is it, sir?' The strange hesitancy here (strange since it was a flagrant and obvious purple, even if a few pupils might not have a word for purple) represents the kind of undermining of pupils' confidence in their own constitutive speech that could be produced by recognizing the precarious status of their contributions. The question might well mean, 'What colour is it appropriate to call it?'. The teacher's somewhat sibylline reply was: 'Something different happened to that.' Then there followed the passage already discussed which I shall reproduce again.

T:  What *didn't* happen to the iodine?

P1:  It didn't form fumes.

T:  Oh, yes, I think it formed fumes. What happened to the naphthalene?

    (Two indistinct but evidently wrong answers.)

T:  Then what happened to the iodine?

P2:  It melted.

T:  No, it didn't melt.

P:  Sir, smoke's coming up the neck!

T:  We'll come to that. Yes, so it's turned straight from the solid to a vapour. And it does this at quite low temperatures.

The résumé on the board was: 'Iodine when heated forms iodine vapour without melting. It is said to SUBLIME.' He accompanied this orally with, 'That's what we say when we mean . . .' and so on, and added a written comment: 'When a substance turns from being a solid into a vapour without melting it is said to SUBLIME', adding, 'Put that in brackets because that explains the first word.'

A pupil then asked, 'Why was that yellow and the others purple?', and was told, 'It's just the state of the glass'.

Finally a diagram was drawn, which the class was to copy, and the title 'Some Effects of Heating' written up. The bell went as the children were drawing the flask.

The double lesson discussed above would amount to about one seventeenth of the teacher's actual teaching time. It is a complex lesson in many ways, but in particular it is highly structured temporally, in an informal way. A plot of the lesson shows this.

Stage  1  Résumé of last week's lesson.
Stage  2  Introduce subject of this lesson.
Stage  3  Sulphur – oral description, with pupils.
Stage  4  Write up 'definition', have it copied.
Stage  5  Heat sulphur.
Stage  6  Oral description of heating at melting stage, with pupils.
Stage  7  Résumé of melting.
Stage  8  Oral description of vaporizing.
Stage  9  Résumé.
Stage 10  Oral description of cooling.
Stage 11  Résumé.
Stage 12  Exit to fume cupboard.

These twelve stages were distinct; the divisions were marked by the teacher's decisions to move on, or divert, what was happening. There were these twelve stages with sulphur, then a further eight with naphthalene and six with iodine. Most of the lesson time (about half) was taken up by the sulphur part. After these further fourteen stages, there followed:

Stage 27  Written notes on 'SUBLIME'.
Stage 28  Drawing and notes on 'some effects of heating'.

What seems striking is the way in which the lesson's structure, rationally derivable from the course of which it is a part, produces – despite its overall 'simplicity' in some respects – such a series of discrete events temporally bounded. I say temporally bounded because while an explicit timetable of stages is not necessary, since no synchronization with others is involved (not within the lesson, though a good deal of synchronization with lab assistants and three other science teachers would have been needed to decide on it originally), the teacher's own decisions about what different things will be done have imposed an informal distribution of lesson time available through the stages. He wants, clearly, all three materials to be heated since 'they're all different'; he wants some discussion to take place; he wants all this gathered together; and he wants a final drawing. Admirably careful and thorough though it is, some of the directional closures commented on are perhaps entailed by such planning. The various learning problems arising (misunderstandings about the conservation of one sub-stance behind appearances, the undermining of pupils' natural ways of speaking about what they see) could only have been con-fronted at the expense of the structure as a whole.

Some closures might now be seen more clearly against the temporal backcloth of the lesson's structure. Two striking ones occurred at crucial times. The editing out of 'green', 'lime' and 'lumps' occurred during the very first preparatory stage, when the teacher was presumably anxious to get his 'definition' on the board so as to start the experiment proper. (A sloppier teacher might not have troubled about this piece of preparation, and so not produced the closure.) A second occurred towards the end of the double period, when the teacher was moving towards the general notion of subliming. To say, in apparent contradiction, 'It didn't melt', was perhaps for him merely, after three sets of observations and some time spent in discussion, a nudge to remember, a trivial correction of some thoughtlessness. That was not, though, how it appeared; it is as if the directional set itself allows the teacher to see what may be profound misreadings as merely superficial hitches in communication; and as if focusing on the approaching future involves not adequately reading the pres-ent. At any rate, to take this 'wrong' suggestion that it melted as problematic, not just a slight snag, would have compromised the lesson at a crucial time; the bell was getting nearer. The pupil's comment appears less significant perhaps *because* the bell is get-ting nearer and it cannot be attended to if we are to go to 'sublim-ing'. Teachers often see their lessons as dramatically constructed, and the handling of time towards the end is especially crucial.

There were other closures. A pupil saw the naphthalene 'turn red', and the teacher commented that 'if it did, it must have been the bunsen'. Later, right at the end, after 'sublime' had been explained, a girl asked 'Why is that yellow and the others purple?' and was answered, 'I think it's just the state of the glass'. These fringe effects in practice, therefore, come to be defined as irrelevances, whatever the teacher might believe about the value of discussing them. Again, it seem that the crowded agenda of the lesson makes it likely that the non-typical, non-central event is edited out.

The dilemma perhaps then is in 'curriculum' itself, as it is expressed in structures down as far as the lesson unit, and beyond. It is not surprising that radical attitudes to content entail radical attitudes to time, and vice versa. Fines and Verrier, in *The Drama of History*, argue for 'the rejection of content as a governing factor in lesson design'.[4] That a lesson has a design is not in question; in practice their designs, the structures of their lessons, are organic. 'Structure' in this sense belongs not objectivistically to knowledge itself before a lesson is performed, but is what issues in performance. The future-within-the-lesson is not a mechanical progress, manipulable to some extent but essentially closed; it is rather the space which exists for the development of emergent possibilities, not least those of the self (pupil and teacher), and of relations between those selves. In the lesson just analysed, the mistakes and 'wrong' observations (such as 'water' and 'it turned red' when 'it did not') might have been possibilities that emerged, rather than being erased, and they might have been organically developed into content.

Fines and Verrier stress the need for 'openness of eye', suggesting that 'the teacher whose mind is clouded by the significance and multifaceted nature of his material cannot observe properly'. This involves 'the willingness to slow the action down sufficiently for the children to find what they need'.[5] The question for teachers is how far slowing the action down is a possibility for them in any consistent way, and whether the slowing-down of the rate of passage through content events does not wait on, for instance, a change in the nature of the ideas 'curriculum' and 'syllabus'; and whether, without this basic change, it is conceivable that teachers can work with minds that are not 'clouded by the significance and multifaceted nature of their material'. The clouding of the observation of what happens to learners here described seems to derive from teachers' need to bring forward prematurely items from the constituted forms of school science.

## Digressing

Another teacher, confronted in a similar lesson at first-year level by a fringe effect, chose to confront it as an interesting problem that could be exploited. Pupils here were working in small groups heating various materials. A pupil had asked, 'Where did the black coating come from?' The teacher suggested that 'ideas' be collected about the possible source of this effect.

T: Let's think of *all* the items involved. What were they?
P1: Flame . . . foil.
T: Yes . . . what else was there? What else could it have been?
P2: The tongs.
T: The tongs. . . . All right . . . let's put that down . . . maybe . . . the tongs . . . let's put that down as a possibility. It may be *unlikely*, but it's still a possibility until we've proved that something else was responsible. Right, are there any other possibilities?
P3: The air.
T: Yes, the air. What else is in the vicinity? Have we got all the various agencies involved?
P3: Gas?
T: It may have come from the natural gas . . . let's put that down. It may have. It's a possibility. Now – who would like to summarize what these possibilities are for causing the black coating on the tube?
P1: The copper coating, flame, tongs, gas, air . . .
T: Right, now how do we find out which was responsible?
P4: By an experiment?
T: Right, we need to design another experiment after half term. What should we do?
P5: We could scrape off the coating . . . and work out why . . .

T:    We could do . . . we could analyse it. . . . Good, right now
      . . . who found it weighed more after it had been heated?

Here, a general principle about science is enunciated and acted
on. Science is possibilities, hypotheses that attempt to explain
things. Everything is 'a possibility' until 'we' have proved something. 'We' is a different 'we' at this point from the 'we', in the
other lesson, of 'We can say that "sulphur is a pale-yellow fine
powder".' It was the flaw, the unforeseen contingency, which
produced this broad meta-communicative statement about
science. Whereas the causal connections of the successful routine
experiment are somehow made to seem unproblematic, here the
need to choose amongst different causal explanations demands a
theory to handle the observations. The theory is: all explanations
are equal, initially. Paradoxically, it seems as if it is the temporary
suspension of the routine science lesson that allows this basic
feature of scientific activity to be revealed. It becomes clear, at
least at such points, how in typical lessons the routine directional movement of 'science' can undercut science itself. The
typical experiment associates a and b and proceeds to a pseudo-
causal explanation of a relation which for pupils is essentially
associationist. The digression from routine 'science' to discover
what caused the coating is atypical in that no planned association
exists initially (between coating and cause) to make a later causal
connection readily identifiable.

In a real sense, then, the pupils have been responsible for reconstituting the topic of part of a lesson. This has another implication
for teaching what science is. Normal school science seems to
proceed through a given sequence of activities prescribed by a
course and chosen by a teacher. The connection between one
experiment and 'the next' is likely to be objectivistically 'logical'.
Here, rather than this kind of connection, one experiment is seen
to demand another; there is the human uncertainty of searching
for an *ad hoc* solution to a problem arising. Arguably, the learning
involved in thus stumbling on something problematic and having
to improvise the next experimental step, in that it creates a kind of
existential continuity between normally discrete, if 'logically
related', activities, offers a more authentic version of science

as a practice. The routine whereby, as in the lessons observed earlier, conclusions seem to emerge rather too easily – even enthusiastically – from observations seems to deprive experiments of the character of search. The boy whose tape-recorder doesn't work searches for an answer. The children in the subliming lesson seem to be waiting for science to provide one.

The teacher here, however, made the proposal that they should design another experiment after half-term. It was not followed up. It may be that if the hypothetical digressive experiment had been constructed it would have led sideways again to another off-course investigation, and the time scale for first-year science would have been disrupted. It may be that the logic of moving forward by *ad hoc* changes of direction and digressions cuts too obviously across the directional logic of the course. It is perhaps foreshadowed in the talk that it might be difficult to follow through this digression. 'Good, right now', seems to signal that we have stopped talking about what 'we' could do, and we return to 'the lesson': 'Who found it weighed more after it had been heated?' It is as if this briefly authentic mode of relating to the future seems ironically to envisage its own suspension.

## Giving out time

As long as the 'black coating' problem and others like it are thought of as digressive, one can speak of topics themselves necessarily 'taking two weeks' and so on. If, on the other hand, they are thought of as constitutive of pupils' science, one can only say things like 'the way these pupils are proceeding with this topic it seems likely they may take two weeks', or longer. What Thompson describes as 'task orientation'[6] is a mode of handling time that proceeds essentially from its subordination to the character of tasks as human beings 'naturally' (that is, without a clock to instruct them) have performed them through history. In this relation one is oriented primarily to tasks, and time is, as it were, consumed incidentally, or rather it passes incidentally. When tasks are timed – time itself being now a commodity rather than a context, and the orientation being to that commodity – task orientation 'appears to be wasteful and lacking in urgency'.

Saying this topic takes two weeks and this course a term, pre-supposes a relation between time and task that is opposed to that reconciliation between human needs and the temporal demands of work that the term 'task orientation' was coined to describe.

It is perhaps not surprising, then, that in personal and insti-tutional terms time can be difficult to think about clearly, for it lies at the point of intersection of conflicting interests. This may be partly why, though teachers appear to talk and think so much about time, and particularly about how much to allow for this and that task, they none the less seem to make routine mistakes with time and frequently criticize themselves for having done so, par-ticularly for not having allowed enough of it. A double lesson in first-year Nuffield science taught by the teacher who digressed to deal with the black coating suggests how unlikely it is that even the best and most experienced teachers will make accurate predic-tions about how much time pupils need to deal adequately with particular tasks, and to understand them.

The lesson, which was run in small groups, was a matter of weighing a series of liquids and 'runny solids'. Groups had to make an estimate of each before weighing and recording both, and copy up the individual estimates and group measurements in their best books at the end. I taped one of these small groups, leaving the tape running for the double lesson, going in occasionally to the storage cupboard where they worked (because it was quieter there) but mainly leaving them unobserved. Having listened to the tape, I handed it to the teacher without comment for his com-ments, which he wrote out for me. Some of what he wrote related to their sense of the task as a whole, and to considerations of time:

> They seem to progress along the lines of the experiment through discussion, but the plan of action provided by me tends to be partly forgotten once the practical work had begun.
>
> Timing. The boys were constantly under pressure where the timing is concerned. Possibly I should have set a slightly lower target, where the number of items to weigh is concerned.
>
> The boys tended, possibly due to lack of time, to miss out certain procedures.

Other comments related to problems he had not anticipated.

They have more difficulty reading the figures on the scales than I thought they would have. (At four points in the lesson, there were arguments lasting from ten to twenty-five seconds about what the readings actually were.)

I underestimated the children's management of the simple practicalities.

This further complicates the picture, in that unanticipated problems with the sub-tasks will involve pupils in considering these separate components for more time. Difficulties with readings and other 'simple practicalities' would make it harder to sense the logical narrative, so to speak, that threads the parts together. In his classic work *The Psychology of Time*, Fraisse, summarizing experimental evidence, suggests that the sensed duration of tasks 'decreases as the tasks are less broken up . . . the more unity a task has, the less time it seems to take, for the partial changes are no longer in the foreground of our attention.'[7] He also relates absorption in the elements of tasks to a diminished sense of overall purpose: instead of considering each element of the task itself we can concentrate on its purpose. For pupils, then, retaining sub-tasks 'in the foreground of their attention' is likely itself to diminish the possibility of their grasping the essential point of what they are doing. But this problem is complicated by the ensuing lengthened sensed duration of the overall task. Since the unity of this, and the sense of its purpose, is initially implicit only in the teacher's time sense or 'temporal horizon', the increased duration of sub-tasks for pupils serves perhaps to accentuate the discreteness of the stages and further disguise the basic point of what is happening. For the teacher's carefully woven plot we might well substitute the pupils' picaresque adventures.

It was very striking that in their talk there was no single speculative comment about the relation between weight and original estimate. This may be partly what the teacher had in mind when he said, 'the plan of action . . . tends to be partly forgotten . . . they missed out certain procedures'. There was merely a good deal of reminding each other that they 'had to guess', for they continually forgot to. There was only one general comment: 'This is a solid. Solids are heavy.' That was not elaborated or qualified then or later. Since it bore on the central point of the lesson, which works to undermine exactly that commonsense prejudice, it is a strange failure to pass it over as obviously true; it also controverted the evidence offered by their earlier weighing of runner bean seeds which they noted were light.

The sub-tasks' discreteness was reflected in their talk. 'Right, we've finished this one.' 'We've done paraffin now.' 'Right, we've weighed dry sand and peas.' Between weighing, as one of them went for the next item, the talk was about various things to do with the tasks – 'We've got five minutes' – or about things like the dripping tap, or there was silence, as if they were taking a badly needed breather. But there was nothing in general terms about what they were doing, about their surprise that certain substances were heavier or lighter than they had expected; just, 'Cor, it's heavy'. Much of the talk was a matter of deciding who should go out, coping with crises – 'There's not enough rivets!' – reminding each other what to do, checking on what they had done, gossiping about the next lesson, looking for things and borrowing things, having quarrels, and accompanying themselves as they wrote ('Name . . , of . . . material'). Towards the end there were frequent exhortations to 'get a move on' because of the bell, and when it rang, 'Oh no! an' we 'an even started!' (writing up the last bit). Very frequent, and in indication of their absorption in the practicalities of the sub-tasks, were remarks like 'Now we've got to . . .' and 'We have to' do this and that.

Equally revealing in terms of this absorption was the way in which they handled their suspicion, right at the end, that the readings might be flawed.

P1:   Eh, you two! We've been gettin' the wrong readings! That wasn't on 0.
      (The arm which pointed upwards was bent, the lower, longer part pointed up towards 10.)
P2:   Why?
P3:   Ah, no . . .
P4:   So?
P2:   Oh, yes.
P1:   Look, that was bent look. . . . Oh, so that's all right then.

P2: Yeah – cor, that was lucky . . .

P3: Oh, no, I've put kilogrammes not grammes, 600 kilo-grammes!

They find reassurance with enviable but necessary alacrity; the bell was due in two minutes, and they had started writing up their results and conclusions. It was 'all right' because the upper part of the bent arm pointed at 0. They overlooked the fact that this meant that all the readings were out by about 10 grammes. The teacher's comment was:

> I was slightly disappointed that they did not try to adjust the results through an assessment of the error. Perhaps they appreciated that a comparison of weights was not hindered greatly by the error, but probably that is wishful thinking on my behalf.

I think anyone listening to the tape would have an impression of cheery lads busy on something that interested them, chatting in a lively way and hurrying themselves along, and having a certain amount of fun. What is not there is any sense of what the estimat-ings and weighings are slowly uncovering, or even a sense that they might be uncovering something. Certainly, they are not using language to express interest or enquire, or compare or theorize with. They are using it to help them get through the tasks. They may well have learned a good deal on that level about how to handle tasks, equipment and each other. Barnes and Todd make a comment on small-group talk that seems relevant.[8] They suggest that some groups do demonstrably 'build up hypotheses', 'handle evidence' to come to 'insights', 'construct their own questions', 'are capable of reflexive awareness of their own and others' thinking', and so on. Equally, some groups do not: 'These chains of first-hand experience are not utilized to cast light on the question: "Why do boys fight like this?"'

This group's talk may be typical of many in its failure to get off the ground. Part of the reason for the limitations of the talk seems to be shortage of time. But what this expression may mean is precisely what is at issue as well. This teacher is, it seems, less inclined than either the other science teacher or the history teacher to proceed so directionally as not to sense some of the problems that arise for pupils' understanding and true involvement. None the less, the way in which the course is laid out in parcels of time – a double lesson for measuring liquids and runny solids – itself entails a directional movement which seems partly responsible for the closure both of general speculation about the meaning of the results and of matters like the flawed readings at the end. This isn't to suggest that the group would have handled the questions with more time, only that without it they had no chance of doing so. In other words, for this teacher working with an objectivistic conception of 'the course', the inclination to be 'open' is frustrated not just by the objective existence of the course, but perhaps also by the way in which its epistemology – which doesn't envisage contingencies like arguing over results and what that may contribute to learning – tends to usurp the individual teacher's less confidently authoritative phenomenological style. The teacher's drawing-back from following up the 'black coating' digression might be seen in either light, or both.

But 'shortage' of time seems not to be the whole answer. The pupils' not seeing the lesson as piecing together a pattern may also reflect the absence of that longer-term temporal horizon that a teacher who knows the topic possesses. Pupils encountering a lesson that for them is a series of discrete 5- or 10-minute passages may even be described as experiencing a variant of what Minkowski calls 'a-temporal actions, actions with no purpose, no tomorrow',[9] since the separate weighings did not seem to link up conceptually and so point forward to other experiences. The inference would then seem to be that somehow the purpose implicit for the teacher in the parts needs to become continuously explicit for pupils if their temporal horizons are not to be restricted to a series of brief present moments, and their labours somewhat trivialized. Without this longer horizon which overall purposefulness offers, the inductive-seeming activities they pursue lack the questioning, hypothetical orientation that makes sense of them as inductive science.

## Accelerating science

An examination of one pupil's note-books over a three-year

period suggests that the directional impetus of the first-year lessons may not only be a routine feature of science but that it may be more marked in succeeding years. In a period of two months from 16 October to 11 December in the second year E was introduced to these topics: 'How shape affects movement in water', 'Streamlined animals', 'Hot water heating systems', 'Water pressure', 'Surface tension', 'What happens when water freezes', 'Problems ice causes and solutions for them', 'Drying paper', 'Investigating how fast water cools down', 'Dehydrated foods', 'Estimating surface areas', 'Looking at plants that live on water and on land', 'Stages of development of land vertebrates', 'Making and testing bridges', 'Is water formed when fuels burn?', 'Calcium reacting with water' and 'Hydrogen'. Twelve of these involved experiments with conclusions.

The topics are closely related to pupils' everyday worlds, and their small-group experiments exploit and extend action-knowledge curiosity by inviting their observation of objects falling in water, constructing bridges and overloading them, and so on. None the less, the 'involvement' that might be expected when action-knowledge content is handled in small-group experiments is likely to be limited by the temporal structure of the work; the pace is brisk, and each problem seems quickly to produce its solution. Thus, in the written-up experiments the conclusions seem to be the clear conclusions of a defined science, and to bear no constitutive marks of qualification, uncertainty or tentativeness. The 'conclusions' about air, for instance:

Facts about air.
We have discovered these facts from our experiments:
(a) Air expands (gets bigger) when heated and contracts when cooled.
(b) Air is needed for burning and oxygen gas is used up during burning.
(c) Hot air rises.
(d) Empty bottles contain air.
(e) Air can be squashed (compressed). Water cannot.
(f) Air has a pressure – one unit of pressure is Newtons/Square Centimetres.

In this section, none the less, the tone of voice is often personal:

> You will notice on my diagram that the lower the hole is drilled in the side of the tin water-container the further the jet goes, because there is more water pushing down on the lower holes than on the higher ones.

The voice is confined, though, to occasional sentences and paragraphs. At these times E seems to employ everyday language constitutively to endorse and grasp bits of knowledge, and a personal 'voice' is perhaps audible.

(1) These were orange crystals at the start. They were heated directly, sparks appeared at once and a sizzling noise was heard. The bunsen was removed but the reaction went on. More sparks flew above the reaction.

(2) [A wallflower] has four petals as opposed to the bluebell's six. Each petal has a stalk which attaches it to the base of the flower. For the wallflower instead of having a stalk and pollen bag per plant there are (I counted) six pollen bags. (Specimens were attached.)

At one point, 'looking at specimens to see if they are insects', there are three entries to the effect that she 'couldn't see them' in the column referring to number of legs.

(3) New pasteurized milk smelt all right – fit to drink. Our pasteurized milk smelt a bit off. The test indicated OK to drink but I wouldn't like to drink it. Untreated milk smelt horrible. I would *never* drink it.

A voice is discernible in the bracketed 'I counted', and in comment like 'I would *never* drink it'. She is free to say she 'can't see' the number of legs, and to dissent from the indication that 'our pasteurized milk' was 'OK to drink'. In different respects – syntactic, semantic, tonal – such writing seems to be 'hers' as well as, and in being, science.

At main school in the third year she encountered a more academic science, and the earlier general science became chemistry, physics and biology, each with two periods a week. She summed up the change in talking about chemistry: 'Lower school's more relaxed. With Mr P I just used to write. With Mr F I just write the sentence bits clearly and leave the fussy bits out.' One such 'fussy bit' is the 'I' and 'you' that litters earlier second-year pages; these words are quite absent from the fifty-four pages of the third-year chemistry work which filled up the second-year book, except on one page where answers to 'Do you agree?' questions were sought. Her style becomes formal, without the personal touches that characterized the earlier manner. In June of the second year it was possible for her to write, reflectively: 'This creature [a pond snail] moves occasionally at a leisurely pace. The snail is a greeny colour, quite dark, an olive green.' Accounts of what happens in chemistry three months later are generally somewhat more brisk and bald: 'After ten minutes there was a ring around the inside of the tube. The ammonia had travelled 56 cm and the hydrogen chloride solution had travelled 36 cm.'

Absent, or finally expunged, are hints of any emotional accent. In June untreated milk 'smelt horrible'; from September responses like that are absent. (I sometimes heard 'Cors' of amazement from pupils watching practicals; these notes seem never to be transposed to written accounts.) Such 'objective' non-emotionality establishes, of course, an emotional field of its own. She perceived this shift in terms of what she called 'style'. Talking about dictation early in the third year, she said, 'What they try to do is get you into a style by dictating, but by the time you're in the fourth year you're expected to do the style yourself.' The dictating, of which there seems a good deal early in the third year, accompanies – and seems partly a result of – another shift, towards experiments at the teacher's bench, and away from small-group experiments. E felt there were three reasons for this change: it was expensive working in groups; chemistry was more dangerous than lower school general science; and, significantly, 'maybe the results would be inaccurate'. Paradigmatic ideal experiments imply ideal results. If the value of this science is seen to lie in the objective accuracy of its results (and conclusions, even), rather than in the experiential attempts at being accurate in the process of doing an experiment, it is not incongruous that, in the teacher's single experiments, method, results and conclusion are often dictated.

To be 'got into' a style in this way seems to mean there can be no clear understanding on the pupil's part as to why the 'personal' features of style, the 'voice', have been discarded. The radical formalism of this slenderizing shift is then apparent. And what seems also to be discarded is a tentative linguistic reconnoitring which makes particular bits of science 'precise' for particular children by situating them in the passing moment. The exclamations of surprise, the hesitations, the emotional nuances, are properly to be seen as working for 'precision', as recording an individual's state of self-knowledge about his knowledge of 'facts'; this running meta-communicative clarification seems to be what is abandoned in the imposition of the new, properly 'scientific' style.

In the interests of 'objectivity', then, the time-consuming personal dimensions of the earlier science were slowly relinquished to make way for higher concentrations of content. And, as a result, it seems that there is less of a problem about handling time, since the tension between the temporal demands of 'the course' and the temporal horizons of pupils struggling to understand – a tension that seems to surface only occasionally even in the first- and second-year courses – is no longer as manifest. The conflict has been solved by the teachers' stronger endorsement of objectivistic conceptions of science, to the point where, perhaps, there is no longer a conflict either about time or definitions of subjects, or – by extension – the kinds of subject language appropriate for holding open access to pupils' constitutive involvement.

### Detail and time

E herself, by implication, raised the problem of time in commenting that one problem was 'not going into enough detail'. When questions are raised, she said, a teacher will 'often' say 'Let's not go into that now. You'll be doing it at "A"-level.' She made a pertinent observation on 'method': 'A lot of the scientists who discovered things, they weren't trained in a method, they did their own experiments. If you stick to one method you don't discover things.' In this, perhaps, is discernible a perception of the essential conservatism of 'method', and 'method' realized as 'style'. 'You don't discover things' if the method, or the ritual, is essentially what is practised. Since 'style' here involves a discarding of 'voice', of qualification, speculation, uncertainty, and so on, it seems that method and attendant 'style' necessitate the relinquishing of means for reconstituting content. In order to retrieve what 'method' and 'style' caused E to relinquish, one precondition would be that the time-frame within which she could 'go into detail' would be different from that of the increasingly densely packaged science course. In the previous year she had at one point established her own time-frame for some work done spontaneously at home. Her time was as much her own as the work she did seems to be. The practice of her normal school science contrasts interestingly with this episode of seemingly self-motivated science. She had been bought a microscope, and at one point some two months after its purchase, she made impromptu observations on pond water from her back garden. These observations were painstakingly written out, for her own satisfaction, on sheets of drawing paper. Her style reflects to an extent school science – she clearly feels it suits a private scientific investigation – but it also often departs from it in interesting ways.

*Pond Water from Our Garden*
(Spring – quite good weather)
This thing* under the miscroscope was an opaque yellow and stationary.

Pandorina                Scenedesmus

These were mainly orange and yellow, opaque. They were very active and appeared to have a mass of cells moving about inside its body.

*Figure 20*

Further down she writes: ' "Thing" is a very unscientific word but I don't know what else I can use.' Then, after consulting the *Observer Pond Life* book, she writes 'Algae' and crosses out the above, substituting 'algae' for 'things'.

The private directions in which speculation takes her – including changes of direction and digressions – are hardly replicable or

anticipatable: 'In water there are remains of these ~~things~~* algae
which showed that they eat each other.' 'Some of them had three
segments not four; this is probably due to injury rather than
natural growth.' So far she has discovered the term 'algae' for
herself, and produced a personal hypothesis about the fact that
some have three not four segments. This speculation distinguishes
her writing here from anything in her science notebook, where
'answers' seem readily available. She goes on:

> Another thing I discovered was that if the algae are brought
> from the cold pond water in which they live into a warmer
> atmosphere they die *slowly* . . . if a glass slip covers the water
> they die quickly. With no trapped air bubbles they die almost
> *immediately*. I'm not sure yet but I think this is probably due
> . . . if the algae when they have died are left in the warm
> atmosphere they seem to disappear altogether . . . the smaller
> of the pandorina seem to last the longest, though to be honest I
> haven't the faintest idea why, perhaps its because they don't
> use up as much as the rest of the algae. I've no idea how many
> single algae live in one pond . . . it must run into millions judg-
> ing from what I can see under my microscope in only a drop of
> water.

Another hypothesis about why the algae die attempts to relate
warmth, air supply, and size to her observations about their dying
and disappearing. And all of it is written as if she were proposing
questions to herself; the passage's brisk tentativeness is preliminary to a formulation of questions. The highly provisional possible
answers are woven in with the observations and puzzles; no
schematic progress from 'observations' through 'results' to a
'conclusion' breaks the stream of this consciousness; the use of
'seems', 'perhaps' and 'I've no idea' are precise means of marking
degrees of uncertainty, and crucial parts of her explanation of it to
herself. The confidence of the normal 'conclusion' in the school
notebook is in marked contrast.

To some extent, of course, she may be drawing on school
science. The existence of the microscope, in particular, conduces
to a style of examination where she removed organisms from a
habitat to the 'laboratory' in order to observe them, and (rather

coolly) 'watch them die'. And there is no way of telling how far the activity of producing hypotheses, observations and conclusions is a reflection of her socialization into school science. Though the manner is different, that science may be 'there'. And yet, since a phenomenological view of language and subject contents does not reject a subject's constituted forms, but looks rather to the constitutive negotiations of the 'speaking subject' with those forms, it could be said of E's negotiations here that they so far imply openness and constitutive involvement as to make possible not just the personal reconstruction of this piece of scientific content but the personal reconstruction, through further involvement of the same kind, of the epistemological grounds of that reconstructed content. In other words, here, such authentic practice raises the possibility that questions like 'Why did I remove organisms from a habitat?' might eventually be raised, precisely because E is here travelling freely, so to speak, with her own purpose, rather than on an errand for someone else.

## References

1 M. Young, 'The schooling of science', in G. Whitty and M. Young (eds), *Explorations in the Politics of School Knowledge* (Driffield, Nafferton Books, 1976), p. 54.
2 A. Schutz, 'Phenomenology and the social sciences', in T. Luckmann (ed.), *Phenomenology and Sociology* (Harmondsworth, Penguin, 1978), p. 131.
3 J. Hardy, 'Textbooks and classroom knowledge: the politics of explanation and description', in Whitty and Young, op. cit., p. 95.
4 J. Fines and R. Verrier, *The Drama of History* (London, New University Education, 1974), p. 17.
5 ibid., p. 12.
6 E. P. Thompson, 'Time, work-discipline, and industrial capitalism', *Past and Present*, vol. 38 (December, 1967), p. 60.
7 P. Fraisse, *The Psychology of Time* (London, Eyre & Spottiswoode, 1964), pp. 224–5.
8 D. Barnes and F. Todd, *Communication and Learning in Small Groups* (London, Routledge & Kegan Paul, 1977), pp. 53–75.
9 E. Minkowski, quoted in Fraisse, op. cit., p. 197.

# 7

# THE CONSTRUCTION OF WRITING

## Creating people

In her last year at junior school, the same girl (E) wrote the following piece about the school yard, where the pupils had gone after rain.

*After Rain*
Cold, icy air and lush green grass, scattered with shining droplets of water. A caterpillar sheltering under a leaf and a spider's web decked with transparent diamonds. The boggy, brown mud marked with small channels where the water has been. Wet apples strewn forlornly over the mud and lush grass. Browny yellow leaves lying wet in the grass and green leaves turning a browny gold at the edges but still thriving. Small droplets of water sliding from the leaves to the ground. The

tree's bark vaguely shining in the weak sunshine. The swimming pool a forbidding green colour with leaf stalks sticking up rather like tubes that you breathe through under water. Muddy puddles containing freezing cold water. At the bottom of the trees trapped water lies stone still until a breeze comes and disturbs it.

Most teachers would be very gratified to be given this in response to something they have asked children to do. It seems to be the kind of writing which carries the imprint of one child's special way of looking, thinking and speaking. There is no trace of any formalistic encounter with language 'placed before language' or any sense that aspects of her engagement with what she examines have been selectively closed off or edited. The product has her own stamp. I wish to look at the idiosyncratic structure of this piece later, but for the moment simply offer it as an example of what teachers often aim towards when they do 'creative writing', and in more general terms of what they hope may be realized through a stress on pupils' own experience and ways of handling language.

Teachers are drawn to those open styles of working which creative writing perhaps most obviously represents because offers of 'genuinely personal' learning are made through them. At the same time, the inheritance of opposed ways of handling knowledge – of the kind that I have tried to exemplify in operation – might be expected to carry over at times into contexts that are explicitly and particularly designed to be open. This is perhaps by now an almost trite observation. Yet an examination of lessons where there is a particular intent to avoid closure of the pupils' knowledge world not only seems to suggest how difficult it is to effect the change, but also hints at the possible role of the teacher's own constituted structures of awareness in displacing pupils'. Again, it seems, we are up against the difficulty of redefining how children come to gain knowledge in situations where the teacher is not as clearly called upon to redefine the manner in which he proposes to relate to those of his own awarenesses that are to be used to generate response in the child.

An English lesson at first-year level was to be mainly given over

to creative writing about 'An Old Lady'. The teacher explained
to me that the work had begun the day before, and that she was
working on this kind of thing because it was 'part of their experience'. (This sentiment, in almost those words, was also expressed
by a geography teacher and an RE teacher at about the same
time.) The previous day the class had, through discussion, collected notes on the old lady, and written them in their exercise
books for homework, and now the discussion that was preparatory to the writing was resumed. The headings they had made
were first recalled; one heading was 'One old person, sitting by
the fire'. The teacher then asked questions such as 'How old is
she?', 'Is our old lady well dressed?', 'What is her walk like?',
and so on. What was soon evident was that the image of an old
lady was being constructed out of the questions and answers, so
that for each pupil she was about 70, didn't wear ragged clothes,
walked slowly, and had old furniture, dusty photographs and
cream-coloured walls in her room. There was the one shared
image for everyone, and it was being defined and clarified during
and by the lesson. This became particularly clear at one point,
when the teacher reminded the class that there were to be two
paragraphs, and that in the second the lights go out, at which
point our old person had to get up slowly, cautiously (as had been
demonstrated by one boy in a piece of impromptu role-play). The
old lady was not in fact emerging out of individual pupils' recol-
lected experience of actual old ladies but was being assembled
communally by agreed-on structures of words and phrases that
would fit together – a grammatical but perhaps less empirical old
lady. The generalized image created out of consensus seemed to
work to prevent the formulation of those different images of 'an
old lady' that would arise from spontaneous reworking of 'their
own experience'.

The teacher seemed to be attempting openness through seeking
pupils' personal recollections: 'How might an old person light a
match?' Yet there had to be matches, a candle, a flame and
shadows; and the teacher's approval of pupils' contributions
('flickering' for flame, 'gnarled' for her fingers) had the effect of
endorsing kinds of things that might permissibly be said. Thus a
stereotype – a cliché even – was gradually produced; the gnarled

fingers, wrinkled skin, trembling hands and flickering candles occurred in many if not most pieces, and this grammar was only intermittently touched by what really did look like observation issuing from experience.

It was striking that in the version they began to write several pupils employed a usage which undermined the existence of their old lady, whether it were factual-documentary existence or a fictive one. They said, 'an old person *would*', not 'was' or 'is'. This conditional mood perhaps expressed an awareness that they were dealing with a structure that might – probably would – later come to fit the facts of experience. This 'would' be the case if the experience were to occur; the language might be 'right'. This then seems like a gathering of information more suitable for discursive writing, and one thing that is clearly missing is at the meta-communicative level of saying what such writing is for, what it does.

Some pupils, rather than write up their notes for homework, had produced a second draft of the initial rough sketch they had written before the notes. Their alterations, which were often interesting, revealed how they had reoriented themselves to writing 'well' about the old lady, by taking into account the discussions that occurred in the second lesson, in which the teacher's formalizing stereotypical version displaced whatever constitutive beginnings had been made. Thus one first version promisingly began: 'One Sunday afternoon I thought I'd go for a walk so I went out and said to my mum, I'm going for a walk and I went.' That rhythmically follows the movement of his thoughts, it is unselfconscious and crisp, the boy himself. His second version began: 'The old person sat by the firelight. She had wrinkled hands so the fire shone on her hands.' The voice has gone, it no longer expresses a coherent perception; one does not sit by 'firelight'; it is not hands in the idiom that are 'wrinkled' but skin; and the 'so' is gratuitous. The editing out of the original beginning results in fragmentation and loss of feel.

The teacher pointed out to me some boys at a corner table who were not writing much. I talked with them a while about old people they might know. All four had sharp recollections of grans, aunts and strangers, but none of them seemed to be making any use of this fertile vein in their writing. One of them pointed out that his gran did not have gnarled hands and was particularly mobile – and so on. Another gave a quick, detailed description of his gran's room, and said he would find it easier to do *his* gran.

The teacher explicitly adverted to the notion of using 'their experience'. And yet when, just prior to the enquiries made of the four boys, I remarked on the number of 'would' constructions, suggesting that it indicated a reluctance to endorse such a record as either solid fact or solid fiction, she replied that it 'wasn't really in their experience', and that this kind of writing was very difficult because it was to some extent 'imposed'. She then instanced the four boys I spoke to, commenting that they found such work difficult; they were 'rather weak'.

This is puzzling. But the apparent contradiction is perhaps explicable if by 'experience' the teacher means – as the lesson suggested she did – some generalized conceptual version of 'old lady', a constituted form abstracted from particulars of experience, though not, of course, these children's. She would then presumably mean that the 'weak' pupils have not had enough particular experiences to be in possession of the general 'experience'. Though it may seem odd to find writing in English failing to recognize the significance and value of particulars she is, arguably, only doing what I have described other teachers as doing, namely substituting a formalizing abstract schema for a personal empirical encounter. If she is construing 'experience' in this way, she commits no greater distortion of the teacher's language than those occurring in those contexts where words like 'observe', 'evidence', 'find out', 'conclude', and so on were made to relinquish at least some of their 'open' connotations.

## The man on the promenade

Before describing a second creative writing lesson, it will be useful to outline some of the guiding ideas of the teacher in charge of lower school English. Her emphases form a context for the work described above, and that of the young teacher whose lesson is considered next. Primarily, she seemed concerned that pupils should not be left to write 'as they please', but should be 'guided': 'If I don't tell them how to begin, I get pages and pages that might be nothing to do with it, just getting started.' She stressed the dangers of 'writing too much, as in junior school projects'.

In one of her own lessons that I observed, pupils were being prepared to write on 'what it is like to be hunted'. They had to 'write carefully', and do the piece 'in a few paragraphs . . . not getting carried away . . . in half an hour'. The preparatory discussion was initially in the form of a string of anecdotes from pupils. This was very fertile, and the stories seemed to possess a vitality often missing from their finished writing – perhaps because they were simply telling, not 'using words'. In the lesson itself there seemed to be a change of focus from language used unselfconsciously for telling stories to language gathered to create a structure of, or display in, words. The change occurred when the teacher stopped asking questions about what had happened when they were chased (she seemed very skilled at drawing out children's stories and somehow ensuring there was a good audience for them), and began to talk about how to write, about the difficulties of describing a hunt or chase, about 'finding words' and 'using the right words'. Listening to their anecdotes, she had said things like 'Good heavens, what on earth did you do then?' Now, on several occasions, she began: 'A word you could use is . . .'. She had not 'prepared' their talking, or interrupted to help them find 'the right word'. They were warmly and considerately listened to, and they talked. But now they were not somehow to persist in relating to their own language in that fashion. They were not merely to write; they were to learn things about how to write. In part the shift of interest seemed to be from the empirical to the grammatical. The relations between words and the world seemed to count less in this part of the lesson than the relations between words and words, their 'grammar'. It seemed that the teacher's very concern to develop the pupils' writing tended to edge what was valuable in their talk to the periphery of their concerns when they wrote.

Of course, writing is more difficult than talking for 11-year-old children, and the problems of what Smith calls 'transcription' (the transfer of ideas from the head to the page) are still considerable.[1]

That the shift from talk to writing is seen as crucial seems appropriate, but the teacher's interpretation of how to handle it seems neither to look for constitutive features of their talk nor to ensure that they are somehow preserved in writing. She explained that she was 'interested in quality', as revealed by 'the sort of words they use':

> There are some people who enjoy writing and if they're not careful they go on too long, and forget all about punctuation and spelling. And the weaker children need a structure. If they do have long stories to tell, I get them to tape them or talk from notes . . . in junior schools they do all this writing, pages and pages no matter what it's like.

It seems that 'structure' is the means of guiding, or restraining, those who 'enjoy' writing and 'go on too long', as they did in junior school. Such 'structure' produces 'quality', which is related to 'the sort of words they use'. This latter criterion is expressed somewhat objectivistically. It seems as if, like the words in the lists that were often given to help pupils write on certain subjects, the 'appropriate' word is less the contingently expressive word for the particular situation, than the perennially appropriate word in the grammar of the general situation.

It is for this reason, perhaps, that such a 'structure' is suitable for pupils of varying ability; it is in itself a possibility of 'quality' for all pupils. But producing lists of words, apart from the particularized experiences that call them forth, seems to drive language towards formalism, and ultimately cliché. Thus, in one pupil's preparation for 'A Friendly Fire' the word 'golden' occurred three times in a total of twenty-two words, in expressions like 'golden glow'. The task was to 'describe vividly . . . a friendly fire; your description should include words to convey the appearance, shape and sound and the comfort of such a fire (about half to three-quarters of a page)'. While this might be a structure, it serves to direct attention to discrete components of experience, and might well tend to fragment pupils' accounts, especially if they conscientiously treat 'appearance', 'shape' and 'sound' as things to be dealt with separately. The pupil's interpretation did not in fact do this, but was over-adjectival and hyper-kinetic in tone: 'twisting turning flames, dancing jumping flames. Friendly, bright and gay. What a lovely thing to end the day.'

Similarly, a list for writing about a witch includes: 'Her nose – long, crinkled, knobbly, pointed, lumpy, warted, hooked. Her mouth – crooked, cruel, thin-lipped, toothless, puckered.' The same pupil's version runs, 'she has a hooked nose with a wart on the end. In her mouth there are no teeth worth talking about.' The final phrase is one of only three that seem idiosyncratic enough to escape the implied template; she says her hat is 'tatty' and she 'grins'. Even so, the final form of the piece, seven short paragraphs of one or two sentences each, all beginning 'she has' or 'her', suggests the subordination of the imagination to a pre-coded version.

In the same month three exercises were set called 'The Right Word': an exercise on synonyms for 'looked', 'to describe more accurately what a person is doing' (the fact that 'synonyms' and 'right words' seem here synonymous makes clear the general formalistic nature of the project to write about a person 'looking', etc.); some advice on 'not using the same phrase twice'; and other work on tenses, and singulars and plurals. A good deal of the teacher's marking comment derives from a view of adequate language as being made up of 'good' words and phrases. Thus: 'well-phrased'; '"stuff" is slang – "belongings"?'; 'scrape or squelch' (replacing 'the sound of something being spooned onto a plate'); 'is this a suitable word?' Implicit in this seems to be an 'atomistic' notion of language: language is reducible to its bits or component parts. Words and phrases are first gathered according to a principle, and meaning in writing is then constructed out of the pieces in a way analogous to the construction of 'meaning' in jigsaw puzzles, in that the bits are thought to be meaningful intrinsically (as 'right' or 'good' words or phrases) before they meet other pieces. In effect, a content is constructed in order to give employment to means of expression. This focus turns the relation of content and means of expression inside out. Creative writing is thus formalized into a preoccupation with grammar, and the truth-value of its language may consist less in the way in which it conveys an experienced reality than in some form of appropriateness to a model, or template.

The stress on words, on finding and using them, on a 'clear, orderly account', and on brevity and relevance ('Describe the fire, not the events which led up to it') might well help to push the writing towards 'description'. Hence, perhaps, the frequency of notions like 'word-painting' and 'vividness' in the teacher's language ('we are going to create word-pictures of'). Children's writing, as in long stories where they get 'carried away', often seems to evince little interest in pictorial description; their comments on fiction that is slowed down by 'too much description' are often astringent. Yet pupils' English for the first year started with this dictated note: 'Descriptive writing depends so much on the right selection and use of words. Contrasting word-pictures can be created by careful thought and choice.'

One problem may be that a feeling for description depends on a rudimentarily reflexive appreciation of language in a way that narrative does not. Children seem not to read each others' descriptions, to appreciate their vividness, as readily as they will read each others' stories merely to enjoy them. A tendency to bring descriptive writing to the centre of creative writing thus seems itself likely to formalize it to some extent.

These considerations may be related to the following comments on a creative writing lesson conducted by a young teacher. As in the lesson described earlier, though less markedly, the editorial shadow of the experiential template, her own structures of awareness, seems to be evident. Certainly some of these first-year pupils are aware of the plan of the lesson as coercing, and perhaps even diverting and restricting them – as shown in the transcript of their talk below. They were to attempt to write from the stimulus of a seaside picture of a deserted beach and a man by a lamp-post on the promenade. There was a class discussion, during which words that could be used in the final version were written on the board.

T:    What kind of a seashore?
P1:   Sandy.

T:    What else?
P2:   Lonely.
      ('Lonely' was written on the board, but not 'sandy'.)

The teacher herself added 'and bare', and wrote that down too.

This first interchange about the seashore, for all its brevity, is important. In neglecting the sandiness of the shore and endorsing a particular emotive note through reinforcing it herself with another word, the teacher immediately signals that the picture is to be perceived in terms of a certain mood. The pupils responded to this first indication of the appropriate emotional tone, and contributed immediately to the note of desolation – the more readily, perhaps, because the photograph, a dull one, seemed emotionally neutral. Thus the next contributions were:

P4:   Deserted.
P2:   Empty.
P6:   Isolated.
      (These words were recorded on the board. There was then a change of focus to the man.)
T:    Let's have a look at the man . . . what kind of a figure is it?
P7:   It's an old man.
T:    I'm thinking about him being alone – another word beginning with 's'.

'Old' is put aside as 'sandy' was, and the same mood is ascribed to the man as to the beach. So this is a choice parallel to the initial selection of mood, but a more coercive closure in that a pupil had provided the word 'lonely' originally, whereas the teacher herself provides the emotional keynote here, implying that it is to be found in a word in her head. In response, a pupil found 'solitary'.

The pupils next closed their eyes and pretended they were the man standing by the lamp-post. What did they hear? Seagulls 'screeching' and 'crying' – both recorded. The wind was 'moaning' (not recorded), 'howling' and 'whistling' (both recorded). Then the sea 'crashing'; the waves 'withdraw' or 'retreat'; and the pebbles 'clink', 'move' or 'rattle'. What did they see? They saw the gulls 'hovering', 'swooping' and 'soaring', and the waves 'sending off spray'.

The lesson continued in this way, though contributions came too quickly for all words to be recorded on the board. The teacher's questions were all related to the hypothetical situation provided by the picture. The final part of the discussion was introduced by the question: 'What do you feel?'

P1: The wind.
T: Especially where?
P1: Your face.
P2: You feel your feet sink.
P3: Your hair waving about.
T: When your hair's blown about, what do we say?
P3: Windswept.
(Another pupil then provided the word 'unwanted', and the teacher added 'despised'.)
T: Susan [the pupil] feels unwanted, despised, lonely (said dramatically).

After this there was a little more discussion about the texture of the wood of the post, about gulls and waves, and so on. Then the pupils were asked to write a poem about a man on a beach. It could be 'a poem about things you see and hear, or a poem about feelings, or both'. It didn't have to rhyme.

Even though there was some sharp editing, and though it seemed that the teacher had herself decided on an emotional key-note, she takes the children with her, weaves many of their offers and contributions into the fabric of the version that is being put together, and involves more than half the class in discussion. If she wished them to write about loneliness, why not start this way, with a nondescript, emotionally neutral photograph through which she could engage them in an imaginative reconstruction that would draw on their own experience of loneliness?

But if this is what is being attempted, the stage at which the particular accent of their own experiences might be brought forward is missing. They don't in fact talk about loneliness in this constitutive way, as the other class had earlier talked about being chased. Connected with this is the way the pupils here interpret questions like 'What do you hear? or see?' and so on. By the time these questions are asked, it seems already to be established that they are not, so to speak, going back to their individual private records for answers; and the production and acceptance of the more generalizable and predictable terms for the gulls' behaviour further hint clearly at the kind of general-conceptual account that is being assembled. Questions like 'What can you see?' seem to be handled here as meaning 'What words can you find that will help you picture the gulls?' (a grammatical question) rather than 'What did you see when you last saw gulls?' (which seems more empirical). Though creative writing aims to be concerned with the second kind of question, the answers being collected are word-tokens for interchangeable and no longer distinctly realized experiences.

The fact that these distinct questioning procedures go in different directions and produce different results is perhaps worth stressing. A basic consequence of the focus being placed on biographical particulars is, of course, the kind of sharpening and qualifying of usages that comes of their being situated in a personal actuality. The teacher would hardly then stop at the point where the word 'swoop' or the word 'hover' is received. She would ask for more of the situation, would probe further. She might well say, 'What did you see the gulls swoop down towards?' or, 'Did the gull you saw really hover in the way kestrels do?' And the questions will need to recognize the way in which the emotional tone of the initial picture is necessarily made more complex by pupils' own recollections.

I remember some 8-year-olds' impressions of a beach that I had wished them to see in a certain 'creative' light gathering instead round the discovery of a dead black-headed gull that was, they saw, ringed – No. 106. The metal ring, the number, the dead bird looking 'quite fresh' became the emotional centre of at least some children's sense of the beach that morning and could not be gainsaid in our discussion later. Similarly, questions like 'What do you see?' have to be willing to uncover more than just the words that here are placed before pupils' language.

### Writing a poem

In an attempt to sense whether children themselves felt any sense of the closure of their ideas or means of expression in lessons such as these, I talked to one group of pupils at first-year level and three at second-year level (three or four in each group) about the lists of words that were often written on the board and in exercise books before writing. I said I wanted to know if they felt they were a help, or not. Perhaps predictably, given that the required product was related to the list, the consensus in the three second-year groups seemed to be that a list was helpful. However, the first-year group, talking immediately after the man on the promenade lesson, there was some expression of a feeling of being directed.

The discussion with this group started with the idea of a poem, what it is. All the pupils defined it in terms of rhyming or not rhyming, number of beats in line, capital letters at the beginning of each line, verses, and so on. (A story, by contrast, 'has paragraphs and sentences'.) Then, we discussed the man on the promenade. Some comment was made about why he was waiting – he was waiting for his girlfriend; he was a tired criminal pausing for a breather. These ideas had been thought of during the lesson, but not mentioned. I asked why not:

P1:   Miss – didn't sort of ask us what – what – what. . . . Well, she just went on to say how we feel. . . . She didn't describe his personality.
Self:  Yes –
P2:   He could have been somebody from outer space or something, waiting for his spaceship to come down . . .

They were not sure whether they would use these ideas or not: 'It depends —'; 'How it starts depends on how you're going to finish.' There seemed no sense that their ideas about crime and outer space were closed off and would not be used just because they were not dealt with in the lesson; on the other hand, the consensus style of the lesson was not interpretable as a clear invitation to follow up such imaginative ventures and see them as part of their own versions.

I asked if they ever thought of things to write about that they did not get the chance to.

PP:   *Yes!* (chorus).

P2: I'd like to write about something that's ordinary, you know, like an apple, describing a spider going over an apple. (This had been a set topic.)

Self: What do you like to write about?

P1: Well, Miss gives us all kinds of funny things like describe a spider going over an apple. . . . I don't like doing those kinds of things really.

Self: (to P2) You do like that though?

P2: Well, yes if you wasn't told to . . . if you could just pick up a pen and paper and write it down . . .

P3: You have to keep to so many words . . . say, em. . . . she puts all these words on the board . . . she says you can use all these words if you want . . .

P1: It confuses me.

P3: Yea, and it confuses you . . .

Self: Does it?

P2: It does.

P3: Yea, and it depends on the words on the board.

Self: Will you use those words on the board?

P1: No.

P2: Sometimes, not all the time . . .

Self: Do you feel you ought to use them?

P3: No.

P1: No . . . you'll have forgotten them . . .

Self: Well, why will it confuse you?

P1: You're using everybody else's mind, then, aren't you . . . using everybody else's words not *our* words . . .

P2: Everybody else is probably going to use it and by tomorrow maybe you'll have forgotten them . . . maybe you've forgotten which words are on the board and the ones you [indistinct] they might come up . . .

Self: So if you did it *your* way, then, would it be different from the way it was prepared today?

PP: *Yes!* (chorus).

Self: How would yours be different?

P3: Well, I often try and put in the funny side of things . . .

P1: Yes.

P2: Yea.

P3:   . . . instead of making it more solemn . . .

P2:   Yes.

P1:   Yes, I agree with that.

P3:   Putting something funny in it, like saying 'as he crawls across the wet [indistinct]'.

P1:   I'd like Miss to say just 'We've got a lesson, write something that you want' . . . and Miss S talks when you're trying to work and it distracts your concentration . . .

Self:  Yes, I'm sure a lot of teachers do that . . . I'm a teacher and I'm sure I do that . . .

P3:   Mr M does that quite a lot . . . cracks his jokes half way through a sum and you have to start all over again . . .

Self:  So if you were. . . . I notice there's some poems on the side there, about fire . . . was it your class that . . .

PP:   Yes.

P3:   Yea . . . they were just descriptions . . . and I did a poem though.

Self:  Did you see a piece of fire being . . .?

PP:   Yes.

Self:  And did you like that? Did you find it easier to write from that?

P1:   Yes.

P3:   Most of them wrote just ordinary descriptions, you know, with the 'amber flames' and [indistinct].

P2:   . . . the 'crimson edge' . . .

P1:   . . . there again she gave us the words to use and I think it's much nicer if you use your own mind, so everyone's different instead . . .

P3:   I did.

P1:   Instead of everyone's the same . . .

P3:   I used my own words. I wrote a poem . . .

P1:   A lot of people depend on her words on the board . . .

P3:   Yeah.

P1:   . . . and then you don't get their writing or their mind in that and you get her mind in it . . . instead of writing what you think . . . and if you're silly against somebody's clever . . . then she'll find out, but everyone's at the same level by using her words.

Self: When did you first start thinking like that, can you remember when you . . .
P1: Oh, a long time ago, at junior school . . .
Self: Perhaps . . . can you tell me . . . is it something that your mum and dad or maybe another teacher has talked about as well sometime or . . .?
P1: No.
Self: Just out of your own head?
P1: Yes.

Their 'confusion' was not shared by children in the second-year groups; perhaps by the second year this mode of operation is known and accepted. At any rate, it was not there raised as an issue. For the first years, it is hard to say what the confusion is exactly; it exists, it seems, whether or not words are forgotten, and whether or not they are used; it is complicated by the feeling that it might unfairly disguise 'if you're silly against somebody's clever'. But for P1 it seems to be a confusion at a deep level; 'you're using everybody else's mind' might mean 'Is it me doing this?' She does not like the way that the teacher's words and mind 'get into' her own work, with the result that 'you don't get their [my] writing'. Her feeling that everyone is being 'reduced to the same level' is perhaps less a worry that she herself will not be seen to be as good as she is, than a concern that things are not what they seem, that 'using everyone else's mind' is, in some sense, where writing of this kind is concerned, losing your own.

Then the topics that did not come up – the criminal, the waiting lover, the science fiction character. What amounts to a closure here is not the fact that these particulars did not emerge, for if the teacher is to discuss the topic with the whole class, as a kind of chairman, there is no time perhaps, without the rhythm of the task itself collapsing, for all pupils to offer all their ideas and have them endorsed explicitly. The closure flows from the mode of existence of the teacher's version if she said, 'This is what I, teacher, can do – you can do the same thing as well or better', there might be no closure. As it is, the lesson moves quickly to a kind of definitive theme, on which variations are invited. It is a template, and creativity is the freedom to develop or embellish the set theme, more than it is the freedom to make, shape or invent.

It seems interesting that the pupils dismissed the idea that there was anything poem-like about the 'descriptions' of fire pinned on the wall. Although I said 'I noticed your poems', I was informed they were 'just descriptions'. One piece had the expression 'the air crinkled'; a number of others were vitally metaphoric, and several were written in lines like verse, though without rhyme or capitals. Even so, these were called 'ordinary descriptions'.

The pupils did not seem to identify metaphoric power as a defining trait of the 'poem' – not surprisingly, since an appreciation of the difference between vitality and cliché is a subtle matter. In consequence, they lean on the formal features of 'verse' – lining, capitalization, and rhyme. Properly speaking, 'verse' is the category they handle. And yet they are frequently encouraged to call 'poems' those pieces of writing that lack these verse features: free verse is perhaps more widely encouraged than rhyming verse. Teachers call free verse compositions 'poems' because they are aware that such writing often displays metaphoric power and orchestrative richness. Yet it is unlikely that first- and second-year pupils have access to this meta-communicative awareness. They have to take on trust the characterization of free verse 'descriptions' as poems. If their poem is the merely formal verse, their attempt to cope with those features of the teacher's working definition of the poem that go beyond the merely formal to metaphor, orchestration, and so on, is itself a formalism that obscures both their own verse notion and the teacher's poem notion. Further, because a 'poem' for them is formal, it may be that it is within the category 'description' that one might look for a sense of the incipiently poetic, since the term 'description' as compared with (their) poem, implies a reflexive attention to words.

This may point to a meta-communicative problem involved in the production of free verse writing. To children, such pieces may be chopped-up descriptions, which 'pass' as poems for reasons they are not clear about. The poetic vitality of some productions may seduce teachers into thinking that pupils do in fact offer them as poems. Pupils may be keen on them because they are shorter than compositions, and earn approval. Moreover, they are often ungraded, unlike essays. Even so, teachers must accept them as genuine poems because, though they may be aware that there is some ambiguity about the term, once they have set up the (formalistic) situation in which pupils write what are called 'poems' in that way, there is no escape from a categorization of free verse productions as precisely those 'poems' the poetry of which pupils, mostly, are not aware of. There seems to be no other term or phrase for teachers to handle them with, unless it is some such expression as 'chopped up descriptions', which may be slightly demystifying, but still leaves hidden the reasons for the chopping-up. Pupils in such uncertainty may be left unaware of what the poetic does, is for, and so on. Attention to expressive features of their own daily talk, in jokes, mimicry, story-telling, and so on, is perhaps one neglected mode of entry into 'the poetic'. Ironically, to imply the equation of verse and poem seems to erase consideration of the poetic.

## Structures

I suggested that the piece called 'After Rain', which was offered as an example of what teachers might be aiming for in creative writing, exhibited a structure of awareness that was idiosyncratic – peculiarly that child's. The 'structured' lessons about the beach and the old lady, and the 'structured' approach espoused by the teacher in charge, which to some extent may lie behind them, work with a notion of structure which seems, when it is compared with the quite different personal structure of a piece like 'After Rain', to be in itself objectivistic; the 'structured' approach, in that it is 'placed before' the other personal kind of structure, seems not only unlikely to issue in such pieces as 'After Rain', but likely to work against their production.

A closer scrutiny of 'After Rain' lends some substance to this suggestion.

*After Rain*
Cold, icy air and lush green grass, scattered with shining droplets of water. A caterpillar sheltering under a leaf and a spider's web decked with transparent diamonds. The boggy, brown

mud marked with small channels where the water has been. Wet apples strewn forlornly over the mud and lush grass. Browny yellow leaves lying wet in the grass and green leaves turning a browny gold at the edges but still thriving. Small droplets of water sliding from the leaves to the ground. The tree's bark vaguely shining in the weak sunshine. The swimming pool a forbidding green colour with leaf stalks sticking up rather like tubes that you breathe through under water. Muddy puddles containing freezing cold water. At the bottom of the trees trapped water lies stone still until a breeze comes and disturbs it.

There are two general features that seem to me to stand out. One is an empathizing close-upness, which also leads to some interesting constitutive shifts slightly away from customary usage. The other is the sustained balanced tension between a kind of dark wintry or decay principle and an opposing resurgent one. This occurs in the first phrase: icy air and lush green grass. Both these features come clear on close reading. 'Scattered' shifts slightly from usage, in that it is the grass which is 'scattered', rather than the water. The caterpillar 'shelters' under a leaf rather than – unempathizingly – merely 'lies' or 'is' under it. There are balancing transitions from the caterpillar's timid sheltering to the flashy, powerful situation of the spider, and from 'decked . . . with diamonds' to 'boggy, brown mud'. 'Forlornly' registers an emotional colour which is echoed later by other images suggestive of the failing pulse of life – the brown leaves, the 'weak' sun, the 'vague' shine on the bark, the stone-still 'trapped' water, the 'forbidding green' of the pool. And yet this colouring is not singled out, but seems an integral feature of the one unified act of apprehension. At the same time an opposing vitality runs through it – in the 'thriving' leaves (a marked shift from routine usage), the 'lush' grass, the wet apples, upturned leaf-stalks 'like [breathing] tubes' (children's snorkels in the pool – a beautiful and organically situated image), and the animating breeze. And this balance is achieved not by a conscious one sentence for this, one for that principle, but by a quite unforced reconciliation, sometimes occurring within the sentence, that appears to emerge from a constitutive apprehension of nothing less than a basic drama of life. A number of sentences do this, but that beginning 'Browny yellow leaves . . .' will serve as an example. 'Browny', 'yellow', 'lying', 'turning brown' and 'gold' are autumnal, while underneath the 'green leaves' are 'still thriving' and the wetness echoes the fresher images. Wetness seems also to effect its own reconciliation, being part of what is trapped, forbidding, and so on, but also regenerative in 'lush', the 'droplets', the 'channels', and 'disturbed water'.

It is as if she has ordered her experience in terms of this basic conception of a dialogue between dark and light, decay and renewal. And she has done this without being asked to underscore an autumnal or any other 'mood'. Had she been working consciously towards the expression of such a mood or theme, rather than simply absorbing in her own fashion what was there, the emotional ambivalence and complexity of the passage – its truth – would surely have disappeared under the burden of 'good' words for decay, and so on. It seems clear also that her capacity for ordering this experience is in part a capacity for full and unimpeded sensory response. (Which is not to say that it is unselective in this regard; clearly, the structure of her awareness imposes its own selective criteria.) The account seems to be read straight off the vibrating senses. The closeness of 'boggy, brown mud marked with small channels', the accuracy of 'thriving', the harshness of apples strewn over mud, all of these are less 'good words and expressions' (though they are that) than language which becomes more than usually truthful and revealing by being pressed into the service of a vision which remains genuine and integral, not composite and constructed. The idiosyncratic nature of the observed particulars of this wholeness gives it, indeed, a particular sense of the authentic. The very unusualness of the accents testifies to the strength of the intuitive grasp in which they are caught up.

The structure of this child's awareness – the structure of the piece, then – is clearly not the 'structure' of the lesson or the course. The quasi-magical confusion of the two in teachers' minds is likely to result only in the effacing of the former, and in formalistic negotiations with forms of language deriving from an objectivistic conceptions of creativity. This is not to suggest that all pupils habitually display in writing such personal structures, or that the degree of shaping recognizable in 'After Rain' is encountered in every lesson. Rather, it is to suggest that creative writing may be more a matter of trying to find out what is really there in children's heads than providing structures (or stimuli or ideas) to write with. The value of these will lie in their capacity to elicit the children's own worlds, the structures in their heads.

The writing lessons I have commented on seem structured only – or at least primarily – in the objectivistic sense. In this they resemble the programme that the girl who wrote 'After Rain' was engaged on for the first two years of secondary school. What is visible in her writing is at least the demise of the kind of writing that seemed so personal and genuine. The first-year creative writing that she did consisted of set subjects: A Friendly Fire, An Unfriendly Fire, A Normal School Day, Sounds I Heard When Mummy Was Making My Tea, Unfriendly Sounds at Night, Sounds I Enjoy Hearing at School, Sounds at The Fair, The Hunt, The Witch, The Witch's House, The Witch's Chant, The Storm, The Bus Queue, Spring is Here. The thematic links give them at times the character of exercises. All the pieces were prepared, and often there was a limit imposed of two paragraphs or three-quarters of a page, and, normally, a list of 'words to be used'. The writing is often flat, but at the same time frenetic. When she writes about fire, there is no *thing* burning, only a generalized abstract fire itself. 'Flaring and spitting, devouring everything in its path. Leaving behind it a trail of destruction. It terrorizes and kills. It leaps and dances, taunting the firemen who cannot get at it.' In 'Sounds at The Fair', objects are predictable props: 'As I draw nearer the fair I hear the sounds of gay organ music. Children's excited shouts as they spin round on the whirring roundabout. . . . I walk on past the gayly coloured organ.' The organ is twice 'gay', the shouts 'excited', somewhat tautologously. The kind of writing that seeks to grasp reality becomes, at such moments, an evasion of it.

'The Storm', written in January of her second year, may be interestingly compared with a poem, 'The Storm', written three years earlier.

Outside the wind is howling like a pack of hungry wolves. Whistling round the house it sends shivers up my spine. Suddenly I hear a loud pattering noise against the window. For a moment I am not sure what it is and I feel scared and frightened thinking the window is broken. I then realize that the noise is just hail driving hard against the windows. Just then a flash of lightning lights up my whole room for a split-second and following it in a few seconds is a thunder clap, almost deafening me which sounds like a giant clearing his throat.

The teacher writes '6 – Good'. Equally, one might find it false and over-written, lacking the unforced emotional coherence of 'After Rain'. The fear seems suspect, the sense impressions not sharp and too highly coloured, though the image of the 'giant clearing his throat' is vital and engaging.

Three years earlier, at the age of eight, she was woken up by a storm, drew the curtains back, and scribbled these words.

*The Storm*
An angry pack of wolves howling round us,
Spears being thrown at us from every side,
Angry giants hovering above us,
Bright hands reaching out towards us,
And rustling of a witches broom.
Then queer faces peering in,
A gong in the sky sounding,
A tapping of fingers on the window,
It begins to cease,
It ceases and everything disappears.

This metaphoric outpouring – the queer faces, the bright hands, the gong, the rustling – is a startling, urgent vision; like 'After Rain' it seems idiosyncratic but integrally so, a confusing moment grasped almost as a single perception.

Though the later piece was about 'the recent winds' – she evidently had fresh experience to draw on – the writing was prepared from a list of words 'to describe the wind, and rain'. She used 'whistling' and 'pattering' from the list, but not 'howling', 'roaring', 'thundering', 'whirling', 'blowing', and 'flooding', 'swirling', 'driving', 'pattering', 'smashing'. The act of writing is performed in such a way that the self obtrudes its authenticities less frequently. Only occasionally does a prepared subject call out a personal encounter like 'After Rain'.

The next piece was written by the same girl two months after 'The Storm' exercise.

> The earth instead of just being wet and slushy, is drying out on top and shoots of later flowers are beginning to show through. The air has a fresh healthy smell of . . . spring? The buddleia where all the peacock butterflies collect in summer is losing its grey appearance and is sprouting leaves directly from the branch. The cherry tree at the end of the garden is opening its fist-like clusters of buds. The apple trees have buds which look more like fungus with their covering of fur. One of the apple tree buds are opening, while the other ones are still tightly shut. As well as the domestic flowers coming through many wild flowers are showing as well. Down one side of the garden is a place where there have never been any domestic and where there are a host of wild flowers. Including red and white dead nettles, button-hole flowers, shepherds purse, and many more.

The homework had been simply to write about the garden, and this was a result of walking round it, just looking. It is clearly in the 'After Rain' vein and has the same immediacy. 'Fist-like' would not be remembered, or 'invented'; 'grey' for the buddleia that sprouts leaves 'directly from the branch' is precise; the 'fungus' simile is unselfconsciously apt; 'domestic' (the teacher altered that, substituting 'cultivated') reveals a classifying alertness, and a neat constitutive use of a familiar term for a novel purpose. In general, the knowledgeableness of the passage in botanical and other ways, the matter-of-fact, engaged tone, very different from the meretricious enthusiasm of the fire and the storm, make it not merely better writing, but a different kind of statement.

I shall sum up what I have tried to suggest may happen to close off the possibilities inherent in creative writing by using existentialist terminology, drawn this time not from Merleau-Ponty, but from Heidegger. For Heidegger, poetry is what 'discloses' the

world to man, while the opposing tendencies towards 'inter-
pretedness' result in a mere 'passing the word along' in that kind
of 'idle talk' which 'covers up' the world.[2] Heidegger, no doubt,
needs much elucidation, but here I should like just to point up the
contrast between the revelatory 'disclosures' of 'After Rain',
'The Storm', and 'The Garden' and the other exercises in 'inter-
pretedness' which hide from her the world that her language
enables her to reveal to herself. The urge towards disclosure
needs, though, to be continuously endorsed. When she re-read
'After Rain' recently, she said, 'I wouldn't bother about that
kind of thing anymore . . . they wouldn't be interested . . .
wouldn't appreciate it, the reason we write now is to get high
marks, it's the only reason we bother.' Even allowing for some
cynical hyperbole, there may be a connection divulged in this
remark between the foregoing account of teachers' attempts to
work in an open way with language, and her perception of the
relation between herself and such work.

## References

1 Frank Smith, *Writing and the Writer* (London, Heinemann Educational, 1982), p. 20.
2 M. Heidegger, *Being and Time*, trans. J. Macquarrie and E. Robinson
  (London, SCM Press, 1962), p. 213.

# 8
# THE PLACE OF READING

## The teacher's voice

I have noted ways in which children seem not to be drawn in to constitutive involvement in what they learn in school. The extent to which they participate in observing and producing ideas in science, speculating about lives in earlier times, thinking about the physical fabric of the world, writing about what they see and feel, seems more limited than, for instance, teachers' ways of talking about learning would lead one to believe. Some of the explanation of the way in which children's concerns often seem almost inevitably to drift towards the fringes of relevance lies, I have suggested, in that objectivistic conception of knowledge which turns language into a depository of information and ideas assembled in essentialist or simplified versions that children negotiate with as formalisms.

One might accept some of this as a description of certain features of school learning but still argue that reading, at least, interposes no barrier like the teacher's editing of responses or the directional impetus of prescribed courses between the world of the subject and the pupil's mind and interests. The books are there, they are better written these days, the library is well run, they're continuously encouraged to read, and told reading is important. There might seem to be little warrant for suggesting that in school reading often resembles other modes of learning in not being defined in ways that represent an openness to the constitutive involvement of the learner.

I should like to compare two pieces of prose that describe the same process (the emergence of a butterfly from the pupa): one is a school fourth-year textbook account, the other is from David Attenborough's *Life on Earth*.[1] A comparison of the kinds of reading offer that the passages represent might serve to open to consideration the question of the nature and purposes of school reading. First, the textbook:

> Many of the parts of the future butterfly – the antennae, eye, proboscis, leg and wings – can be seen pressed close to the thoracic region, and the segments of the abdomen are visible also. The pupa does not feed, and remains still except for occasional twitchings of the abdomen. Inside the pupa changes are taking place, for most of the larval tissues are being broken down and re-organized to form the adult organs.[2]

Attenborough's version might seem less 'biological' but it is more alive:

> But now, inside the pupa, their moment has come. The giant cells of the caterpillar's body die and the dormant cell-clusters suddenly begin to divide rapidly, nourishing themselves on the soup of the disintegrated caterpillar body. The insect, in effect, is eating itself. Slowly it builds a new body of a completely different form. Its shadowy features can be seen on the outside of the brown pupa like the anatomy of a mummy, vague beneath the wrappings. Indeed, the name 'pupa' derives from a Latin word meaning 'doll', for at this stage the insect within seems to be wrapped in swaddling clothes.[3]

While the textbook is like a store of information awaiting retrieval, Attenborough is *telling* us, bringing knowledge out to the reader, presenting the prelude to emergence as a drama, investing his narrative with a sense of events happening in time, moment by moment, and gathering its stages together in a series of metaphors. The textbook lacks any aspirations to such a voice: 'These changes last from ten to fourteen days, and then the cuticle splits in the region of the thorax, and the adult butterfly or imago drags itself out. At first the wings are small and crumpled, but they soon harden. The body of the imago is divided into a head, thorax and abdomen.' The writer then describes these features atemporally: 'The head has a large compound eye', and so on. The textbook's drama, such as it is, is over. The contrast in the writers' aims seems clear at this point. Attenborough is eloquently detailed about the dramatic moment of emergence that the textbook quickly passes over:

> The actual emergence usually takes place under cover of darkness . . . legs come free and begin clawing frantically in the air. Slowly and laboriously, with frequent pauses to gather strength, the insect hauls itself out . . . it begins to pump blood into a network of veins within the baggy wings.

And there is a detailed and sensitive paragraph on this 'half hour' of the butterfly's life:

> Blotches swell into miraculously detailed eye-spots . . . the veins themselves are still soft. If the tip of one of them were damaged now, it would drip blood. But gradually the blood is drawn back into the body and the veins harden into rigid struts that will give the wing its strength.

Attenborough's text resembles the voice of a knowledgeable, deeply enthusiastic teacher precisely because it carries that voice; in its enthusiasm it seems to seek contact with the reader, as if a dialogue were latent within it. The other merely states; its lack of voice derives from a static knowledge structure which seeks no contact, but waits to be entered. Attenborough's text reaches out; the other has to be reached. Nor is it just good versus indifferent writing. The quality of Attenborough's text emerges from its primary purpose, to teach and speak vitally to the reader, not neutrally and passively to embody and represent constituted forms.

It is this purpose which seems to produce the craftsman's care for the persuasive shape of sentences, and the moments of metaphoric illumination in 'soup' and 'struts', and to account for the way in which the technical word 'pupa' is clarified and vivified by the images of the doll, the mummy and the swaddling clothes. Similarly, it conscripts the genuine writer's intense, empathizing vision as it watches the insect 'haul itself out', grasps that 'it is, in effect, eating itself', and imagines – almost fearfully – how 'if . . . one of [the wings] were damaged now, it would drip blood.'

It is not, though, the enthusiastic teacher's written language but the voiceless neutral manner of the biology textbook that prevails in the reading material in other subjects at fourth-year level. The manner is so persistent as to amount to a kind of housestyle. From a geography book:

> There has been a marked increase in the cultivation of peanuts and in some places near the coast it has replaced cotton as the chief crop. It does best on sandy, well-drained lands, and is grown mainly for fodder or vegetable oil. Cultivation is becoming increasingly mechanized except for harvesting, which requires a lot of labour.[4]

And the first paragraph of the chapter on electricity in *Exploring Physics*:

> The dependence of modern life on electricity is very great. Our homes are lit and often heated by it. Electric kettles, cookers, irons, blankets, washing machines, vacuum cleaners, refrigerators, television receivers and record players work off the electricity supply. In industry and commerce computers and other machines are either all electric or have vital electrical components.[5]

Next the opening paragraph of a chapter on soil in a fourth-year 'O'-level biology text:

> Soil, which is present as a thin layer over a large area of the earth, provides the water and mineral salts which plants require

as food material. It is through the roots, which are firmly embedded in the soil, that plants take up this food material. The soil, therefore, is highly important to man, who relies on it for producing so much of his food.[6]

Since teachers know their audiences, and are aware of the ways in which each class's experience of meeting topics is idiosyncratic, one might expect that worksheets would 'speak' to pupils by referring to incidents in the history of the class's work, such as the black coating digression described earlier, or the thatch episode in the Anglo-Saxon village lesson. And yet the speech of worksheets seems to be as much 'torn out of history' and situation as the textbooks quoted above. Being written by teachers, they might be expected to have the same manifest purpose as the Attenborough text, and to refract something of the enthusiastic teacher's voice. And yet they seem not to, whether at first-, second- or fourth-year level. For example:

> Climate
> The Climate of Denmark is Maritime. The average annual rainfall is quite low – 600 millimetres. In Copenhagen the average January temperature is 0°C and in July is 17°C. (second-year)

> In Figure 1, a and b are SUPPLEMENTARY angles because a + b = 180 degrees. (180 is the degrees in a straight line.) (first-year)

> The Anglo-Saxons were heathens and they had occupied Britain for about 150 years before Christianity came again to Britain. There were Christians in Ireland because of the teaching of St Patrick and St Columba. St Columba and his monks also set up a religious centre on Iona off the coast of Scotland. (first-year)

This voiceless desituating occurs also when topics are introduced, so that the text makes no signal about the novelty of what it brings forward:

> Yeast as we know it consists of millions of single-celled plants. You may grow yeast plants by placing some yeast in a weak solution of sugar. Under a microscope each yeast plant can be

seen as a small oval mass of protoplasm. Sometimes several yeast plants can be seen in a chain.

Assuming that 'we know it' seems to result in a failure to reach out to the reader so as to evoke the process of growth, or to dramatize the picture in the microscope: it becomes compressed, 'difficult'.

Rare attempts at speaking seem to be quickly undermined by the need to inform:

> It is the year AD 126 and you are at Hadrian's Wall. It has just been completed by order of the Emperor Hadrian, and runs for about 73 miles between Bowness, on the Solway Firth, and Wallsend, at the mouth of the Tyne. It has been built by the 20th legion from Chester and the 6th legion from York, and is intended to keep out the fierce Picts from Scotland.

Worksheets like these thus edit out any hint of what the knowledge means to the writer in terms of feelings, values, and so on; there remains no sense of fascination or drama, or of the teacher's own relation to his knowledge. It might be said that the teacher's voice will present knowledge anecdotally and dramatically, and so 'speak' as print does not. This may be true, but need not imply that print should be confined to the referentially informative and succinct. The implication is rather that 'speaking' – that is to say, all forms of dramatic, anecdotal, generally human modes of telling – are realizable in written text, and that the tone of the worksheet could be closer to the teacher's way of speaking to a particular class. Ironically, it seems that the unspeaking neutrality of textbook text can take over the teacher's voice, to such an extent that dictated notes, for example, may lose all semblance of emanating from particular enthusiasms and moments of awarenesses.

The following was written on the board for first years after a lively, experimental small-group session: 'In the early nineteenth century Alexandra Volta made the first battery. It was called a voltaic pile and consisted of alternate copper and silver coins, separated by salt-soaked paper.' As the teacher wrote, he acknowledged its unsatisfactoriness as appropriate reading in saying, 'Here's that word "alternate" again. What does it mean, Paul?'

During the lesson pupils had expressed amazement – 'It's gone up to $1\frac{1}{2}$ V!' – and curiosity – 'How did you cut open the battery?', 'What would happen if you drank that?' – but the notes dictated for revision reading discarded these and similar moments, suppressing much of the vitality of the lesson and leaving only the distilled text. Similarly, a fourth-year CSE dictated note on sedimentary rocks states: 'These rocks are formed at the surface of the earth by the accumulation of particles of sorted matter and by the precipitation of dissolved material.' It then lists types of 'fossils': 'Hard parts, petrifaction, carbonization, moulds, trace fossil'. A dictated note for 'O'-level pupils in the fourth year informs them about their own town as if it were a distant place: '_____ is situated on the coast in _____. This is in _____, England. To the north of _____ there is a ridge of high land', and so on. A first-year science dictated note headed 'Conifers (gymnosperms)': 'This group includes the "evergreen" trees, pine, spruce, larch, birch, etc. Reproduction is . . .'. (Larches, of course, are not evergreen, and alders are cone-bearing trees; both are common in the area. An empirical base for pupils' work might expose such problems earlier.)

Teachers perhaps often assume that their notes and worksheets should focus more or less exclusively, as the textbook does, on the informative functions of written language, and that they should discard idiosyncratic features of written discourse – its local enthusiasms and difficulties. And in this they would receive support from views of written language which so underscore points of difference between written and spoken language as to produce a sharp dichotomy between them. In their influential book *The Effective Use of Reading*, Lunzer and Gardner generalize about written language in ways which seem more appropriate to voiceless text than to the Attenborough text quoted earlier.[7] They first suggest that 'Differences between spoken and written language are central to a discussion of reading and it is worthwhile considering them in more detail because they constitute the principal background to all that follows.' One very crucial difference pertains to 'situation': 'unlike spoken communication there is no common situation to which written communication can refer.'

It is hard to be sure what this means. In one sense any language which is not private and 'communicates' appeals to a shared context of some kind, and often text appeals to social situations shared by writer and reader: notes passed in class do, and letters can, and so on. The teacher's dictated notes on the Voltaic pile had a shared social situation to which greater reference could have been made. Written text is not necessarily desituated, therefore. Instructions for the public communicate through shared situations: 'Pay as you enter', for instance. I saw two identical red buckets side by side on a railway station, one labelled 'Fire', the other 'Water'. Situation resolved the ambiguity.

Lunzer and Gardner treat other features of written and spoken language as well-nigh universal, though they seem characteristic only of certain kinds of text and speech. Thus they say that written language is 'more complete than utterance and tends to be more dense'. 'Moreover, there is no opportunity of feedback'; 'the readership of a text is not known to the writer'; 'the impersonality of written language underlines the separation between reader and writer'; and 'the written version will generally lack an element of warmth.'[8] These features are contingent rather than necessary. Most of the generalizations are either readily falsifiable – thus, a lecture on Eliot may be 'denser' than a gossip column, a church magazine readership will be known to the writer – or they lean on narrow senses of the words 'feedback', 'known', 'separation' and 'warmth'.

I shall labour this point somewhat because it seems crucial that a defence of the voiceless neutrality of certain written texts can appeal to the presumption that they are attributes intrinsic to written language as a whole, when this particular feature may derive from its necessity to the packaging of bits of knowledge defined objectivistically. The Attenborough text, and examples like it, make it difficult to argue for some necessary 'lack of an element of warmth' in written text.

The notion that text lacks opportunities for 'feedback' and emphasizes the 'separation' of reader and writer is perhaps more central, however. It is particularly hard to see imaginative literature as being 'impersonal' or 'underlining separation'. Sartre suggests, rather, that in one sense it 'has no other substance than the reader's subjectivity',[9] and that the obliteration of the distance between reader and writer is part of the experience of reading. Greene suggests that there has been a tendency in English literary critical theory to stress the notion of the poem or novel as 'an object', a structure of words with its own internal organization and its own life.[10] The problem with this, she suggests, is that, as theory, it does not sufficiently account for the presence of the reader and the reader's subjectivity. She proposes with Sartre that an alternative, more complete, view would be that 'the reader's subjectivity is the substance of the literary object.' This view seems to account for what one senses is the pupil's need not just to respond to text in a passive way but to construct 'its' meaning through his own. Clearly, this is a view of reading in general, not just of the reading of literature. I do not make sense of the sentence '$E = mc^2$' because I have no subjective meanings with which to take it over; I have no meanings which would for me be constitutive of that constituted form. Pupils' capacities for making meanings through encounters with text are thus dependent on the extent to which their 'subjectivity' becomes the 'substance' of text. Sometimes, as for B reading 'cake in an oven in a bowl', there is little subjectivity that can be gathered together to colonize a text.

A second theoretical point relates to the idea of 'feedback'. In commonsense terms, what occurs through the tonal alertness of good writing is a sensitivity to the reader's presence which acknowledges that he is there, and might get bored, excited, rebellious, moved, and so on. Jakobson suggests that there are six aspects of a speech event – addresser, addressee, context, message, contact, and code – and associates each aspect with a function, labelled respectively: emotive, conative, referential, poetic, phatic and metalingual.[11] A 'focus' on one aspect, such as the message (the language itself) entails the predominance of a certain function – the shaping or poetic function. A text may carry several functions, though one predominates. Thus, the Attenborough text may be said to demonstrate a conative impulse to arouse awareness, an emotive field that contributes to that, phatic allowances for the reader's position as he follows the process moment by moment, and metalingual extensions and clarifications of some of the language he uses, as he uses it.

At the same time, the predominance of a function can tend towards the exclusion of other functions, so that where the writer's focus is exclusively on context, the text will have an exclusively referential function. The other functions that so humanize the Attenborough text are then excised; the text has no voice. Lunzer and Gardner do appear to equate text that exhibits this exclusive predominance of function with written school text generally, but clearly, in terms of Jakobson's scheme, the degree to which a text can be successfully referential is not affected by its assuming other functions. The absence of such functions, then, can not be defended on the grounds that text then becomes more efficiently informative.

## Understanding the text

It is worth stressing, predictably perhaps, that much of this voice-less, predominantly referential material may not be open to pupils in the primary sense that it may only be intermittently comprehensible. The point has often been made, tellingly by Katherine Perera for instance, in her work on pupils' acquaintance with school terms.[12] I have noted already that the questions asked of text, once an assumption of its basic accessibility is made, may be no help in revealing the extent to which it is not. It may also be that text's very voicelessness, its exclusively referential function, which implies something of the 'separation', 'impersonality' and 'lack of warmth' that Lunzer and Gardner refer to, itself contributes to attenuating that part of the teacher–pupil relationship which flows through talk about the subject, and makes it less likely either that pupils will notice when they gather no adequate meanings from their reading or that they will mention it if they do. It would be ironic if the text's focus on content made it more difficult for questions to arise about how pupils handle content, but if the nature of the reading pupils are offered implies something about the relation between the learner and learning it seems possible.

I shall describe an episode that shows some first-year pupils' difficulties with routine reading and reveals how they stay hidden even behind the questions they are asked. The possible complicity

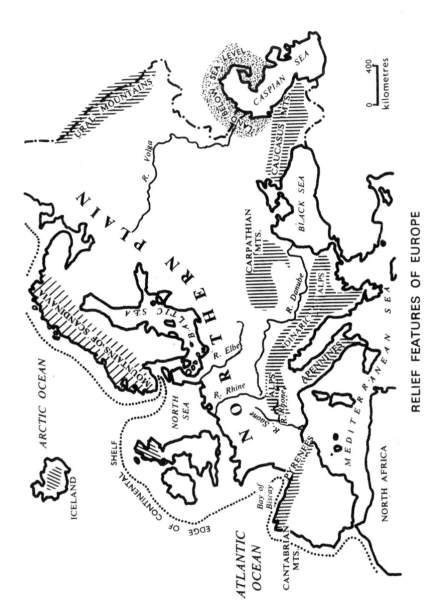

RELIEF FEATURES OF EUROPE

Figure 21

of text in inhibiting talk that goes beyond the referential might perhaps be read into what happens, but there are no overt signs of such talk developing.

A second-year geography class was working on 'The Relief of Europe'.[13] A section of the textbook (Figure 21) was being read, and the questions at the end had to be answered. On the board was the heading 'The Physical Structure of Europe'. The pupils were instructed to read the short chapter before doing the missing-word answer questions at the end. They were to write the title 'Relief of Europe' in their note-books. The teacher also referred to 'looking at mountains'. I talked to groups as they worked, which they did zealously and quietly. It was clear that the map was itself not being easily read. One pupil was uncertain about what the 'R.' in 'R. Elbe' meant, for instance. I asked another what 'Europe' was, as he worked on the 'Relief Features of Europe' map:

P1:     A place.
Self:   Can you show me?
P1:     (Points to England.)
Self:   Is that part of Europe? (pointing to Spain)
P1:     No.
Self:   That? (Italy)
P1:     That's Italy.
Self:   Is it in Europe?
P1:     Not sure.
Self:   Is that? (pointing to the Carpathians)
P1:     Not sure.
Self:   That? (West Russia)
P1:     Not sure.

We next looked at the climate map (Figure 22). I asked another pupil what the border lines were between, and were dividing up. He was not sure. The teacher had asked them to copy the climate map and 'wanted them to see the borders', and at home 'go over the borders in red'. He had, understandably, assumed pupils would see the relation between the borders and climate, for instance by reading the phrase 'Climatic Regions'. His

CLIMATIC REGIONS

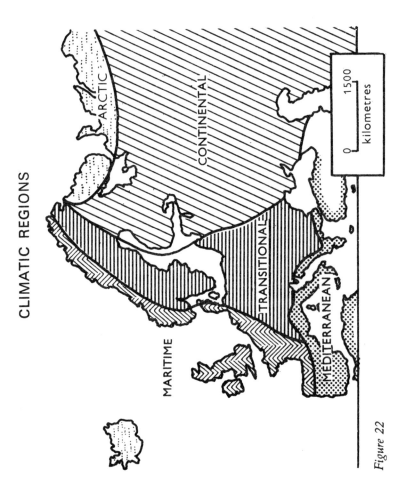

ARCTIC

CONTINENTAL

MARITIME

TRANSITIONAL

MEDITERRANEAN

0    1500
kilometres

*Figure 22*

instructions to 'copy out the climate map' and 'go over the borders in red' could be followed to the letter by pupils not making the assumed connection between 'climate' and 'borders'. Similarly, they could choose 'navigable' from a list of missing words to complete the sentence reproduced from the text ('there are many navigable rivers') without knowing what 'navigable' meant.

I then asked pupils what 'relief' meant. The first three asked said they did not know. I devised a set of questions and gave them, two weeks later, to the teacher's two second-year geography groups. The first question asked what 'relief' meant. Only 16 answers (out of 46) referred to aspects of structure, like highlands and lowlands, land feature, and physical structure. Eleven answers related to climate, or climate and temperature, and 10 to 'divisions' of a country or how it was 'split up'. In this context nearly all pupils knew that 'R.' was short for river, and what climate meant. I also asked them why they had not asked about 'relief'. Many answers invoked shyness or a fear of being shown up or shouted at. Five referred to a distressing junior school experience. Others said they had not asked because 'it did not occur to me that I did not understand it', 'because I think I should know', and 'because I already know one meaning and it didn't seem to fit in.'

A fourth-year 'O'-level English group commented on the difficulty of this text and on the problem of not knowing terms and not asking. One quoted 'Mediterranean (warm temperate southern marginal)' and said, 'I have not the faintest idea what they mean', but interestingly, 'the exercises are very easy'. As to her own uncertainties: 'I was making notes . . . and quite happily writing down the word "flax" not knowing what it meant, when someone asked the teacher, and the teacher was not too sure. I would have written it down in an exam without knowing what it meant.' Another girl said: 'I came across several words that I do not understand, e.g. precipitation, temperate, marginal.' Another commented that 'things could be written in the simple form first and the hyper-intelligent geographical jargon afterwards.' Another said that 'recently, in history, difficult words have come up and I felt embarrassed to ask the teacher in case he, and other pupils, made fun of me . . . also the teacher seemed to be in a hurry to get on with the lesson.' Several referred to being afraid or too embarrassed to ask.

It seems clear that though pupils are told to 'ask if they don't understand', they tend not to, perhaps through fear of exposure. More pertinently, if pupils can succeed in school terms, or 'get knowledge done', by reproducing from the text 'There are many *navigable* rivers' the meaning of 'navigable' may not seem relevant to the purpose in hand. Teachers' requests that pupils should ask if they do not understand seem to be requests that pupils should be unilaterally responsible for raising questions about access to text, and implicitly are claims to continue to deal with knowledge in the way they do without questioning themselves closely about what they know of pupils' understanding. Even if pupils do attempt such a unilateral restoration, there is still the question of their awareness of their own uncertainty. Pupils in the fourth year who were asked whether they understood their textbook tended to believe that they did.

I asked three fourth-year groups whether they felt they understood their textbooks. Most of them said they understood textbook language 'most of the time', 'usually', and so on. But it was common for them to say this even when they demonstrated uncertain grasp of the meaning of textbook words and phrases. Thus, a girl who said she understood most things in textbooks said 'harbour' (in 'Animals harbour insects') was 'collect and eat', 'navigable' was 'easy to follow', 'infant mortality rate' meant 'birth rate', and 'initial stages' was 'middle'. Some of this confusion may be remedied when sentences occur in richer contexts – such as the textbook as a whole, or the teacher's commentary. Such contexts were available for pupils working on the climate and relief of Europe, however, yet basic uncertainties persisted undetected. I also asked them what they would do if they felt they didn't understand:

When you do not understand something in class, what do you normally do? Do you:
(A) Keep quiet and not worry?
(B) Keep quiet but worry?
(C) Ask the teacher?

(D) Ask friends later?
(E) Ask friends in the classroom?
The responses were:

|  | 'O'-level pupils (26) | CSE pupils (52) | Total (78) |
|---|---|---|---|
| (A) | 1 | 3 | 4 |
| (B) | 1 | 7 | 8 |
| (C) | 10 | 6 | 16 |
| (D) | 4 | 8 | 12 |
| (E) | 10 | 9 | 19 |
| (C)/(F) split double responses | 1 | 8 | 9 |

In both 'O'-level and CSE groups most pupils said they would not ask the teacher. And of the pupils who did not answer with (C), there were numerous references to exposure (being shouted at, thought stupid, being embarrassed or shy) – 39 pupils spoke in such ways, 12 in the 'O'-level group of 26, 27 in the two CSE groups.

It is possible, then, that there were a number of reasons why many second years accept a situation where their reading didn't make sense. They were reluctant to ask. They were unaware of their own uncertainty. The working assumptions that 'relief' and 'Europe' were known terms made asking questions about them particularly difficult. The text's lack of emotive or phatic functions, in particular, made other than referential questions unlikely. Children also perhaps feel – as one girl put it about another matter – that 'If they're not teaching it you you don't think it's important.' And by doing the missing-word and other answers successfully, they were 'displaying knowledge' appropriately; knowledge was still 'getting done'.

It seems important to have some rough background sense of the extent of pupils' success with the school text they read. I devised a reading test using both sentences and phrases drawn from books and worksheets in use in the school, and some drawn from other textbooks for comparison. I intended that the reading tasks should be relatively discrete, as in a typical school questioning. I asked questions about words and phrases that belong not to the language of a subject, but rather to the language in which such terms are embedded. Barnes makes distinctions between 'specialist language presented', 'specialist language not presented', and 'the language of secondary education'.[14] A distinction might perhaps also be made within the category 'specialist language' between what might be called the specialist-conventional and the specialist-conceptual. Thus the verb 'harbour' in 'Animals harbour insects' is a conventional metaphor, and of course replaceable, and yet it occurs frequently enough in biology to have acquired a specialist flavour and be part of a grammar. Similarly with terms and phrases like 'navigable', 'western leaders', 'a water surface', and so on. It seems that school subjects can, by conventional usage, colonize a good deal of 'ordinary' language that comes, thus, to be handled as grammar while remaining outside recognized specialist registers.

The asterisked items were drawn from text in use in the lessons I observed. The other items, included for comparison, came from similar school texts used elsewhere. This was the test as set to three fourth-year groups.

*Fourth years' reading of typical subject sentences*

(A) Write down a word or phrase *of your own* that could be used instead of the words and phrases underlined in the following sentences, without altering the meaning. You can write out a whole sentence if you like.

  1 Animals harbour insects.

  2 When two black guinea-pigs are mated, their offspring are invariably black.

 *3 On the east coast are a number of navigable rivers.

 *4 There were a number of factors responsible for the high infant mortality rate.

  5 Ever since 1917 western leaders have looked on Russia as a menace to freedom.

  6 Ghent is the lowest bridge-town on the river.

 *7 A random sample of 100 villagers were asked to say how many refugees they would be prepared to accommodate.

*8 A <u>representation</u> of base two numbers can easily be made by punching holes in a piece of paper tape.

*9 The natural wealth of Finland <u>lies chiefly in her coniferous forests</u>.

10 Men's <u>dreams of</u> <u>peace</u> after 1918 were <u>dashed</u> by the rise of Hitler.

*11 They fought well <u>in the initial stages</u> of the battle.

*12 What <u>assumption</u> did we make about the size of the acid particle?

*13 Why was the solution dropped onto <u>a water surface</u>, and not onto a bench-top or a plastic tray?

*14 Explain what tests you would perform on an unknown gas to discover its <u>identity</u>.

In coding answers to the reading questions, 'Bl' means blank (or word-for-word repeat); '1' means 'adequate'; '2' means 'less than adequate'; '3' is 'inadequate'. Since this is very subjective, some illustration is needed of how some typical replies were assigned.

Harbour:
(1) collect, support, carry, house
(2) look for
(3) eat

Invariably:
(1) always
(2) nearly always
(3) sometimes, usually, often

Navigable:
(1) passable, sailable, big
(2) navigatable
(3) charted, small, known

Factors:
(1) reasons
(2) things
(3) people

Infant mortality:
(1) high death rate

(2) danger

(3) birth rate

Western leaders:

(1) Prime ministers and Presidents of European countries

(2) NATO, government officials

(3) People, America

Lowest bridge-town:

(1) Town with a bridge nearest to an estuary

(2) Nearest town with a bridge

(3) Small town with a bridge

Random sample:

(1) A selection made by chance

(2) Choice, selection, a few

(3) People, everybody.


Table 2 indicates the striking extent of failure with such tasks. CSE pupils in particular, but 'O'-level pupils as well seem to have difficulty assigning adequate meanings to this text. All but 5 of the 19 items were in this sense 'failed' by at least a quarter of the 'O'-level pupils, and nine were failed by at least a half of the CSE pupils. It seems that typical subject sentences containing conventional terminology like 'harbour', 'factors' and 'identity', 'lowest bridge-town', 'dreams of peace', and 'in the initial stages' are not readily accessible when handled in this relatively discrete way. Such language is routinely 'taken as read', with the result, for instance, that even common errors can go undetected. Of this kind would be the reading of 'assumption' as 'conclusion' (5 'O'-level and 10 CSE pupils) and of 'infant mortality rate' as 'birth rate' (1 'O'-level and 12 CSE pupils).

I shall not dwell on these 'results' since I do not wish to treat them as that, but only as a way of further articulating the possibility that pupils may be habitually engaged in reading encounters that are, to some extent, sterile. The problem that seems to arise is whether this is due to the intrinsic difficulty 'of' text, or whether it is a difficulty produced by the structure of relations in school between text, knowledge and the pupils' world. If knowledge is conceived objectivistically and presented in essentialist grammars

Table 2   Degrees of adequacy in assigning meaning to 'environing' language in reading single sentences

| | 'O'-level group (29) | | | | CSE groups (47) | | | | Total (76) | | | | % adequate answers | | |
|---|---|---|---|---|---|---|---|---|---|---|---|---|---|---|---|
| | Bl | 1 | 2 | 3 | Bl | 1 | 2 | 3 | Bl | 1 | 2 | 3 | 'O' | CSE | Total |
| Harbour | 1 | 24 | 3 | 1 | 6 | 31 | 3 | 7 | 7 | 55 | 6 | 8 | 83 | 65 | 72 |
| Invariably | 0 | 5 | 3 | 21 | 2 | 4 | 8 | 33 | 2 | 9 | 11 | 54 | 17 | 8 | 11 |
| Navigable* | 4 | 19 | 2 | 4 | 12 | 16 | 1 | 18 | 16 | 35 | 3 | 22 | 66 | 34 | 46 |
| Factors* | 4 | 23 | 1 | 1 | 13 | 25 | 4 | 5 | 17 | 48 | 5 | 6 | 74 | 53 | 63 |
| High infant mortality rate | 6 | 22 | 0 | 1 | 23 | 5 | 2 | 17 | 29 | 27 | 2 | 18 | 76 | 11 | 35 |
| Western leaders | 6 | 15 | 4 | 4 | 9 | 15 | 17 | 6 | 15 | 30 | 21 | 10 | 52 | 32 | 39 |
| Lowest bridge-town | 16 | 5 | 1 | 7 | 20 | 0 | 4 | 23 | 36 | 5 | 5 | 30 | 17 | 0 | 6 |
| Random sample* | 4 | 15 | 9 | 1 | 7 | 9 | 21 | 10 | 11 | 24 | 30 | 11 | 17 | 19 | 18 |
| Be prepared to accommodate* | 9 | 20 | 0 | 0 | 8 | 35 | 3 | 1 | 17 | 55 | 3 | 1 | 69 | 74 | 72 |
| Representation* | 16 | 10 | 0 | 3 | 27 | 11 | 3 | 6 | 43 | 21 | 3 | 9 | 34 | 23 | 27 |
| Lies chiefly in her coniferous forests* | 4 | 15 | 10 | 0 | 10 | 14 | 21 | 2 | 14 | 29 | 31 | 2 | 52 | 30 | 38 |
| Dreams of peace | 5 | 20 | 4 | 0 | 11 | 26 | 7 | 3 | 16 | 45 | 11 | 3 | 69 | 55 | 60 |
| Dashed | 6 | 21 | 1 | 1 | 12 | 32 | 2 | 1 | 18 | 53 | 3 | 2 | 72 | 68 | 69 |
| In the initial stages* | 2 | 27 | 0 | 0 | 5 | 24 | 0 | 18 | 7 | 51 | 0 | 18 | 93 | 51 | 67 |
| Assumption* | 6 | 10 | 8 | 5 | 12 | 16 | 6 | 13 | 18 | 26 | 14 | 18 | 34 | 34 | 34 |
| A water surface* | 13 | 13 | 3 | 0 | 8 | 22 | 11 | 6 | 21 | 35 | 14 | 6 | 47 | 47 | 46 |
| Identity* | 4 | 19 | 5 | 1 | 8 | 27 | 5 | 7 | 12 | 46 | 10 | 8 | 66 | 57 | 60 |

Bl – blank, 1– adequate, 2 – less than adequate, 3 – inadequate.   * Items drawn from text in use in the lessons I observed.

it may be that the difficulty that children seem to have with reading school text emerges from the way it is instrumentally defined as simply a means of access to knowledge so conceived and presented. For all its potential openness, it becomes another formalistic encounter with language and, as in the other encounters that have been described, the constitutive features of children's language seem not to enter into the process of producing knowledge. Their subjectivity seems seldom to be the substance of the things they read. Such a structural 'difficulty' is a fundamental closure. Reading is then likely to be continuously precarious, and if little or no other reading of subject content takes place, the pupils are held again in a formalistic impasse.

It might be as if – to offer a rough analogy – one looked at a picture from which some of the foreground, as well as most of the middle ground and nearly all the background, had been withdrawn, leaving a few selected items thus further unnaturally foregrounded and shorn of relations with other items and with most of the rest of the picture. In this analogy the fragments of essentialist language are the foregrounded items, the middle ground is ordinary environing language, and the background is the pupils' own language for their empirical realities. Isolated foregrounded objects thus lose their relations not only with what supports them and gives them (situated) meaning, but, in consequence, with each other. Then, the apparent paucity of objects in the picture (or the curriculum) leaves space for other things, which are of course other similarly isolated, foregrounded objects. The gathering together of such isolated objects produces a clutter, routinely not noticed as such because the objects tend to be handled as if they were part of a picture, primarily because for the teacher they are. Yet while for teachers the foregrounded objects or terms do normally represent whole pictures, for pupils not able to read so much into essentialist referential text, they do not. For them it is as if a junk shop window had to be seen as a set of interiors.

To exemplify again this basic point, I shall consider briefly how a typical school technical term might be handled. Alliteration is a word that 'needs to be known'. It comes to be 'taught', and its teaching may often take the form of a definition or explanation with a list of examples. For example, a teacher produced some duplicated 'O'-level notes on poems, headed 'Descriptive Techniques', in which pupils were advised to 'Remember these headings when dealing with other poems'. The headings included 'onomatopoeia', 'metaphor', 'rhyme', and 'alliteration', examples of all of which are listed for each poem. Thus, for 'Breathless', by Wilfred Noyce: 'Alliteration – repeated ''s'' sounds imitate the sighing sounds that might escape the climber's lips (glasses, breathless, swings, swallows).' The poem is much less effectually alliterative where these particular words occur than the collection of examples suggests – and interestingly, it is 'swallow', not 'swallows'. The list creates an impression of the unambiguous out there-ness of the entity called 'alliteration'. It becomes a fact, and the reader's job is, implicitly, to grasp it, cognitively.

This strategy seems to be the beginning of a foregrounding towards formalism, in that attention is immediately turned towards alliteration in a way that begins to stabilize and reify it, instead of being drawn into awareness of the alliterative behaviour of words *in situ*, in poems or in ordinary speech and as one confronts them, in relation to words' rhythmic or metaphoric or other behaviours, all of which interpenetrate in actuality and lose their isolated and unequivocal character in relations, and in the context of, and subordinated to, the primary fact of the reader's activity. The idea of alliteration may then articulate a dimension of emerging awareness rather than function as a to-be-known entity, a commodity which poets *use*, and so on. As a dimension of awareness, alliteration retains its relations with ordinary language, and with the experiencing of poems, so that the danger of slipping towards formalism is avoided. In terms of the analogy just offered, alliteration then represents a part of a complete picture, and when pupils read the isolated term, as they are likely to at least in exam papers or commentaries on poems, no formalizing of the language of poems need occur, since the word recalls not merely grammatical expressions and examples but a permanent feature of one's personal knowledge of poems. And it need hardly be said that for this to be possible, pupils' encounters with the empirical reality of poems will necessarily be rich. Other constitutive everyday language will function as middle ground and background, and other poems will stand alongside and behind this poem. Such objects, no longer foregrounded, will perhaps tend to resume their relation to contexts and to each other, and no longer resist the learner's attempts to see meaningful wholes by means of them.

## The importance of reading

It would be surprising if teachers did not become aware at times of the way school text foregrounds subject language to the point where ordinary language disappears, and with it pupils' capacity for constructing meaning. I observed a fourth-year technical drawing lesson in which pupils had a written instruction to 'Draw what you see in sectional elevation'. The teacher had explained this orally, and later said to me: 'Of course, if you just say "sectional elevation" they say "What's that? We haven't heard of it".' The perception that technical language needs embedding in ordinary language has consequences only for his own talk, however, not for the text he writes. His own exam, like the worksheet, merely states: 'Draw these two elevations and add a sectional plan.' The convention seems to be that written text does not make the connections or concessions that the teacher's voice does; the teacher's voice explains the text which embodies the subject, but text does not itself attempt this.

It becomes possible to have two distinct attitudes to this convention; one can accept it, even embrace it as 'part of the subject' which 'they have to accept', or chafe at it as a possible hindrance to learning. The former attitude, which can seem more 'academic', seems represented by the physics teacher who commented that third-year physics was 'too descriptive, too wordy, not down to basic physics enough'. He also approved of the multiple-choice examining of physics because it was 'tough', and 'you could examine the whole syllabus in three hours'. An alternative attitude to the toughness of concise question text is espoused by the head of lower school, in the maths department meeting referred to in Chapter 3. Commenting on two versions of a question I had asked first years to do (A and B, p. 203), he said,

The short concise question is strictly in teachers'-type language

– it's very concise, not normal pupils' reading-book learning at all. Furthermore, it hasn't the style of the other version. That's more the style of the general readers they use. It also guides the logic problem in a way the concise form does not. The intellectual level of this sort of language is years ahead of this longer form.

## 'Concise' and 'wordy' versions of a maths question

### A VERSION – 'CONCISE'

John measures how long paths A and B are, using a walking stick. Then he measures how long paths C and D are, using a metal rod which has a different length from the walking stick. The answers are:

Path A: 13 walking sticks
Path B: 14½ walking sticks
Path C: 15 rods
Path D: 12½ rods

For each of the sentences below put a tick in one of the columns, to show that you think the sentence is true, or is not true, or is something you cannot be sure about.

|  | True | Not true | Cannot be sure |
|---|---|---|---|
| 1 Path B is longer than Path A |  |  |  |
| 2 Path C is longer than Path B |  |  |  |
| 3 Path D is longer than Path C |  |  |  |

### B VERSION – 'WORDY'

John is measuring the paths in his garden. He hasn't got a tape measure. Instead he is using a walking-stick. That has no measurements on it, so he doesn't know how long it is. The first path he measures in this way is *13* walking sticks long.

(This is path A.) The second (path B) is *14½* walking-sticks long.

Then his brother steals the walking-stick. John wanted to measure two more paths, so he gets an old piece of metal rod from the garage and uses that. The third path (path C) is *15* metal rods long, and the fourth one (path D) is *12½* metal rods long.

So which of the three sentences below can you be sure is right? Which can you be sure is wrong? What is it impossible for you to be sure of?

1st sentence:

> Path B is longer than Path A. True/Not true/Can't be sure.

2nd sentence:

> Path C is longer than Path B. True/Not true/Can't be sure.

3rd sentence:

> Path D is longer than Path C. True/Not true/Can't be sure.

TO ANSWER: draw a ring round either 'True' or 'Not true' or 'Can't be sure'.

Others argued against 'wordy' versions – in particular on the grounds that slow children would have difficulty reading them. One teacher said they had 'no idea at all' about this question in set 3: 'there must be a cut-off point', he suggested, beyond which dull pupils get lost in long questions. And yet, as the teacher in charge of lower school maths had said earlier, what was found both surprising and interesting by some teachers was that, judging by their scores, 'the wordy one' seemed 'less difficult'.

Whether in fact, for those particular children, they were is not discussed here. The point is rather the crucial divergence of view about the kind of text that makes for accessibility. The 'tough' view, which presumes that wordiness will confuse, and resembles other views that equate the simplified with the accessible, speaks for the strong predominance of the referential function. The dissenting view, which suggests that such conciseness derives from the teacher's achieved perspective and prefers language which 'guides the logic of the problem', speaks against that predominance. Toughness and wordiness are not linguist's categories, clearly. At the same time they clearly enough indicate here an assumption on the one hand that text emanates from and encapsulates bits of subject content and is thus exclusively referential, and a perception, on the other, that the text which children encounter as learners needs to carry other functions that humanize it; that it must somehow involve and reflect their everyday language.

There is a reflection here of the basic conflict that I have tried to describe between what might be termed the ruling orthodoxy of objectivistic assumptions and formalistic practices, and the moments of dissent that attempt to break its hold. Though reading might be thought open enough to do this, the kinds of text that have been examined so far suggest that it frequently does not. An impressionistic view of reading as it is practised in the school – its enacted 'importance' – seems to endorse this rather pessimistic account. With the exception of three situations, the reading I observed was of textbooks, 'class readers', worksheets, blackboards and question papers (tests and exams). The exceptional situations were English lessons in the library where books were being exchanged and read, some RE lessons where RE class library books were similarly used, and some project work where library books were in use. In addition, particularly in English lessons, pupils occasionally read their library books. These were, however, atypical situations. Overall, by far the most frequent encounters children had with print seemed to be related to discrete tasks on worksheets, and in question papers and textbooks.

In one RE classroom there was an open cupboard of class library books which the teacher used. In English rooms the books on the few open shelves were generally class sets, though there were some individual titles. In other teaching rooms, the most that was visible were class sets and small collections of reference books. The classroom itself, as a visual message, did not suggest that pupils encounter subjects through the reading of books.

Teachers' classroom talk seemed to reinforce this impression. It is curious that even open and easy classroom talk does not seem to lead towards books and private reading. In one observation period, comprising some forty lessons, I recorded only one occasion on which a title was recommended; this was in first-year RE, in class library time. In English lessons in the lower school library, teachers seemed to talk to individual pupils at the shelves, but the library had to be used for English lessons as an ordinary classroom, and often the library's particular resources were unused. The most frequent and noticeable mode of teachers' talk about reading related to negotiations with the particular texts being worked on.

I talked on many occasions to teachers about reading. I mentioned to two teachers, an English teacher and the head of the remedial department, the Bullock Report recommendation that pupils should read more for pleasure in school. In response both, separately, said that pupils were instructed to bring books to read in registration, but mentioned no other situations in school where 'reading for pleasure' might take place. Perhaps reading needs to be described in tougher terms before it counts as educative. I asked about the place of reading in lower school science. The teacher felt that 'reading isn't important here', and added that in the Nuffield science course which he taught the duplicated material was sufficient in itself – it had survived for several years. A classical studies teacher, talking about the value for children of reading stories themselves, said that he preferred to '*talk* the stories to them; it gets over the literary problem, especially with mixed-ability groups'. Another English teacher associated 'reading' with comprehension work, and instanced the 'SRA' boxes (graded cards with varied reading matter and multiple-choice comprehension tasks) as ideal material: 'It does away with writing whole sentences, which is time-consuming. They're invaluable. Where else would you find such a wealth of reading?' Reading is here implicitly defined as a 'doing comprehension' kind of activity, a cognitive struggle with print.

No claim was made in these conversations for the liberating effects often associated with reading – pleasure, wonder, imaginative involvement – nor was any particular claim made for its value in gathering information generally. In one situation, a distrust for reading was expressed. A chemistry teacher said of a fourth-year boy who had tried to read up a subject on his own and attempted an explanation to the class, that 'reading things on your own often confuses you and then you don't understand when it's done in class.'

Other reflections of the peripheral status of reading are perhaps visible in documents like the head's report (for Speech Day) and the options booklet. Books are mentioned in the library section of the report, which refers to the 'intensive' use made of books, especially paperbacks, but nowhere else in the 27-page report are books or reading mentioned. The options booklet, which in 26 pages describes the work done in years 4 and 5, omits any reference to books and reading. On the other hand, a document giving advice to tutors about registration, which of course can be a difficult half-hour or so of the day, reminds them that 'reading is always worthwhile and pupils should be encouraged to have library books at hand'. A document on 'The Gifted Child' circulated and under study in the school, produced by 'ten heads and senior staff' in three counties, nowhere specifically mentions reading or books, though reference is made to 'premises and other facilities', 'programmes', 'resources', 'enrichment', 'hobbies', 'group projects', 'in-depth interests', and so on.

Nothing I observed about the amount of time spent reading or the kinds of reading that took place, or what teachers said and did about reading, seems discrepant with Dolan's general findings as these are recounted in 'Teachers' perceptions and children's reading in secondary schools'.[15] Dolan points out that before his research there had, surprisingly, been 'no extensive empirically-based investigations' in this country of 'the reading demands made by teachers' in the last year of junior school, and years 1 and 4 of secondary school. He hints at a radical inconsistency in teachers' attitudes to reading: 'One assumption the project team made . . . was that teachers have high regard for what children may learn from reading. Another was that this expectation would prove in many cases to be unrealistic.'[16] Asked how much reading was involved in their subject, secondary teachers 'feel that reading often plays an important part in their lessons, but are reluctant to rely on it as the chief vehicle for learning'. This, apparently, is because 'many teachers consider that children in the lower years of secondary school are not very skilled as readers.' Clearly, being 'reluctant to rely on' reading because children 'are not very skilled at it' seems likely to help perpetuate that lack of skill. But, apart from this, the contradictions between teachers' high regard for reading and their low expectations of what it accomplishes, and between belief in its importance and a reluctance to rely on it, seem to give expression to the basic contradiction between the need to read to gain access to subject knowledge and the closures that flow from defining it objectivistically.

The subservient, technicist role envisaged for reading is apparent in his report of teachers' comments: 'A commonly expressed view was that one of the least effective ways for children to acquire information is through reading alone.'[17] And: 'Some teachers drew attention to the fact that syllabuses are often so content-packed that they are compelled to "feed" children with information rather than let them discover, perhaps through reading . . . at their own pace.' For this reason the purpose of reading is 'to allow pupils to do something' rather than to read 'merely for pleasure'.

Much the most common type of reading material in the secondary schools he surveyed, as in the one under consideration here, is the 'textbook' (in Dolan's research this includes the English 'class reader'). His tables are reproduced here.[18]

*Table 3*  Percentage of types of reading material in first- and fourth-year secondary school lessons (S1 & S4)

|  | English | | Maths | | Science | | Social studies | |
|---|---|---|---|---|---|---|---|---|
|  | S1 | S4 | S1 | S4 | S1 | S4 | S1 | S4 |
| Textbook | 66 | 71 | 37 | 59 | 30 | 13 | 34 | 42 |
| Reference | 5 | 16 | 0 | 0 | 7 | 1 | 25 | 7 |
| Library | 1 | 5 | 0 | 0 | 0 | 1 | 3 | 0 |
| Exercise book | 15 | 5 | 14 | 23 | 14 | 43 | 16 | 10 |
| Blackboard | 12 | 1 | 4 | 18 | 22 | 25 | 12 | 6 |
| Other (work cards, etc.) | 0 | 3 | 47 | 1 | 27 | 18 | 9 | 36 |

Dolan sets this in the context of other language activities (Table 4). Having earlier asked teachers about their perceptions of how

*Table 4* Time spent on *language* activities in secondary school lessons (averaged out in terms of a forty-minute lesson)

|  | English | | Maths | | Science | | Social studies | |
|---|---|---|---|---|---|---|---|---|
|  | S1 | S4 | S1 | S4 | S1 | S4 | S1 | S4 |
| Listening | 15 | 17 | 6 | 7 | 10 | 12 | 10 | 10 |
| Reading | 9 | 12 | 4 | 3 | 4 | 4 | 6 | 6 |
| Writing | 5 | 5 | 2 | 4 | 4 | 8 | 4 | 8 |
| Discussion (child) | 2 | 2 | 4 | 4 | 4 | 3 | 2 | 3 |
| Discussion (teacher) | 1 | 1 | 1 | 1 | 2 | 2 | 2 | 2 |
| % of lesson | 80 | 95 | 42 | 47 | 60 | 72 | 60 | 72 |

much reading takes place in their lessons, Dolan comments, significantly, that 'teachers may be overestimating the amount of reading which children complete'. He also tabulates information on 'continuous reading', and concludes that most reading in secondary schools takes place in short bursts of less than fifteen seconds; that is to say, of the total time spent on reading, a high overall percentage accumulates from tiny increments. And he notes that 'Most teachers greatly overestimated the continuous reading in their lessons.' He found that 'reading for pleasure is comparatively rare in secondary schools', and that there is 'little reading of library books in class'.[19] Overall, 'one might infer that reading is not generally regarded as a well-developed learning skill in secondary-school children, and is not to be trusted as a reliable information-gaining activity, particularly in the case of first-year pupils.'[20]

Some of these generalizations echo the impressionistic comments I have made. I made no measurement of the lengths of time children spent reading and the teachers' comments, except in the one instance, do not so much convey overt scepticism about the reliability of reading as fail to endorse its value. But Dolan's points about the paucity of reading for pleasure, the peripheral status of reading in general, the dominance of the textbook, the small amount of reading compared with other language activities, and the sense that the crowded syllabus restricts reading, seem further exemplified by what I have noted.

It also seems to follow that teachers' criteria for evaluating children's reading should reduce to 'efficiency' and 'reliability'. Reading in the school was continuously assessed for informational uptake, in questions such as those in the geography book, in worksheet questions, tests, and exam papers. These appeared to be the only kinds of question that were asked of text. Perhaps this is only to be expected. If text is reduced to the referential function, questions are similarly reduced. The only question to be asked, in effect, is 'Has the information been reliably transported into pupils' heads?' The Attenborough text, of course, would permit other questions. If after reading it a teacher were to ask, 'Isn't it amazing?' he would be perceived by pupils to be responding to the mood of the account, more specifically perhaps to its emotive function – though that seems to be closely involved with the conative and the phatic. To ask the same question of the biology textbook at that point would produce an emotive focus that was private and intrusive.

In short, efficiency and reliability become objectivistic criteria if they are exclusive and unaccompanied by criteria corresponding to the other functions of text. When pupils' difficulties with voiceless text become apparent, the exclusive focus on content ('context' in Jakobson's scheme) produces two distinct responses, both objectivistic, each dependent on the other. One locates difficulty 'in' text itself, and looks to measure the 'difficulty levels of' text. The other locates the problem in the pupils' inadequacies, characterized as a lack of reading 'skills'. Both perspectives tend not to look at the network of relations that exist in particular institutions between text, other language, the pupil's world and the teacher; rather, they sever the relation between the pupils and their language and the subject and its language in order to look at each 'objectively', when it is the confrontation between the pupils' constitutive speech and the constituted forms of the subject that is crucial. The value of trying to see the 'intrinsic' difficulty *of* text or the 'intrinsic' lack of skill in pupils lies in whatever usefulness each might have as a preliminary to the scrutiny of the relation between pupil and text in particular situated encounters.

To postulate a body of reading skills as being needed before reading is trusted for academic work is also to propose a new deficit-model of the pupil, as someone lacking the basic tools with which to approach subject content. A recent book for teachers, *Language Skills through the Secondary Curriculum*,[21] is continuously concerned with the teacher's need to focus explicitly on a very wide range of reading skills – sufficient almost for a curriculum in itself – but nowhere emphasizes the possibility that the prescription of such an array of qualifications for entry might indicate a problem about how pupils encounter knowledge rather than in pupils themselves.

## Ordinary language and extraordinary language

One might say that a formidable range of skills is needed to read the textbooks and worksheets I have briefly examined. Or rather, one might say that what often makes them readable is less a set of skills than a particular perspective – that of the reader who is able to see contents as succinct, formalized versions, essentially the teacher's achieved perspective. To re-read paragraphs and pages from a collection of textbooks without a series of such perspectives – without contributing one's own gathered meanings to them – or to glance through worksheets picked up at random from a pile of 200 or so conveys, to me at least, a sense of clutter. So might glancing through books picked at random off a shelf. But pausing with books often produces the intimations of some relevance, the promise of a meaning that will unfold within the confines of the one narrative or the one argument. And smaller statements – a limerick in an anthology, or a single, resonant photograph – seem capable of establishing, despite their compass, a transient field of relevance which makes the encounter meaningful. The same experiment tried with worksheet and textbook produces for me only the possibility of a meaning that waits on some richer encounter, of which this is a kind of abstract – maps without terrain.

Clearly, if there is evidence that children so frequently fail with school text that their experience might be comparable to this, some explanation is needed of why such a version of reading in academic subjects continues to be offered to them. One answer might be that a particular view of language, which generally goes unexamined, underpins decisions about what children may be usefully given to read. This view or basic presupposition seems to be that written language is essentially an instrument for carrying messages. The strong emphasis on its instrumental character means that a distinction is nearly always and often unwittingly made between the message and the language 'used to get it across', between the 'facts' and the words that carry them. This seems to entail that language can be altered in various ways, by compression, or the editing-out of non-referential features, without really changing, provided that it still embodies the 'same' information. This, in turn, implies that the facts, the nuggets of essential information, are somehow stable and do not depend for their meaningfulness on the way they are organized in particular minds or how they emerge in particular lessons.

In thus taking facts out of language, as it were, this view becomes schismatic, and gives language a kind of split personality – facts over here, what are not facts over there. In this account, the constitutive power of everyday speech, to return to Merleau-Ponty's terminology, is a power that functions only in regard to what is left when language has finished dealing with the objective and neutral. Stanley Fish argues powerfully that this 'disastrous model' accomplishes only the 'trivialization' of ordinary language, and leads to 'an inadequate account' of both ordinary language and what it is severed from, which becomes, not surprisingly, the domain of 'literary' language.[22] In his view, 'the trivialization of ordinary language is accomplished as soon as one excludes . . . matters of purpose, value, intention, obligation, and so on – everything that can be characterized as human.' The definitions of ordinary language that flow from this exclusion necessarily, then, focus on its capacity for carrying messages, or making logical structures, or picturing the world objectively. Whatever the definition, 'two things remain constant: (1) the content of language is an entity that can be specified independently of human values . . . and (2) a need is therefore created for another entity or system in the context of which human values can claim pride of place. That entity is literature'.[23]

A belief in the capacity of an objectively neutral language to describe the facts of the world as they are, and specify them independently of human values – including the child's – seems exactly to be what supports the faith that voiceless referential text can offer to the learner satisfactory biological, geographical and historical accounts of the world. But if, as he suggests, 'ordinary language is extraordinary because at its heart is precisely that realm of values, intentions, and purposes which is often assumed to be the exclusive property of literature',[24] then a reductive purge of language in favour of essential facts makes problematic what precisely is thought to be 'essential' about the facts that remain. For instance, one wonders what is essential in these few lines. 'I found the circles which the red light made to be manifestly bigger than those which were made by the blue and the violet. And it was very pleasant to see them gradually swell or contract accordingly as the colour of the light had changed.'[25] If the second sentence is omitted because it is a tautologous, merely emotive colouring, something about Newton's relation to his work is effaced. It may be argued that for certain purposes at certain levels this may not matter, and may be necessary. What cannot be argued is that the omission does not alter the facts as they are presented in the two sentences of the first version; to hide the fact that something different is being said after the omission makes it likely that children will encounter text which is divested of that particular human accent. Drained of such resonant ordinariness, text becomes 'essentially' sterile, an extraordinary written language contrived as if in a spirit of irony especially for educational purposes.

## References

1 D. Attenborough, *Life on Earth* (London, Collins/BBC Publications, 1979).
2 K. G. Brocklehurst and H. Ward, *A New Biology* (London, Hodder & Stoughton, 1978), p. 213.
3 Attenborough, op. cit., p. 92.
4 F. R. Dobson and H. E. Virgo, *Canada and the United States: New School Geography 5* (London, Hodder & Stoughton, 1970), p. 76.
5 T. Duncan, *Exploring Physics, Book 4* (London, John Murray, 1970), p. 136.

6 Brocklehurst and Ward, op. cit., p. 36.
7 E. Lunzer and K. Gardner (eds), *The Effective Use of Reading*, Schools Council Project (London, Heinemann Educational, 1979), pp. 8–15.
8 ibid., p. 21.
9 J. P. Sartre, *What is Literature?*, trans. B. Frechtman (New York, Harper & Row, 1965), p. 39.
10 Maxime Greene, 'Curriculum and consciousness', *Appendix to Unit 6: Schooling and Pedagogy*, in OU Course E 202, 'Schooling and Society', ed. M. Esland (Milton Keynes, Open University Press, 1977), p. 34.
11 R. Jakobson, 'Linguistics and poetics', in T. Sebeok (ed.), *Style in Language* (Cambridge, MIT Press, 1960), p. 350.
12 K. Perera, 'The assessment of linguistic difficulty', *Educational Review*, vol. 32, no. 2 (1980), p. 151.
13 N. Jackson and P. Penn, *Groundwork Geography: Europe* (London, Phillip, 1974), p. 3.
14 D. Barnes, 'Language in the secondary classroom', in D. Barnes, J. Britton, H. Rose and the LATE, *Language, the Learner and the School* (Harmondsworth, Penguin, 1969), p. 46.
15 T. Dolan, 'Teachers' perception and children's reading in secondary schools', in J. Gilland (ed.), *Reading: Research and Classroom Practice* (London, Ward Lock Educational, 1977).
16 ibid., p. 171.
17 ibid., p. 172.
18 ibid., p. 179.
19 ibid., p. 180.
20 ibid., p. 180.
21 W. A. Gatherer and R. B. Jeffs (eds), *Language Skills Through The Secondary Curriculum* (Edinburgh, Holmes McDougall, 1980).
22 Stanley Fish, *Is There a Text in This Class?* (Cambridge, Mass., Harvard University Press, 1980), p. 101.
23 ibid., pp. 101–2.
24 ibid., p. 108.
25 K. G. Irwin, *The Romance of Physics* (London, Weidenfeld & Nicolson, 1966), p. 160.

# 9
# INTRUDING ON MONOLOGUE

One young teacher of English in the school described the burden of her work in these terms: 'My problem is how do I get what's inside my head into theirs?' If the teachers whose lessons I observed had explicitly based their work on the same assumption, that it was concerned essentially with the efficient distribution of intellectual products from the store of their heads into pupils', the foregoing accounts of their lessons might well have been presented more or less as they stand. This Gradgrindian legacy exists despite the fact that teachers often believe that they are engaged in something different, and despite the fact that many attempt to do something different. And there are others who are aware that they come to be his spiritual heirs entirely against the grain of what they are themselves.

At the same time there have been clear intimations in this account of a world that lies somehow behind the world of school knowledge and its preoccupation with the art and technics of distribution. This preoccupation seems to be interrupted from time to time – almost like a hitch in the planned proceedings – by the urgency of some questions about atoms, by a sudden interest in thatched roofs, by a puzzle about why a test-tube turns black, by curiosity as to whether Achilles' mother knew she hadn't been thorough, by private speculation about pond water, and so on. For an observer, these moments do not merely stand out as almost abruptly atypical, though they certainly do that. Their atypicality is of a particular order, and what I wish to focus on is not their significance for learning but an aspect of their social character.

In the lesson the contexts that reveal these intimations are intrusive; socially, they resemble other intrusions, like humour or mild impertinence, in that they seem to suspend the action and produce some uncertainty as to what will happen next. Teachers have few ideological scruples about inflicting closure on impertinence, but the way they handle humour may resemble the way they often appear to handle intrusions from the world of the pupils' own intellectual concerns, since in both cases there is some pressure to accept what pupils offer.

When boys and girls are witty or amusing with words, it seems as if they have established – to put it solemnly – a constitutive involvement in the lesson. At the beginning of the lesson about atoms that is described in Chapter 5, a boy came in 5 minutes late and said, 'Sorry I'm late, sir, but I was on my bike and the wind was against me and I'd had a big lunch.' Everybody laughed, but the teacher's faint discomfort (as I interpreted it) signalled anxiety about control. In some way, the social initiative had been taken by a pupil, and the teacher seemed uncertain how to allow this to happen without signalling that similar initiatives could be taken by others. In pupils' terms, he didn't seem to find it easy to 'take a joke', he construed as impertinence what looked like pure humour. One might say that he didn't handle well a particular type of constitutive involvement which the skilled teacher not only knows how to handle, but positively values. This valuation is social: the teacher who knows how to handle pupils' humour so that it is seen to be socially relevant is not normally conveying the idea that it has a further relevance as content; a distinction is preserved that is essential to the lesson's resuming as a lesson and not continuing as a joke-session.

Impertinence is normally unambiguous and an overt threat, though, of course, it can be disguised as humour. Humour is often ambiguous and a latent or potential threat; it can be construed, appropriately or not, as impertinence. And perhaps there is a similarity between the need to define the joke as having a merely social relevance, and so prepare for its extrusion, and the need to treat intrusions of interest from the pupils' own intellectual world as having a transient, predominantly social value, which implies a restricted area of relevance like that allowed to humour.

The metaphor of an intellectual world that lies behind the working world of school knowledge is perhaps a trite one, but it may serve to put the atypicality of pupils' questions and speculations in a particular light: one in which they are seen as fragments of an alternative world of discourse as large and significant as the established world. These fragments of speech do more than make statements acknowledging the receipt of goods. They have little to do with distribution, and if a metaphor were needed to express their character, it would have to be some organic or vegetative one to convey a sense of intellectual pressure and growth, of awareness pushing towards light, or questions groping for niches of meaning. Such a characterization might be dismissed as another version of a dubious pre-lapsarian child's world, or another over-ripe romantic distortion of the child as 'best philosopher and eye among the blind'. But it might also be seen as one coherent interpretation of a daily social encounter in which the world of established knowledge confronts the pupils' world, and in which established knowledge maintains and reproduces itself by handling the pupils' world as a kind of threat.

If pupils' constitutive speech about knowledge is seen as somehow valuable but essentially intrusive, the kind of relation that maintains such a definition of knowledge might be described as monologic. The lessons I have looked at might be described, then, as monologues which occasionally pause or are interrupted. The questions which teachers ask when they are interested in discovering whether a piece of knowledge has been understood seem, in such a relation, to seek to diagnose how efficiently the subject language over which they have custody has been distributed.

Thus, in the context of 'artesian' the questions 'How does water get into different rocks?' and 'How do farmers get water in artesian basins?' may be seen as requests to reproduce a particular formulation, to confirm the receipt of goods. They are thus themselves parts of the monologue, checks on the quality of the distribution system at this point.

Clearly, the language practices I have noted in writing, talking and reading imply an underlying monologic relation in which the teacher functions as repository and the pupil as empty vessel. The basic operational assumption or presupposition, that language is essentially a means of conveying information – the view described at the end of the last chapter – seems to make ultimately necessary the maintenance of a monologic relation in the distribution of knowledge, because the pupils' constitutive awareness and speech are not 'in at the beginning of the process', so to speak; their awarenesses and speech are not part of the original store of information, not part of the notion of what knowledge is. A reductive, instrumentalizing view of language ultimately cannot say that 'knowledge' is constructed in part through the acts of knowing and speaking of particular pupils, since it has a prior existence – in the teacher's head, textbooks, worksheets, and so on.

Many teachers would find it difficult to agree with the suggestion that their pupils are subjected in learning to a relation that in essentials has the character of monologue. They would find it hard to reconcile this notion with their awareness that so much of teaching seems to consist of offers of patience and sympathy, attempts at understanding, and the frequent neglect of personal time. But precisely what seemed observable in lessons in different subjects is that certain fundamental taken-for-granted notions of the kind I have called objectivistic – relating to what knowledge is, and learning, and the language we use in school – can press into service a wide range of admirable professional virtues, and that teachers do seem to exhibit at one and the same time a deeply solicitous regard for children and, paradoxically, a strange unconcern about what might really be happening in their minds.

I shall try to illustrate from my own teaching a failure of awareness – an unconcern – which seems, in retrospect, to have emerged from an objectivistic tendency to see knowledge as preceding the encounter with content and which issued in a relation with pupils that was essentially monologic, despite an informal context designed not to be over-guided.

I was teaching English to a mixed-ability class of third years in a comprehensive school. I decided to take them for a day out to a particularly pleasant spot in the country; we would walk down a hill and through woods, have a look at a stream, stop for a picnic lunch in some fields, then see the old mill and the mill-pond, and finally go along the disused railway line. We would film and tape things as we went, and when we got back the pieces of films would give us some ideas for writing and, when they were edited (it was Super-8 cine-film), they might be the basis for further work, perhaps something on streams and rivers, or water generally: it would depend on how the film looked.

The day was meant to be 'open', and although we took paper and pencils to record some impressions of the woods at one point where we stopped, there was little overt direction – though that phrase might mean that it was just inadequately prepared, or vaguely thought out. However, the point I wish to make here is that, despite this, I had a preconceived view – a preconceived *open* view – of what the place represented as knowledge. In advance of the event, it seemed that there were several interesting features that we should encounter: the mill, the mill-pond, the disused railway line, the trout farm, the stream itself. There would be bird life on the pond that we could look at, and we might see fish; and the nest or two that I had found earlier would be interesting as well.

Laudably interdisciplinary and uncoercive though this might have been in some respects, it suffered from an objectivist approach to content which necessarily pushed the teaching relation in a monologic direction. First, I assumed that certain objects were intrinsically interesting; a personal interest in the mill and the railway as historically significant and aesthetically pleasing things was confused with the hope, or assumption, that pupils would find them interesting. I had thought of interestingness not as reflecting judgements that might emerge in talk, as something like an emotional colouring that might be present in talk and reveal a relation taken up by the pupils to what they confronted, but as an attribute inherent in old mills, streams and disused railways. So that the attempt to talk about these things, despite the ease and informality of the outing, was essentially monologic. This was especially so in the case of the railway line – perhaps because it bore no particular marks of having been one – and the imaginative *frisson* which comes with thinking 'once small steam trains passed along here' was not available to them.

The 'nature' side of the enterprise fared only a little better. To think in advance that there would be grebe, various species of duck, moorhens and coots is one thing; to say, *in situ*, 'Look, there is a cormorant on a pole' is another entirely. Had one been working with totally objectivistic assumptions, there would have been less of a problem, on one level, in that no reservation would have made itself felt about setting ruthless tasks with worksheets. As it was, that was precisely what I wanted to avoid. At the same time, neither the residue of objectivistic ways of defining the place as knowledge had been appreciated, nor the problem of how to justify the act of observing birds for several minutes at a time when the cruder objectivistic justifications have been removed and one is saying, in effect, 'We're watching that duck go under water', not 'You need to be able to say how long that duck stays under the water for the work we shall do later in school.'

The other, greater problem with the pre-written view of the place as knowledge was that it failed to prepare itself for the kind of endorsement that the pupils did manifest. This isn't to suggest that the ways in which they responded were predictable, but to say that the pre-written view also disposed one towards a lack of alertness about what might, and did, so to speak, just turn up.

Four things in particular did turn up and were, in various ways, endorsed by pupils as being worth their interest. One was a dead deer that two boys found. It was in long grass by a stream, and there seemed to be no injury to account for its death. Two girls noticed that a stretch of the disused line a few yards away had been treated with something that had killed weeds and other plants and left a brown swathe of dead grass and other greenery for a hundred yards or so. They connected this with the dead deer, and were indignant. From the way they talked about it then, and when they put the film together about two weeks later, it was evident that this experience was not simply the focus of that day, but in itself a significant emotional encounter. The second imponderable was the way in which a large-ish group of about seven or eight (mainly boys) became preoccupied with locating some fish they saw in the stream, which they said were chub. This absorbed them for a 10-minute period or so, during which time the knowledgeable fishermen instructed the others. Both these episodes were filmed by pupils with some enthusiasm. When, in the same place, I drew their attention to the disused line and suggested someone should film that, there were no takers.

The other two things I became aware of only when the film came back from processing a week later. The first was their entertainment with the stream itself. It emerged that they had had a good deal of amusement in the water as well as on the banks, and that they hadn't just 'fallen in', which was the official version. Also on the film was an episode where two boys discovered a shell – a freshwater mussel shell, apparently – in the bed of the stream, and had themselves filmed taking it out and inspecting it. Neither of these two episodes had been properly dealt with at the time, so for the sake of having a film with some shape to it we decided to go back with a small group and take some more film. The girls who originally said they had 'fallen in' were keen to re-enact their romp in the water. I had taken some 'atmospheric' pictures where the stream flowed through a dark part of the woods, and one of the girls said she'd like to take more pictures of that sort.

What seemed to have happened was that the original version I had of the usefulness of the place as knowledge had revealed itself, perhaps because of the attempt not to coerce but to work from an idea of relaxed enjoyment and interest, as quite as objectivistic in its own way as the trip to the beach, say, recounted in Chapter 2. On that level, various anticipated contents like the mill simply didn't work, and were virtually ignored. Being engaged at this point of the visit itself in monologue, waiting for pupils to notice how interesting the mill and the railway line were (waiting until what was in my head arrived in theirs), this seemed like failure; the pupils weren't joining in. This failure within a monologic relation looked, of course, like a failure with dialogue.

At the same time, pupils' endorsements of the place had begun to appear. They found the deer, and the drama of this took over for ten minutes or so. I remember having two responses to this. One involved perceiving it as important and potentially instructive; the other was an obscure restlessness that it would distract and detain us from the encounters I wanted to take place. This directional pressure must have made me a poor listener at this point. The other endorsement was the search for fish. This caused less tension because it was 'about the stream'. In these two ways knowledge of the place articulated itself through pupils' own awarenesses and responses, and there was a good deal of talk about both the deer and the fish. They talked about how the deer died, who owned the line where the spraying was done, what laws there were about spraying near streams, and so on. The anglers talked about the habits of chub, and the kind of fish that might also be found in the stream, their breeding habits and close seasons. So that this more dialogic passage was made possible by two sets of responses, and two events, that were not in my pre-visioned version. At the time, my concern about the fate of this version made responding properly to their responses less aware of itself than it should have been. The two other endorsing responses which I have mentioned I was not yet clearly aware of, beyond knowing – and hearing – that they had a good time down at the stream during lunch.

Going back for a second visit to take more film clarified further the pupils' perception of the place and its meaning for them. The romp in the water made clear just how much physical exuberance and uninhibited fun had been released there. They swung from branches, went in waist deep, threw water round, screamed and fought. I'd thought of the woods and stream as being seen by them as a good leisure-time place, but they had fun, not tepid leisure with walks and picnics. It had been monologic even through the idea of relaxed enjoyment. Then the episode where two of them found the shell was filmed again more carefully, and during this it became clear, somewhat late it seems, that the fascination this exerted was quite enough to initiate an exploration of what the stream might mean in terms of wildlife.

Looking at the first bits of film, and then returning to take more, seemed also to act as a means of making clear to the pupils what had been the central concerns of their experience of the place. The girl who filmed flowers by the stream, and sunlight and reflections and shadows on the second visit, did so without prompting and in an absorbed self-aware fashion that would hardly have been possible on the more crowded first visit, or without having seen in the first film a focus that catalysed her interest. There also seemed to develop a sense of the idyllic feel of the place – something I had assumed would be readily available to all on the first visit: that there were conscious attempts made on the second visit to catch this on film, I found particularly interesting.

In three days' hard work at the end of term, four or five pupils put together an eight-minute film from fragments shot during both visits. Even at this late stage, my own instincts for what to leave in were coloured by my original conception. The pupils' own selection criteria were in general more ruthless; no shots of the railway line (there was nothing happening), no shots just of the pond or the mill, fewer atmospheric bits, more of people. They wished to order episodes quite differently. I do not remember the points at issue, but do recall thinking, after they had assembled it, that they had found a sharper and more arresting narrative than it would have been.

The core of this experience, for me, was the subsequent realization of having been a reluctant listener to the finish. There had been brief periods, one might say, when a genuine dialogic relation took over, but the initial, unwitting assumption of monologic rights at first put the whole idea at risk and then made adaptation to their perception of the place so grudgingly slow as to undermine possibilities of a more sustained dialogue. Almost as revealing was the sense that the articulation on film of the content of the place, defined as it finally had been by their responses and endorsements and selection criteria, and consisting essentially of the deer and the shell episodes, the romp in the water, some atmospheric sense of shadow and sunlight and flowers by the water, and the search for fish, was not only satisfying aesthetically and as a record, but was in itself a version with enormous potential for deeper exploration. Two girls intended to write to the RSPCA about the deer, and one or two of the boys wanted to go back to look for more fish. It seemed as if, at the end of the summer term which cut short the venture, the intellectual lineaments of the place were on the brink of revealing themselves along the tracks of interest that had opened up. But it had taken two or three weeks, two visits, and some pieces of revealing film to uncover a dialogic version of that content, and thus a way, or a series of ways, of beginning to look at it.

It seems worth stressing that the possibilities that now presented themselves, however uniquely assembled or, in the first place, arbitrarily encountered, did so in ways that were interpretable as representing subject worlds. The dimensions of their experience articulated themselves as historical, geographical, biological and so on. Having a question about a shell, or a poisonous chemical or an animal's feeding habits means entering into colloquy with the culture one inhabits, which not only classifies knowledge in subjects and makes such structures as filmed accounts available, but produces minds 'so that they are alike in fine detail'[1] to the extent that their enquiring constitutive speech already seeks expression through these categories.

So this is not to follow Postman and Weingartner, in their *Teaching as a Subversive Activity*, in suggesting that the pupils' questions, once they are discovered, will themselves structure curriculum. They may be right in suggesting that 'the art and science of asking questions is the source of all knowledge',[2] and their emphasis on the importance of careful listening to pupils could only conduce to a more open, less monologic teaching relation, a less objectivistic handling of knowledge. But in their disagreement with Bruner, because 'he sees no reason to abandon the abstraction called a subject'[3] and in stressing the way in which the learner produces knowledge without the assistance of the interpreted world, they argue towards an extreme idealism which not only seems burdensome for the child whose task is then essentially to reconstruct the world through questions which the teacher refines and re-articulates in more complex forms, but also seems likely to issue in another monologic relation in which there are only the learners' questions. Some attempts to allow pupils to 'work on their own' and devise 'their own' projects seem to have reversed the monologic relation from content controlled by the teacher to content controlled by the pupil.

But their emphasis on pupils' questions may be put in a less merely subjective light if emphasis is at the same time placed in the 'out there' world that their questions confront. In other words, there is a position somewhere between that objectivistic view which 'reduces consciousness to being a reflection of the world' and the idealist position 'which reduces the world to being a construction of the subject'.[4] In the episode described earlier in this chapter, the position finally reached seemed to be this kind of phenomenological refusal of both reductions. Their questions did begin to produce knowledge of the world for them, but it was knowledge of a world already interpreted and constructed – and not least through other pupils' knowledge of fishing, their attitudes to wild animals, and so on. Perhaps one could say that their constitutive speech about things like the dead deer worked to produce – or rather might have done had there been time – knowledge of the chemistry of chemical sprays, of land ownership and rights, knowledge that exists apart from those pupils, but which here implicates them in a particular and potentially fruitful way. This phenomenological version implies, in Bolton's terms, 'not that reality is constructed in a series of interpretations, but that interpretations take place within the context of a world that transcends them.'[5] But here the pupils do at least make their own interpretations.

The attempt to reconstruct a monologic relation as dialogue meant, in the episode I have described, that their interest in fish and shells, and their comments and questions about them seemed to be crucial. In general, then, expressions of interest that are articulated as questions may be seen as revealing where a dialogic learning relation may begin, or be resumed. But when children do ask questions, they are often seen by others as merely revealing a lack of knowledge, and this social interpretation of the meaning of questions means that crucial questions may be censored and go unasked. If there is to be a dialogic relation through learning, the teacher needs to know what ideas and questions a pupil has, how provisional or developed they are, how urgent, genuinely personal, or quietly speculative, and so on.

To return to the point made at the very beginning, questions that issue from some pressing or central aspect of the learner's present situation often seem peculiarly revealing. For example, a 12-year-old girl, observing high tide on a river 4 miles inland from the beach where she had done the field-trip work referred to in Chapter 2, asked: 'Is the tide in at the sea as well?' and added, 'It's logical, but often teachers expect something more than logic, or simplicity. . . . It makes you not sure whether you know or not.' On the field-trip she had observed tide-marks, and had written about gravitational pull and neap and spring tides; but her own question is at a different level, that of the elementary mechanics and mystery of tides. And clearly her uncertainty, which might well not be exposed in a monologic relation (and may only have been because she was not involved at that moment in such a relation), carries a purposeful desire to know. In a monologic relation a decision as to whether to presume that 12-year-old pupils know that one tide is in at different places is likely to be made out of notions of appropriate concepts and levels of content. A dialogic relation, having not presumed this, and instead uncovered certain questions that are in some way personally important, would take them up as constitutive of content. And it is worth noting the fertility and the importance of the questions. She asks not only whether the same tides are in at different places, but why teachers seem to expect something other than what seems logical, and even how one knows whether one knows anything.

In such situations the exposure of an uncertainty that might have been self-censored gives release not just to the pupil but also to the teacher, allowing him to speak directly in response to the demands of that uncertainty, so that the statements he then makes come to seem especially purposeful. The pupil's release from uncertainty or difficulty thus becomes the teacher's release from the intellectual structures he normally inhabits, and the effect is of a renewal of human and intellectual contact, a restoration of the power of both teacher and learner to speak back and forth. Socrates suggests in the *Meno* that teaching is as much an affair of speaking to, as of speaking about: 'Perhaps it is more like friends talking together, not only to answer with truth, but to use only what the one who is questioned admits he knows.'[6] Objectivistic structures use only what someone else knows or has known;

Socrates' point might be seen as an emphasis on the fact that unless the learners speak through their own questions and awarenesses there is no dialogue, no real conversation. So that if a secondary school is to attempt a dialogic relation through learning with pupils, for instance as they enter from junior school, it might well attempt to discover what ideas and questions they actually have as a necessary prelude to 'speaking' pedagogically to 'persons-holding-ideas'.

This, however, seems not to be what occurs. The socially valued knowledge about children that the secondary school takes up from the junior or middle school seems most frequently to be psychometric information. In the school under observation, for example, junior school teachers' broad judgemental comments were accompanied by IQ and verbal reasoning scores, reading and spelling ages, and details of sight and hearing tests, but very seldom by particulars of the child's social biography, and not at all by narrative or other accounts of significant moments in the child's encounters with learning. And yet teachers have direct access, through the child's talk and writing, to some awareness of the living actuality, the significant contours and pressures of individual minds. A question like 'Is the tide in at the sea as well?' reveals a segment of this actuality, and compared with the kind of knowledge such moments offer, psychometric information is remote and insufficiently precise, uncovering by means of normative assessment only a set of dimly predictive possibilities that are of no immediate dialogic use in a teaching relation.

But such knowledge forms an institutionalized currency of awareness in a way that teachers' own daily observations and insights do not. It is a preferred form, valued because it is objective not intuitive, to do with essential capacity not contingent performance. Its positivist virtues, that is, undercut the values inherent in the more immediate knowledge available to teachers through direct contact with pupils, and it seems that a fantasy or mystification sets in not with the use *per se* of psychometric information, but with its valuation as an intrinsically superior and more illuminating knowledge than that which is itself superior and more illuminating. Moreover, it is the latter, directly human kind of knowledge which makes a dialogic teaching relation possible, in that when the actuality of children's minds is given expression, teachers have something to say which is part of a dialogue: they need no longer speak monologically out of stores of knowledge. The objectivistic preference for summative 'solid facts' about children only serves to prevent such a beginning being made.

And, of course, the facts uncovered in tests are not so solid as all that. For one thing, to extrapolate from a test result to a 'capacity' is to proceed intuitively, in conflating the known test domain with the unknown larger domain that it is supposed to represent. Even at its most controlled, the IQ or reading test indicates only how well a child performs that test, or rather has performed it on that occasion. Even this, as Cicourel shows very clearly, is claiming too much, for the test results often demand interpretation, and the tester often interprets responses in the light of his expectations of performance, so that scores only reveal how the child is interpreted as performing.[7] (Interestingly, in the personal record for B, the boy whose struggles were recounted in Chapter 4, there were two conflicting expert judgements relating to his hearing.)

A dialogic relation clearly depends on knowing children and their minds in a different, more precisely human way, and on drawing continuously on this knowledge. Both an initial awareness and an unfailing reciprocity are implied by the metaphor. That the idea does seem somewhat metaphoric might itself suggest how far from resembling people talking together the teaching relation has become. Dialogue, as a species of conversation, clearly cannot absorb a fundamentally assessive posture on the part of the teacher, or even begin if pupils can only say what they have not yet learned to say. It seems as if it is finally the coercive etiquette of subject languages and their minimal grammars that keep teacher and learner from speaking openly about the things that are in their minds.

## References

1 H. Sacks, quoted in Stanley Fish, *Is There a Text in This Class?* (Cambridge, Mass., Harvard University Press, 1980), p. 333.
2 N. Postman and C. Weingartner, *Teaching as a Subversive Activity* (Harmondsworth, Penguin, 1971), p. 84.

3 ibid., p. 81.
4 N. Bolton, 'Reflecting on the pre-reflective: phenomenology', in A. Burton and J. Radford (eds), *Thinking in Perspective* (London, Methuen, 1978), pp. 204–5.
5 ibid., p. 205.
6 Plato, *Great Dialogues of Plato*, trans. W. H. D. Rouse (New York, Mentor, 1956), p. 34.
7 A. Cicourel, *Language Use and School Performance* (New York, Academic Press, 1974), p. 215.

# INDEX

# ETHICS AND THE
# NEW TESTAMENT